Conversations with Robertson Davies

Literary Conversations Series

Peggy Whitman Prenshaw
General Editor

Conversations
with Robertson Davies

Edited by
J. Madison Davis

University Press of Mississippi
Jackson and London

Copyright © 1989 by the University Press of Mississippi
All rights reserved
Manufactured in the United States of America
92 91 90 89   4 3 2 1

The paper in this book meets the guidelines for permanence and durability of the Committee on
Production Guidelines for Book Longevity of the Council of Library Resources.

Library of Congress Cataloging-in-Publication Data

Conversations with Robertson Davies / edited by J. Madison Davis.
     p.   cm. — (Literary Conversations series)
  "Books by Robertson Davies": p.
  Includes index.
  ISBN 0-87805-383-2 (alk. paper). — ISBN 0-87805-384-0 (pbk. :
alk. paper)
   1. Davies, Robertson, 1913- —Interviews. 2. Authors,
Canadian—20th century—Interviews. 3. Authorship. I. Davies,
Robertson, 1913- . II. Davis, J. Madison, III. Series.
PR9199.3.D3Z64 1989
813'.54—dc19   88-39305
                                               CIP

Books by Robertson Davies

Shakespeare's Boy Actors. London: Dent, 1939.
Shakespeare for Young Players: A Junior Course. Toronto: Clarke, Irwin, 1942.
The Diary of Samuel Marchbanks. Toronto: Clarke, Irwin, 1947.
Overlaid: A Comedy. Toronto: French, 1948.
The Table Talk of Samuel Marchbanks. Toronto: Clarke, Irwin, 1949.
Eros at Breakfast and Other Plays. Toronto: Clarke, Irwin, 1949.
Fortune, My Foe. Toronto: Clarke, Irwin, 1949.
At My Heart's Core. Toronto: Clarke, Irwin, 1950.
Tempest-Tost. Toronto: Clarke, Irwin, 1951.
Leaven of Malice. Toronto: Clarke, Irwin, 1954.
A Jig for the Gypsy. Toronto: Clarke, Irwin, 1954.
A Mixture of Frailties. Toronto: Macmillan, 1958.
A Voice from the Attic. New York: Alfred A. Knopf, 1960.
A Masque of Mr. Punch. Toronto: Oxford University Press, 1963.
Marchbanks' Almanack. Toronto: McClelland and Stewart, 1967.
Four Favourite Plays. Toronto: Clarke, Irwin, 1968.
Fifth Business. Toronto: Macmillan, 1970.
Stephen Leacock. Toronto: McClelland and Stewart, 1970.
The Manticore. Toronto: Macmillan, 1972.
Hunting Stuart and Other Plays. Toronto: New Press, 1972.
Question Time. Toronto: Macmillan, 1975.
One Half of Robertson Davies. Toronto: Macmillan, 1977.
World of Wonders. Toronto: Macmillan, 1979.
The Enthusiasms of Robertson Davies. Ed. Judith Skelton Grant. Toronto: McClelland and Stewart, 1979.
The Rebel Angels. Toronto: Macmillan, 1981.
Brothers in the Black Art. Vancouver: Alcuin Society, 1981.
Robertson Davies: The Well-Tempered Critic. Ed. Judith Skelton Grant. Toronto: McClelland and Stewart, 1981.
High Spirits. Markham, Ont.: Penguin, 1982.
The Mirror of Nature. Toronto: University of Toronto Press, 1983.
What's Bred in the Bone. Toronto: Macmillan, 1985.
The Papers of Samuel Marchbanks. Toronto: Irwin, 1985.
The Lyre of Orpheus. Toronto: Macmillan, 1988.

Contents

Introduction

This collection of interviews with Robertson Davies should prove valuable to scholars looking for new ways of assessing his achievement and to general readers who would like to know better the man behind *Fifth Business, What's Bred in the Bone,* Samuel Marchbanks, and the wide world of wonders that constitutes Davies's writings. All of these interviews reveal various aspects of Davies's character and career, of course, but particularly illuminate such questions as the conflict between the media image of Davies and the reality, the religious and philosophical assumptions in his work, and his view of the Canadian identity as a nation and people.

Few people can aptly be described any more as men or women of letters and of those few many would be uncomfortable with being called so. Yet no term seems more apt when discussing the life and works of Robertson Davies, and, as at least one of the following interviews indicates, he is flattered to be thought so. His writing is an armory of talents. His recent world-wide recognition has led him to be called Canada's best novelist and provoked Anthony Burgess, one of the most flamboyantly critical commentators of our time, to recommend Davies enthusiastically for the Nobel Prize. However, his novel-writing is but a part of a lengthy and prodigiously fertile career as a writer in many forms. Beginning on the eve of World War II with his scholarly study *Shakespeare's Boy Actors,* Davies has adeptly juggled several lives as a writer. He acted, directed, and wrote plays, several of which were offered and treated seriously by such major figures as Sir Tyrone Guthrie, Dame Sybil Thorndike, and Sir John Gielgud. Davies's success was modest, limited mostly to Canada, but far greater than most playwrights achieve anywhere. He received a number of awards and significant recognition as one of Canada's best talents.

Meanwhile he supported this "pastime" by journalism, becoming part owner and editor of the *Peterborough Examiner.* He wrote editorials and book reviews. He created a crusty Tory columnist called Samuel Marchbanks and regularly delighted readers in a number of cities with the fictional Marchbanks's wry observations and acid wit. Later, these pieces were anthologized into popular books. He was also the regular book reviewer for *Saturday Night*. Because he had a number of ideas that suited neither journalism nor the stage, the novel beckoned and Davies began the 1950s with the publication of *Tempest-Tost*. It is in the novel form that his writing has become best known, though it would take nearly another twenty years before *Fifth Business* would raise him to global acclaim.

Meantime Davies was active in the Stratford (Ontario) Shakespeare Festival and received his greatest theatrical disappointment when his adaptation of the novel *Leaven of Malice* failed on Broadway in 1960. The collaborative compromises to which the commercial playwright is subject grew oppressive compared to the creative freedom and absolute control of the novelist. He did not cease writing plays or being involved in the theater, but interviews with him suggest a mental change from "I am a playwright who writes novels" to "I am a novelist who writes plays." A decade after the failure of *Love and Libel* he published *Fifth Business,* which would be translated into many foreign languages, including French, German, and Polish, and which would change Davies from a major Canadian writer to a significant figure in world literature.

Merely writing extraordinary novels, essays, and plays was not enough for a juggler and prestidigitator like Davies, however. The newspaper was sold and in the early 1960s he moved into academic life. He was appointed a professor of English and Master of Massey College, a new graduate school created by a gift of the Massey Foundation, at the University of Toronto. Moving into the Master's quarters in 1963, Davies essentially designed Massey College, delineating its character, its rituals, and its standards. He administered, taught, advised, and did all of the things that such a position entails so successfully that one can only marvel that he had time for his writing. Finally, in 1981, Davies retired as Master and has spent the years since then lecturing and writing, recently publishing his most commercially successful novel *What's Bred in the Bone.*

Were Davies relatively untalented, if he had not come to be recognized, the story of his life as a scholar, teacher, playwright, essayist, novelist, and newspaperman would be nothing less than phenomenal, if only for his incredible capacity for work. Yet, the high level of that work puts him in the category of a wonder, and taking account of the many facets of his writings and personality is a daunting undertaking for the scholar or interviewer. No one envies the task facing Judith Skelton Grant of Toronto, who has spent many years on a biography of Davies. Often a careful reader of this collection of interviews will recognize that Davies seems to be politely toying with those interviewers who are searching for a single thread in what is a batch of very mingled yarn.

In the age of mass media famous writers become celebrities who are known more for their personal idiosyncrasies than for having been read. A simplistic conception substitutes for the complexity of artist and human being. Again and again interviewers ae surprised that Davies does not fit their categorization of him. Davies's media image has been of a crusty Victorian who built Massey College into a quaint simulation of Oxford with its "high table" meals and snuff-taking. He has been portrayed as an aristocrat. His novels have provoked the adjective "Tory," and the term "man of letters" has been used not so much to describe his versatility as to dub him a throw-back. Interviewers have often remarked they were apprehensive about meeting him because they expected him to be pompous and condescending, and his charm and openness came as a great relief. Still, unfortunately, readers and interviewers are frequently so blinded by the image, they fail to see the man. The famous beard becomes a mask, the voice of Samuel Marchbanks deafens the listener's ears to Davies himself. We see more than one interviewer trying to draw out jeremiads against the decline of western civilization, or implications that the form of his novels, his beard, his conservative clothes, and the university rituals he initiated are the last bulwark against a new Dark Ages.

Davies refuses to take these baits. He likes his beard and his clothes, he says casually. Young people of college age enjoy rituals. He is irritated by many features of contemporary civilization— parades to raise money against diseases, inattentive book reviewers, creative work being supported by government grants—but he plainly is more concerned with his personal identity than in dictating a new order for civilization. In a public panel discussion recorded in 1956 by the Canadian Broadcasting Company, J. B. Priestley, Ira Dilworth,

and Davies consider the effects of mass communication upon
Western culture. Priestley strongly attacks the media for pandering to
the lowest common denominator, Joe Dokes, an untutored and
unsophisticated viewer or listener who is bored by the finer aspects of
civilization and makes no effort to grasp them. Dilworth, an executive
of the CBC, unpretentiously defends the positive possibilities inherent
in radio and television. Davies, who might be expected to take
Priestley's reactionary view, does not do so. He not only defends Joe
Dokes for having made many wise decisions at the ballot box in the
major democracies, he pooh-poohs some of the major losses that
Priestley mourns, such as the British music hall, which (like American
vaudeville) is remembered with a reverence that it rarely deserved.

Davies's warm sense of humanity also reveals itself in these
interviews, putting the lie to his seeming aloofness. Peter Gzowski, a
popular radio personality, interviewed Davies for the first time in
1972. Initially, Gzowski seems somewhat awed by this formidable
man he has read but never met. He begins by testing Davies on how
he should address him. Gradually, however, in this interview and in
those that follow, they become relaxed to the point that they
frequently talk over each other, interrupt each other, chuckle, and
laugh freely, and one comes to see a Davies who is anything but aloof
or pompous.

Ironically, the image of Davies as some sort of professorial aristocrat
has contributed to his fame. Although the image is largely misleading,
there are clearly some explanations for it. His father rose to the
appointed position of senator, although the family origins could not
be described as aristocratic. Davies's voice has the strong sound of
authority and easily withers effrontery. These impressions are
buttressed by his novels. There are not many significant literary
novelists who dare to create works along such apparently traditional
lines as Davies. His two most popular novels, *Fifth Business* and
What's Bred in the Bone, provide pleasures for which audiences have
been nostalgic since the triumph of modernism. Both are lengthy
cradle-to-grave stories with a strong authorial presence. Though
evidence of modernism may be present in certain uses of point of
view or in the use of the demons in *What's Bred In the Bone,* for
example, Davies's modernism is more muted than that in the work of
many of his contemporaries. One critic has argued that even Davies's

style, the structure of his sentences and word choice, more closely resembles nineteenth-than twentieth-century prose, and on other occasions Davies is described as Dickensian because of his knack for curious and fascinating secondary characters, or compared to Thackeray and Meredith. Davies, however, has chosen his style for this age, not to emulate Victorian masters.

As several exchanges in the interviews show, Davies is angered by being compared to Dickens (who he says attacked social ills after they had been cured) and being hailed as some neo-Victorian reviver of the "good old" novel. Rightly, too. Davies is not only more adventurous with form and technique in his novels than most critics allow, he is very concerned with the problems of our time. He does not, it is true, focus on the things usually dubbed "current issues": the women's movement, nuclear proliferation, the ozone layer, and so forth. He may comment on these things, but his interests lie more in the internal realms. How does a person live in this time? How does one address the fact of existence? What does one do to replace the serious loss of the spiritual dimension in living? Eventually, most of the interviews evolve into discussions of these questions, and some of them (such as those with Tom Harpur) are entirely on those subjects. His focus is, and has always been, on salvation by self-discovery or by creating the self. In an existential sense, a human being *makes* him or her self through a series of actions, behaviors, or choices. Almost all of his drama and fiction are concerned with exploring the self, and Davies indicates several times that he sees himself as a man who has probed his own psyche and established a distinctive identity, which may have certain familiar aspects but is certainly not an imitation.

One aspect of Davies's distinctive identity—and a recurring theme in the interviews—is his belief in the importance of mystery. Davies is not a religious person, it seems, in the sense that he adheres to the practices of a particular church, but he is religious in the sense that he has faith that much of what is around us is unseen. He subscribes to the humble view that a person who does not believe in God is putting an inordinately high value upon himself and Davies would never presume to feel he has come to understand what God is. He will not reject the possibility that the Devil operates in the world, and he does not particularly fret that there is no hard evidence for the soul. This is strictly a matter of faith with him, for, after all, the unknowable is that which cannot be known. In one interview, he considers why it is that some writers are lucky enough to publish the right book at the right moment, whereas others of equal or greater talent do not. Why does one man live and another die? These are unanswerable questions which occur in all the world's great literature from ancient Greece to Shakespeare to Isaac Bashevis Singer, and what alarms Davies is the nineteenth and twentieth century's "objective" search for an explanation for everything. Lives may be ruined or made by the sequence of cause and effect initiated by a thrown snowball, but what is it that caused the snowball to strike its target? Why was the wind just right? Why did the boy have that impulse at that particular moment? Luck? Character? The turning of Fortune's wheel? It is impossible for human beings to know.

Davies's sense of mystery is also connected with the shift from Freudianism to Jungianism he describes in several interviews. Freud was appealing to the youthful Davies because he suggested a definite cause for each act. If one only probed enough or knew enough, each life choice could be explained by a number of crucial events early in the formative years. It is much easier to accept the possibility of certainty when one is young. Ultimately, however, Freud seemed reductive, said Davies, whereas Jung seemed inclusive. Whether Davies is right or not about the reductive nature of Freudianism is not really important. What is important in Davies's case is that his interest in Jung has contributed significantly to the creation of his art. Critics have successfully applied Jungian concepts to many of his works, and Davies's comments about Jung in the following interviews will certainly be valuable in appraising the intentions of his past and future writings.

Another important theme readers will note in these interviews is the question of Canadian identity. Davies is frequently asked what is distinctly Canadian about his writings, or what distinguishes the Canadian from people of other nationalities. He remarks in one interview that one can really speak of Canadian authors only as regionalists. Atlantic Canada is considerably different from its neighbor Quebec, or from Ontario or prairie Canada or the Pacific coast. He describes, however, a number of aspects of the Canadian character. The climate, he says, makes Canadians rather similar to Scandinavians in certain ways, and he remarks that the heritage which is closest to the Canadian is that of Ibsen and Strindberg. Superficially cool and aloof, he explains, both peoples have formidable and underestimated passions raging in them, and this inner fire often expresses itself in quite bizarre ways. Since Davies is from Ontario and has written much about the dynamics of the small towns there, he has given much attention to the white "Anglo-Celtic" protestant culture with its accompanying Scottish Calvinist bent and its orientation toward Great Britain. Many interviewers delve into Davies's youth in order to delineate the regionalism and "Canadianism" of his works, particularly the Salterton and Deptford trilogies. To all of them Davies comes across as being assured and confident in his identity as a man and as a Canadian.

What is certain is that all of these factors mingled together have produced the extraordinary writer who is Robertson Davies, and who can far better reveal himself through his own words in his works and in the interviews which comprise this collection. I have presented the interviews in their entirety, unedited except for obvious errors of spelling and typographical mistakes. The transcriptions of taped interviews are presented as literally as possible, and through this I hope that some sense of Davies's distinctive manner of speech can be conveyed by the printed page. Because all the interviews are reprinted as they originally appeared, there is, of course, some repetition among them as Davies answers similar questions in similar ways. The slight variations these passages exhibit may prove to be of interest, as when he discusses the history of *Love and Libel* before it goes to Broadway and after it closes; however, when there is a choice between two very similar interviews, I have selected the most thorough and interesting one.

Many of the interviews in this book are printed for the first time and most have not been readily available, particularly to readers outside of Canada. There are selections from newspapers and periodicals, but especially valuable to scholars and general readers interested in Davies's work are the interviews transcribed from a series of recordings done by Gordon Roper at the University of Toronto in 1968 and transcriptions of radio and television tapes in the archives of the Canadian Broadcasting Corporation. These, and the interview from *Realities,* a TV Ontario program, have never been published before.

I would like to thank a number of people who have assisted me considerably. The cooperation of Robertson Davies himself was essential in the making of this book, and I am grateful for his help, as well as that of his secretary Moira Whalon. The travel needed to research this book was supported by a Canadian Studies Faculty Research Program grant administered by the Canadian Embassy in Washington, D.C., and its Academic Relations Officer, Dr. Norman T. Lloyd. In addition, I would like to thank the staffs of the Robarts Library of the University of Toronto, the Metropolitan Toronto Library Board, and the CBC Archives in Toronto, particularly Dido Mendel and Ken Puley: all were cheerfully cooperative and friendly to a degree that is rare. Also at the CBC Bonnie Brickles, Martin von Mirbach, and Robert Daley. I am also grateful to Dr. Judith Skelton Grant, biographer and critic of Robertson Davies; Dr. Michael Peterman of Trent University, author of the Twayne volume on Davies; to Carol S. Griffiths; and to Dr. Gordon Roper, Professor Emeritus of Trent University. Their assistance has been invaluable. At Pennsylvania State University in Erie, I am grateful to Patty Mrozowski and the library staff for assisting in the location of the numerous books and periodicals needed for a project such as this and to Provost and Dean John M. Lilley and the Behrend College Faculty Research Fund for the generous support. Finally, special thanks is due to Norma J. Hartner, for her fortitude in transcribing hours of tapes.

JMD
September 1988

Chronology

1913   William Robertson Davies born to William Rupert Davies and Florence Sheppard (McKay) Davies in Thamesville, Ontario.

1919   Davies begins school; family moves to Renfrew, Ontario, when father purchases the Renfrew *Mercury.*

1924   Visits Europe on tour organized by father

1928   Family moves after father purchases Kingston *Whig;* Davies attends one year of high school.

1928   Enters Upper Canada College in Toronto. In following years becomes active in drama, edits school newspaper.

1932   Unable to pass a mathematics examination, Davies enters Queen's University, Kingston, as a special student; also active in drama.

1935   Father purchases Peterborough *Examiner.* Davies enters Balliol College of Oxford University; very active in the dramatic society in following years, he meets prominent actors and directors.

1938   Receives B. Litt., acts on provincial tour and in London, and becomes member of Old Vic Company, acting and teaching history of drama.

1939   *Shakespeare's Boy Actors,* his dissertation, is published.

1940   Marries Brenda Mathews, stage manager of Old Vic.
          Rejected by the military, he and his bride sail for Canada.
          Becomes literary editor for *Saturday Night* in Toronto;
          first child, Miranda, is born.

1942   Moves to Peterborough as editorial writer for the
          Examiner. Father appointed to Senate. Second daughter,
          Jennifer, is born. Publishes *Shakespeare for Young
          Players: A Junior Course.*

1943   Begins writing Marchbanks articles

1945   Works on two plays

1946   Becomes vice-president, editor, and part-owner of the
          Examiner

1947   "Overlaid" (a one-act play) wins prize of Ottawa Drama
          League Workshop and is produced. Active with
          Peterborough Little Theatre. A third daughter, Rosamond,
          is born. *The Diary of Samuel Marchbanks* published.

1948   "Eros at Breakfast" (one-act) wins Sir Barry Jackson
          trophy for best production of a Canadian play in
          Dominion Drama Festival; Gratien Gélinas prize for best
          author goes to Davies. *Fortune, My Foe* first produced.

1949   *Fortune, My Foe* wins Jackson prize; Davies wins Gélinas
          prize again, as well as Louis Jouvert trophy for best
          directing (of *The Taming of the Shrew,* starring Brenda
          Davies). *The Table Talk of Samuel Marchbanks* published.

1951   First novel, *Tempest-Tost,* is published.

1953   Discontinues regular Marchbanks column. Writes and
          directs *King Phoenix,* which wins at Eastern Ontario
          Drama Festival. Elected Governor, Board of Directors of
          the Stratford Shakespeare Festival.

1954   Writes *A Jig for the Gypsy,* which is produced in Toronto.
            Leaven of Malice published, which receives Stephen
            Leacock Memorial Medal.

1956   Adapts Jonson's *Bartholomew Fair* for Stratford Festival;
            writes additional scenes for the production of *The Merry
            Wives of Windsor.*

1957   Awarded LL.D. by University of Alberta

1958   *A Mixture of Frailties* is published.

1959   Awarded D. Litt. by McMaster University; writes *General
            Confession* (three-act play.)

1960   *Love and Libel,* a dramatization of *Leaven of Malice,* has
            short run on Broadway. Davies is Visiting Professor of
            English at Trinity College, University of Toronto.

1961   Appointed Master of Massey College, a new graduate
            school of the University of Toronto; receives Lorne Pierce
            Medal of the Royal Society of Canada.

1962   Awarded LL.D. by Queen's University, Kingston

1966   Drafts Centennial Spectacle to be produced by Sir Tyrone
            Guthrie in Ottawa; writes one act and continuity of a five-
            act Centennial play.

1967   Elected a Fellow of the Royal Society of Canada. William
            Rupert Davies dies. *Marchbanks' Almanack* published.

1970   Publishes *Stephen Leacock,* and the novel *Fifth Business*

1971   Awarded D.Litt., University of Windsor

1972   Made a Companion of the Order of Canada, and
            awarded LL.D., University of Manitoba; publishes *The
            Manticore.*

1973   Governor General's Award for *The Manticore;* D. Litt.
            from York University and Mount Allison University (New
            Brunswick).

1974   Writes *Brothers in the Black Art* for Canadian television;
            D. Litt. from Memorial University of Newfoundland, Univ.
            of Western Ontario, McGill Univ., and Trent Univ.

1975   *Question Time* produced; *World of Wonders* is published.

1977   *Pontiac and the Green Man* produced

1980   Elected as the first Canadian honorary member of the
            American Academy and Institute of Arts and Letters; the
            Deptford trilogy is dramatized on Canadian radio.

1981   Retires as Master of Massey College; appointed Master
            Emeritus of Massey College. *The Rebel Angels* and *The
            Well-Tempered Critic* are published. LL.D. University of
            Toronto.

1982   *High Spirits* (humor) is published.

1983   *The Mirror of Nature* (criticism) is published; D. Litt.,
            University of British Columbia; D. Hum. Litt., University
            of Rochester.

1984   Elected Fellow, the Royal Society of Literature; World
            Fantasy Association awards *High Spirits* best anthology/
            collection prize.

1985   Publishes *What's Bred in the Bone* and *The Papers of
            Samuel Marchbanks*; D. Litt., University of
            Saskatchewan.

1986   Honorary Fellowship, Balliol College; Canadian Authors'
          Association Literary Award for Fiction; Toronto Arts
          Awards Lifetime Achievement Award.

1987   National Arts Club, New York, Medal of Honor for
          Literature

1988   Receives Neil Gunn Fellowship from the Scottish Arts
          Council and goes on speaking tour in Scotland. Publishes
          The Lyre of Orpheus. Receives the Order of Ontario;
          D.S.L., Thornloe College, University of Sudbury.

Conversations with Robertson Davies

An Editor, His Newspaper, Its Community

Ralph Hancox/1963

From *Peterborough Examiner*, 8 June 1963, p. 4. Reprinted by permission.

Robertson Davies, who has been at the *Examiner* for 21 years this year, and who has been editor for most of the time, and publisher for the latter part of it, leaves for Toronto this weekend where he is to be the Master of Massey College.

He reminisces about his 21 years in Peterborough in a conversation with the present editor. Dr. Davies remains as publisher of the *Examiner*. During his time in Peterborough he has written 20 books (novels, plays, and commentaries) which have been published in a number of languages, played a large part in the development of the Stratford Shakespearean Festival, and in the establishment of Massey College, the Fellows of which will be engaged in graduate studies at 'Varsity.

Ralph Hancox: When you leave the Master's lodgings at Massey College today, you will have been at the *Examiner*—what 21 years?

Robertson Davies: Yes, I came here on March 1, 1942—St. David's Day as a matter of fact.

R.H.: Knowing your Welsh extraction and your interest in saints, I take it that you regard this as an omen of some sort?

Robertson Davies: Unquestionably the coincidence of dates was very important.

R.H.: You came here from Toronto—from *Saturday Night* . . .

Robertson Davies: Yes, I was literary editor at *Saturday Night* under B. K. Sandwell. I admired Dr. Sandwell very much and learned a great deal from him.

R.H.: Wasn't the change from literary criticism to daily journalism a jolt?

Robertson Davies: The *Examiner* is a family newspaper, as you

know. At that time it was owned by my father. I came here as an
editorial writer and as a subordinate to Wilson Craw—who had been
appointed Managing Editor at the beginning of that year—and to H.
L. Garner, who was the General Manager. I don't think I had any
high-flown ideas about what a newspaper should be. I had a family
interest in the *Examiner* of course and prior to that I had written some
editorial comment for the *Kingston Whig Standard*. The change was
not as abrupt as you might think.

R.H.: How did you find Peterborough in those days?

Robertson Davies: It was the early days of the war, of course,
and much of the life of the City seemed to be in abeyance. The army
was here in great numbers.

R.H.: The fact that it was only half its present size would have
made differences from today.

Robertson Davies: There were a lot of young married people
about—as a result of the City being a military establishment I
suppose. Something like this condition will be returning—with Trent
University.

R.H.: You have said on other occasions that Trent is of great
significance to Peterborough.

Robertson Davies: To my mind it is the most significant event in
my time here—perhaps in the life of the City altogether.

R.H.: Can you think of other developments that approach it in
importance?

Robertson Davies: It has always seemed to me that in the past,
Peterborough has been interested in novelties—like Mosport—and
catchpenny schemes. But Trent University's influence will be radical,
it will alter quite deep-set attitudes and opinions. Inevitably, every
place is influenced by its past and Peterborough, because of its past,
has not had a well-developed inner life.

R.H.: Inner life?

Robertson Davies: Yes, you know, a mental inward faculty. In its
early days this place was a lumbering town—vigorous and lively for
its purpose, but its activities were all external. Its inward aspects have
taken a long time to develop.

R.H.: But there have been strong signs of this kind of thing—
painting, music and so on—your own writing for example.

Robertson Davies: That is true and apart from my work; but the

University will give these things focus and it will give them a coherency and an opportunity to continue uninterrupted. When I came here there were tales about the Conservatory of Music which flourished here at one time, the Ladies Choir under Dorothy Allen Park, and the Little Theatre, but they had all run their course and died.

R.H.: But something of the kind was revived, wasn't it?

Robertson Davies: Yes, but it has been spasmodic, the University will give these things continuity. During my time there has been the Coventry Singers, the Little Theatre, the Summer Theatre, and now the Peterborough Chamber Orchestra.

R.H.: And a number of painters. You think that the University will give these things a stable audience.

Robertson Davies: Certainly. And a supply of fresh blood too. The audience for this kind of diversion will be augmented by the University and it will speak with quite a strong voice in the community.

R.H.: It has been quite clear to those who have read the *Examiner* carefully over the years, that your endeavour has been to assert the importance of this inner life.

Robertson Davies: That is true. The notion of what is a learned man has undergone its inevitable change in this City; it is no longer necessarily a clergyman or an instructor at the teacher's college; soon it will be a university scholar; this is a sign of significant development.

R.H.: Your years in Peterborough have embraced your own development too . . .

Robertson Davies: It would be surprising if they hadn't, wouldn't it? I have been here from the age of 28 to the age of 49. This is much of my working life.

R.H.: Of course, but I was going to ask, as a rider to that, if the City had anything to do with the course your work has taken.

Robertson Davies: You mean in my writing?

R.H.: In your novels and plays.

Robertson Davies: Specifically? Well, if it has I am not prepared to disclose whereabouts in my writing 'it is.'

R.H.: How about your work with the newspaper. What in fact have you regarded as the main object of your editorship?

Robertson Davies: The object of my editorship?

R.H.: Yes I don't want to vex you with the question, but you have taken this newspaper along quite determined lines.

Robertson Davies: I wanted to turn it from the trend of newspapers in communities such as Peterborough—that is to say, not make it so that it could be lifted out of this community and put down in any other with no one noticing that there had been a change. To me, it was not primarily a business. It's the 19th Century idea, if you like, that a newspaper is an integral part of a community.

R.H.: But not necessarily a means to change it?

Robertson Davies: Oh, I am as eager to change people as anyone else. I have taken the attitude that all aspects of the affairs of a community should be commented upon when there is something significant to say.

R.H.: That explains the motto: *Humani nihil a me alientum puto.*

Robertson Davies: Certainly; I chose it for that reason.

R.H.: Would you say you had been successful; was this simply to sit in the office and comment?

Robertson Davies: No, but I did less delegation work than you'd suspect. The reason, of course, is precisely the one Joseph Atkinson of the *Toronto Star* gave. If an editor wants to influence people, he doesn't do it running about doing everyone's chores; he spends a lot of time in his office doing his own job.

R.H.: Could you say that any improvements resulted in Peterborough as a direct result of anything the *Examiner* did?

Robertson Davies: That is for other people to say, not me.

R.H.: Will you regret leaving Peterborough?

Robertson Davies: Yes, of course. But we are not leaving it altogether. I have affectionate memories of the City. I remember that it rallied around me when that awful article appeared in *Macleans*— one which thoroughly misconstrued my opinions about the City.

R.H.: That was by June Callwood, was it not?

Robertson Davies: Yes, she was unable to distinguish between me and Samuel Marchbanks, I remember.

R.H.: Massey College is going to be another change. Will you continue to write?

Robertson Davies: Yes, I shall; I regard myself as a writer by disposition.

R.H.: Did you enjoy the reputation that was current about you as a result of your plays and novels—a sort of angry man of Canada?

Robertson Davies: Angry man of Canada? You are thinking of Professor Lower! Angry? I was born when Mercury was in the highest ascendant, that makes me very frivolous.

R.H.: Nevertheless, you did sometimes comment about Canada—critically shall we say?

Robertson Davies: I must admit that I sometimes thought that it was a dull, ill-rehearsed show that someone should put on the road.

R.H.: Do you mean politically?

Robertson Davies: No. Politically, Canadians are very astute—how else would we have survived? Canada is a planned baby—whereas the United States was ripped from the womb of the greatest empire of the time. That is why it has developed myths and Canada has developed none. Look at Champlain—a great man by any standards—rejected. Lord Durham, 'Radical Jack' a first class aristocratic democrat—rejected. Sir John A. Macdonald— 'Old Tomorrow'—rejected. We have all kinds of heroes, but as Douglas LePan said in one of his poems, Canada is 'wild Hamlet with the features of Horatio.'

R.H.: With what result? I find Canadians to be great deprecators—especially of themselves.

Robertson Davies: We are an ironic people; irony and some sourness is mixed in our nature. It is a matter of climate. We are a northern people.

R.H.: Yes, I have often heard you say that we are like the Swedes in many ways.

Robertson Davies: Shaw said that if you go to live in Ireland the climate would make you an Irishman in 20 years. It's the same here.

R.H.: We seem to have strayed from the newspaper and your editorship. Can you perhaps say something that might conclude this conversation satisfactorily?

Robertson Davies: One thing comes to my mind, which makes me proudest when I am thinking of this newspaper, is that its readers now regard it as a forum for responsible discussion. At one time we got hardly any letters to the editor at all. When they came they were from people complaining about parking and garbage and so on.

Today they are serious contributions to discussion—we receive almost 1,500 such letters a year.

R.H.: Our longest letter debate, at least in my years here, has been about God and evolution.

Robertson Davies: Precisely, this is all part of the inner life we were talking about. If it continues,and grows, and expands satisfactorily. I shall be well satisfied.

Conversations with Gordon Roper

Gordon Roper/1968

From the Trent University Archives, Peterborough, Ontario, reference number 87-002-1-82, Gordon Roper Collection. Reprinted by permission of Gordon Roper, Robertson Davies, and Bernadine Dodge, Archivist.

Editor's Note: These interviews were given to Gordon Roper, a colleague and friend of Davies at the University of Toronto, so that Professor Roper could write a critical study of Davies's works. Illness prevented Roper's completing the book, however, and Prof. Michael Peterman of Trent University finished it for Twayne in 1986. Although these interviews are often rambling, their range and depth are extraordinary; therefore they are presented here with only a few editorial changes from the transcript. Peterman's study cites these interviews as having taken place in May 1967, but Roper recently discovered a personal diary entry which establishes the dates as 23, 29, and 30 May 1968.

GR: When you wrote your first five one-act plays, you were primarily concerned with the problems of the amateur players who would be acting them? You were making plays that would act well, and would please amateur theatre audiences?

RD: To some extent, but not extremely so. This is one of the things which used to give me a lot of concern when I was writing plays, because a great many people who wrote about my plays insisted that I was trying to write like Bernard Shaw. It never occurred to me that it was either possible or desirable that I should do so. One of the things which struck me forcibly was that Shaw seems to be writing so clearly for a particular kind of audience, and with a desire to convince them. I never did that. I was really just writing to entertain people, out to entertain them on a good level, and the sort of thing which occurs to me, though of course it's a stupid analogy, is that I tried to write as

9

Mozart composed. He wrote comic operas of his day as well as he could. I was writing amusing plays as well as I could. But I certainly wasn't trying to change anything, or put forward some particular view.

GR: I suppose that's one of the problems a writer has: you have to have some kind of theme to give a thread, or a pattern to the play, and this may seem to the reader, especially to the academic reader, what the play is all about. Whereas the play often is primarily about its own unfolding, or its moment to moment happening?

RD: Yes, the end is primarily entertainment. Another thing that I think a lot of critics don't pay enough attention to is the buttonholing job the writer has to do. You have got to get hold of the reader, make him listen, make him pay attention, and it's no use sitting fifty years in the university and saying what a pity that such and such a writer exaggerates, or seems to scream in print. He knew what he was doing. If he didn't exaggerate his readers would put him down and read something else.

GR: In the universities we are not the readers we should be; we do not try hard enough to read as did the readers for whom the writer wrote.

RD: This is one of the big problems in the universities. So often the response is about 80% intellectual and 20% emotional, while the writer so often is hoping for a big emotional response, and has written his book in a way that ought to secure it. You want to make people cry or laugh; you don't always want to teach them something, or show how smart you are with symbolic constructions.

GR: Some academic critics freeze their emotions as they read, so they can become more objective, more magisterial. . . .

RD: Yes, and one of the problems of the writer today is that the university critic leads the way in saying what's what and who's who. You can see it all around you.

GR: Now, in that talk of yours which you entitled "The Conscience of the Writer" you talked of the older writer and the necessity of his crossing the bridge from his youthful hopes and notions to a mature view of life and of his work. Of course, you talked in that speech as one who has crossed the bridge or is on his way over it. Could you recollect what you felt a writer was when you started to write? For instance when did you first have the feeling that you wanted to write, or that you had to write?

RD: Well, I never had any particular sense that I had to write. It just seemed to be something which I naturally did. Growing up in the family I did. It was part of the day's work. We all wrote things.

GR You must have talked a great deal. It was a talking family too?

RD: Yes, it was a talking family. And also, you see, we all had to turn our hands to the newspaper job sometimes. In places like Renfrew, quite often there was a lot going on and my mother would go somewhere and turn in a report. My brothers both had training as reporters and we just thought that writing was something you did, we never thought of it as a special kind of accomplishment. Just something you had to do like bakers all knowing how to make bread.

GR: You have published eighteen books—fiction, plays, diaries, critical essays, scholarly argument, a textbook on reading Shakespeare, and more of your writing, much more, never has been put between covers. In all your writing you use a wide range of styles. You are many different kinds of writer. One kind is that of the professional journalist: you observe, you put down what you see or think as best you can.

RD: And you really had to be able to do it. Particularly with my father watching you, you had to do it accurately and concisely, because he was extremely persnickety about that. He insisted on the journalist's integrity of getting the times, dates, names, and offices right, because it meant a lot of trouble if you didn't. And no overwriting, no tricks. He was opposed to journalistic clichés; and I know he was very funny at home, talking whole paragraphs about things that had gone in, in journalistic clichés. He used to come home and say "And who do you think is visiting beneath the parental roof this week-end?" because endlessly, weekly newspapers reported that such and such was visiting in town. And my mother was rather ironic about this kind of thing, although in a different way, because she had been trained as a secretary, and she used to be very weary of the style of business letters which began: "Your esteemed favour of even date to hand and contents noted." So you grew up with a sense that that sort of thing was base.

GR: When you were in school, you still maintained the family notion that writing was a natural thing to do?

RD: Really it seemed to me that there was nothing remarkable or praiseworthy about getting good marks in composition. That was something you ought to be able to do, and I never thought much about it. For I never wanted to be a writer. I wanted to be an actor. And I suppose one of the great educative things in my life was the discovery that I wasn't actually a good enough actor to make a life of it. I think I was all right, but not really first-rate.

GR: When did you feel the first urge to be an actor?

RD: Oh, when I was a very small child. My father and mother were keen theatre goers, and liked performing themselves. We had theatres in Thamesville and in Renfrew. It was astonishing how many travelling companies, often of a pretty poor kind, visited these places. They came up the line from Ottawa to Renfrew. In Kingston when I was going to high school and in the summers, I was a playgoer. It was a number one touring town. The things that were on their way between Montreal and Toronto would do a week at Ottawa and then a split week between Brockville and Kingston. So you see things would play for three nights and a matinee in Kingston. That meant a lot of New York musical shows, and performances. For instance, Martin-Harvey included it in his tours, for it was a very good theatre town. It had an excellent theatre which is being refurbished now. The players from Stratford-on-Avon when they came to Canada played for two weeks once, in a big variety of Shakespearean productions.

GR: Did you see your first Shaw in Kingston?

RD: No, my introduction to what was then somewhat advanced drama was a performance of Galsworthy's *The Silver Box* by the University Faculty Players. But the first Shaw I saw was *John Bull's Other Island*; I saw it in Toronto, performed by Maurice Colbourne and Barry Jones. I saw a great deal of theatre as a boy because my parents were so keen on it, and they usually took me with them.

GR: When you were at Upper Canada College in Toronto you spent your summers in Kingston. You saw professional theatre then?

RD: No, I saw amateur productions such as I described in *Tempest-Tost* later on when I was at Queen's University. That was the Kingston Drama Group. Kingston had three amateur societies, the faculty group, a group made up of townspeople, and a group made up mainly of military people. But they all were interchangeable; everybody acted around.

GR: Could we talk about how you have used your own experiences in your writing—the people you have known, local places, local situations? Many critics have commented upon your use of actual people and places.

RD: Well, they have commented upon it, but what astonishes me is that even quite sophisticated reviewers, such as university faculty reviewers, seem to think that you take a person or an incident right out of your experience, and put it down on paper. It is just not so. It would be for me utterly impossible, for my mind does not work that way. I don't know of any writer who ever did that kind of thing. It is transmuted by memory, and a kind of selectivity. The fact is that a whole number of incidents or people may be telescoped into one incident or character.

GR: Often it is not what your eye sees of a person or place but how you feel about that person or place that is transmuted into a fictional person or place?

RD: Yes, and you have a very strong feeling that you are making something. You are not reporting. This isn't journalism; this is creative. I feel that so often that you can spot works, there are so many of them, that merely report.

GR: Like John O'Hara's books; he seems to be compelled to have his eye on what he puts down, and it must go down because that is the way it is.

RD: Yes, but that is done at a high level. I mean the junk you get at the bottom of the ladder of Canadian fiction where the writer has just put down Old Grannie or somebody they knew, and they think it's great. You can spot it because usually there is an affectionate disclaimer that Old Grannie was an old jackass who fell down the well a lot, but, oh, she was a sweet old character and loved God. Well, this is where they are trying to square themselves with their memory of Old Grannie. I don't think a writer who is worth a damn ever deals with any incident or person they feel they have to square themselves with. I bet you when Dickens wrote Micawber it never occurred to him that he had to put himself straight with his father. Because it wasn't his father; he created something new in Micawber. He may have used a lot of his sense of his father, but he is not pillorying him, or coining the raw material of life from memory. It just isn't like that.

GR: In *Fortune, My Foe* and the Salterton books there are characters who had their counterparts in Kingston life?

RD: There are characters who had their counterparts or who had their germ in actual people. It has been somewhat flattering but irritating too that there are contestants for some of those characters by local people who thought they had been put into a book. I never thought of putting many local people in a book; they are not book stuff.

GR: Professor Vambrace in *Leaven of Malice* is so indignant over being made a public figure in the newspaper; he obviously is deeply pleased to be made so indignant. I have heard Peterborough people identify themselves as models for characters in the Kingston books. In the "Introduction" to the New Canadian Library reprint of your *Almanack* I took the liberty of seeing myself in one of the Marchbanks daily entries.

RD: Well, it *was* you. That was quite a different kind of thing, because in the Marchbanks columns many incidents of daily experience were transferred only slightly touched up. That's what the "Diary" was for. People often like to recognize themselves in something described in print; something they have been part of. The "Diary" was much humbler than a great many people supposed. It was supposed to be an amusing column to help to keep people reading the *Peterborough Examiner.*

GR: Coming back to your desire to be an actor. You went to Queen's for three years and then you went to Oxford for three years. Had you ever thought of going to Oxford while you were at Queen's? This is one of the great problems for we who grow up in small Ontario towns. You yearn to be somewhere else—the great good place—but you don't know how to get there.

RD: No, as a matter of fact that happened in a curious way. You see I went to Queens and did quite well there, but was unable to take a degree, because I was unable to matriculate into the University because of a numbness about mathematics. When I was in my third year my father was abroad, and I remember getting a night cable letter from him, saying "What would you think about going to Oxford? Let me know and I will look into it." I had never thought of Oxford before. And it just occurred to him, I suppose, as he was driving through Oxford. So I wired back that I was indeed interested. It had never occurred to me, for one thing because I assumed it would be immensely expensive. So he went there and interviewed or was interviewed by the admissions tutor at Balliol, who said "Well,

ask your son to send us some records and we shall see." And off I
went that autumn.

GR: Do you remember any notion you had before this happened
of what you might do after Queens?

RD: I was going to have to find a job. I had hoped that I might go
to the States or to England and get a job in the theatre.

GR: Since you wanted to do that, you naturally would think of
somewhere outside of Canada. Or more accurately, outside of
Kingston. Then you didn't think of yourself as a Canadian very
consciously; Kingston was your centre; theatre jobs were in New York
or London. You weren't turning your back on Canada?

RD: Not consciously.

GR: At Oxford you were very busy with work in the drama
society. You worked with some senior professional people from
London there. After taking your degree there in the Spring of '38,
you played in a provincial company?

RD: I was fortunate to know some people connected with a
production of the play *Traitor's Gate*, a play on the same theme as *A
Man for All Seasons*, about Sir Thomas More. It wasn't a great play,
but it wasn't a bad play. It was performed in the provinces, and then
came to London. I well remember the great excitement the night that
Winston Churchill came to see it. But it wasn't strong enough to hold
up for very long, so it folded up after a few weeks in London. I had
previously had a note from Tyrone Guthrie who had seen some
things I had done at Oxford, saying "Are you interested in coming to
the Old Vic? If so, come and see me on such and such a date." I was
a very humbly paid actor, and darted down there and was delighted
to be offered a job as a junior member of the company. This was
exactly what I wanted, for it meant experience in a lot of ways, not
only acting, for I had to do some teaching in the school. I taught
nothing technical about acting; I taught the history of the theatre, and
I also had to do a certain amount of literary work for Guthrie,
research on various things, and cutting texts. I went to the Old Vic
Theatre in the December of 1938. I settled in and worked very hard,
for we worked extremely long hours. You started at 10 in the
morning, and it was nothing at all to be there after half-past eleven at
night. You had rehearsal and work all day, and the performance in
the evening.

GR: Where did you live in London then?

RD: I lived in a flat in Maida Vale which I shared with two other fellows I had known at Oxford. One was a chap who was doing subordinate work in the theatre, like myself, but in the management end, and the other was Philip Stead, who used to boast that he was the eighth London *Times* dramatic critic. They used to send him around to things away out in the provinces, or in the suburbs. At Christmas time he was very busy because there were lots of pantomimes. Stead got a little money that way, writing occasional articles. He was very keen on being a theatre historian, and used to spend a great deal of time with Wilson Disher, who knew more about the popular theatre than anybody else. Maida Vale was a pretty scruffy district, because a lot of harlots lived in Maida Vale. We had a flat in a block of flats. We had very little money. Our wants were few; we were all too busy to have time to spend money. We got a kind of meagre breakfast ourselves, and then lunch wherever we were. I ate usually at the Old Vic in the refreshment room. You caught another quick, cheap meal before the performance, and when you went home you had a lot of bacon and eggs which we ate before you went to bed. It would have killed a goat.

GR: Brenda Mathews; Mrs. Davies had come from Australia at 19 to work in the theatre and had become stage manager by the time you joined the company. So Brenda and you were, in a sense, war casualties when war came and the Old Vic closed?

RD: Yes, oh, yes, because as soon as the bombs began to fall the theatres of London were closed and stayed closed for a long time. We weren't in London. The Old Vic was at that time up in Derbyshire at Buxton where it gave a summer festival. And the news was it couldn't go back to London. So we had to go on tour through the larger cities of England. That was a strange experience—strange and very interesting. We toured from the end of August until Christmas when we were at Cardiff. Here the company was disbanded.

GR: At that time your father had a house in North Wales. He used to come over each summer. So you had the sense of two centres, in England and in Wales?

RD: In a way. Though the house in Wales wasn't really a centre for me because I was a different kind of creature. That house involved money and servants and all kinds of things, and I didn't belong in that world. I was getting three pounds ten a week and living on it. That doesn't include that kind of living. So I never had associated myself with that place at that period, or, indeed, ever, except as a guest.

GR: You and Brenda were married in Wales?

RD: We were married in London, but we were going to come to Canada because this seemed to be the best thing to do. We went for our honeymoon to that house in Wales. It was all closed up; we just got along there for a couple of weeks until the boat sailed. To complicate an already complicated situation they had the heaviest snowfall they had had in years, so the only way to get around was to walk. We used to walk a long distance. We would walk four miles across the valley to visit an old friend of my family's who was very old and who had had a stroke; she needed cheering up. So we would walk over to cheer her up, and she was a real woman of her class. We had walked over there at considerable inconvenience to be nice to her and to cheer her up and her greeting to Brenda was: "Well, it is a good thing that you are not a real London lady, or you would never have walked so far."

GR: That wonderful English tact.

RD: Real tact and charm, you know. Poor old girl. . . .

GR: So when you came back to Canada it was to dig in and find a job?

RD: I tried the *Globe and Mail*. Their drama critic, Mason, had died, but they didn't want to replace him; things were paralyzed because of the war; everything was in confusion and uncertainty. I did however get a job on *Saturday Night* with B. K. Sandwell.

GR: So you were not doing what you really wanted to do—theatre work, but what you had been trained to do—write.

RD: No, what I had to do, and could do, because of course I had to earn a living.

GR: I suppose that both Brenda and you must have felt that someday you would go back to London and the theatre?

RD: I don't know that we ever felt that for long. The war was too intense. Brenda did a certain amount of acting for the CBC in Toronto, and every part she got was that of an English war guest, or a refugee, or somebody in a shelter that had fallen in. A very depressing line of work. She was always being brave in a collapsed house.

GR: A Mrs. Miniver?

RD: That kind of thing. You did not know what was coming. I vividly remember in the June of 1940 Mitchell Hepburn, then premier of Ontario, came to our house in Kingston. I remember him sitting at dinner and assuring my father that, before August, Hitler was going to be in Buckingham Palace dictating peace terms. And of course being Mitch Hepburn and having a government office and having the kind of drive and force he had, this carried a lot of weight. But he didn't know anything about it. Those were days full of confusion and uncertainty. There was the question of whether I was going to be in the army. It was a time when the Canadian government couldn't make up its mind about what it was doing. I was called up twice, and both times told to go home and wait until they really wanted me.

GR: Your own performance as a writer since the early 40's has been thoroughly professional. You must have worked at it full time and overtime.

RD: If you really are a writer, you are at it all the time. There are no holidays; you don't really want holidays. And of course this is something I have not only done by temperament but also consciously. I have always since I was a small boy written in my head. I have always been trying to put things in words. My visual sense is less than average.

GR: It is relatively slim; you hear things much more acutely.

RD: Yes, my ear is relatively keen. I think this may conceivably be part of a Welsh heritage. I am very sensitive to rhythms and speech, not very sensitive to visual things. I used to walk along the street—I do this still—making up speeches in my head.

GR: Not really looking at things.

RD: No, not looking. I have been very conscious of this because Brenda has a very strong visual sense. She will say "Isn't that wonderful" of a landscape or building because of the light and colour. I say: "Oh yes, it certainly is," and then I realize I have been looking at it like an old fashioned movie. It is just grey to me. When she calls my attention to it I see that there is colour there but I haven't been aware of it.

GR: Probably in living together these thirty years she has educated your vision.

RD: Yes, just as she has educated me in a whole world of nature, because I know that this is a very real lack. I have never been very conscious of animals or birds. And also my mother-in-law—I'm very fond of my mother-in-law—she has been very important in this way. She has really taught me that the natural world is interesting, and that it is not just scenery against which people move.

GR: Marchbanks hasn't any sense of nature. Once or twice he gives it a whirl; he tries Nature, usually in his garden, but it overcomes him.

RD: I've never been much on nature. I am not proud of it. It is fact, and this has always been my leaning, and I knew that for a writer it is a decided limitation.

GR: But on the other hand your sensitivity to rhythms and to manners of speech is acute.

RD: Yes, so strong that sometimes it is almost an embarrassment. For people often don't recognize that they have any individual rhythms of speech, that they have a way of phrasing. . . .

GR: As you mention in a number of places in the Marchbanks columns we Ontario people often are the last people to realize that we speak with an accent. Stephen Leacock says somewhere that the most natural, uninflected English is spoken in southern Ontario.

RD: Good Lord! What an extraordinary thing to say! Mind you, that blast about the best English: the Irish claim it, the Scotch claim it, I have heard the Welsh claim it, and of course the English, with all their accents, assume it. It's like thinking you have the worst weather in the world.

GR: *At My Heart's Core* has been performed a surprising number of times for what might seem to many to be a play of particular local interest.

RD: Yes, particularly in the West. I wouldn't have thought it would be as interesting in the West as it seems to have been.

GR: You wrote that for the Peterborough Centennial in 1950. Then you wrote *Tempest-Tost*. It wasn't a play, of course, but I wonder if you had first thought of it as a play?

RD: Yes, I had originally had a notion of a sort of light farce. Then I thought it would be much easier, it would give me much more elbow room in the form of a narrative.

GR: Some of the farce-like form remains, and one of its strengths, it seems to me, is the line by line, page by page engagement of the reader; he has little opportunity to stand off and reflect on the action.

RD: This too was the result of something of my experience in the theatre, which had been very interesting and very pleasing. But I came very strongly to realize that if you wanted to produce particular strong effects, you had pretty much to do it yourself, because you rely on the theatre and the big combination of people who are working together. It may come out as you wanted it or it may not. Now, I think that a real dyed-in-the-wool playwright likes the surprise of the thing taking on quite a different shape in rehearsal. But I wanted that thing to come out the way I saw it. Therefore I thought it would be better in novel form than as a play, particularly in Canada where amateur actors caricaturing themselves as amateur actors might be very distasteful, and really not very like amateurs. That might give a lot of offence, and I have much cause to be grateful to the amateur theatre, and I wouldn't want to seem sneering in a cheap, heavy way. I don't think amateur actors have felt that that was jeering at them, because they have all had experience which in some way touches on the experience presented in the book, and the suggestion was that the actual production of the play was rather effective. It was what went on backstage that was funny.

GR: The book does not end up in a farcical tone. The tone has become quite complex, quite mixed. So it would be accurate to say that *Tempest-Tost* in form and material, came out of your own playing experience? You invented some characters, moved them about as actors, and then found you wanted to convey more than that, so moved into a narrative form. Meanwhile you went ahead with *A Masque of Aesop*.

RD: Well that was asked for by the UCC players. I once was a UCC boy.

GR: Then *King Phoenix* came in 1954 just before *A Jig*?

RD: Yes, that was a play which was never well received on the stage. I have a feeling that if it were given a very good, sympathetic production, and were somewhat reworked, it might be good on the stage. That is a play that John Gielgud was extremely interested in, because what I was trying to do in it was to put forward some ideas about life and how it goes that were very near to me. And still are. But you know when I was writing it I was always conscious that any production it got was going to be limited in scope, and this meant I think that the play was slightly cramped. This is a problem that Canadian playwrights had then that they don't have now. If I had been able to write for the kind of production that James Reaney had for *Colours in the Dark* [at Stratford in 1967] it would have been a very different thing. But there was no question of anything of that sort at that time.

GR: The first time you really had a chance to do that kind of theatrical reworking of a play in first-class professional production was with the Crest plays in 1954 and 1956 and then *Love and Libel* in 1960. *Love and Libel* was reworked under rather special circumstances?

RD: Very difficult circumstances.

GR: Did you share in the planning of Stratford? You became a Governor shortly after the first year?

RD: Well, I tell you the Stratford notion I first heard expressed in my father's house in Kingston by Tony Guthrie at Christmas in 1946 because he was saying then what he would really like to do would be to have a big theatre festival, in an amphitheatre tent, and start that way so that the tremendous initial cost of building a theatre would be avoided. He talked very excitingly about it. This meant that when Tom Patterson [of Stratford] approached him he already had been thinking along these lines. . . .

GR: After *King Phoenix* you rewrote *A Jig for the Gypsy* for the Crest. In 1956 you were involved in three plays, your version of Ben Jonson's *Bartholomew Fair* for Stratford, the "Lost Scenes" from *The Merry Wives of Windsor* for Stratford, and the Crest production of your *Hunting Stuart*. But *Bartholomew Fair* wasn't produced?

RD: Well, the problem was that Tony Guthrie wanted it and then they got a new director at Stratford who didn't want it. So there it was. The real difficulty was getting them at Stratford to pay me $500. I pretty nearly had to go and fight them barehanded to get it.

GR: Is there any hope that they might produce it some season?

RD: No, I think not. I think it would have made a very interesting show. But the problem is whether Ben Jonson ever is going to be quite right. It might be someday, but it still isn't right for Canadian audiences. I remember when Donald Wolfit played *Volpone* here how confusing and difficult a lot of people seemed to find it. The language is so packed.

GR: Yes, I remember the Wolfit production. But it had come after his Shakespeares, and his *King Lear* was such a miserable performance; perhaps some of the audience were too sour to respond well to his *Volpone.*

RD: That might be true. But Shakespeare conveys enormous feeling and Jonson conveys enormous thought. And thought is really tough. In that very difficult, knotted language it is not easy.

GR: It is a pity they did not put *Bartholomew Fair* on at Stratford. But it was in that season that you did the "Lost Scenes" which were inserted in their production of *The Merry Wives of Windsor.* Nobody seemed to notice that additions had been made. In a sense you were doing what you had done for Guthrie back at the Old Vic in 1939.

RD: Yes, tinkering with the text, patching.

GR: In 1959 and '60 you wrote what seems to me is one of your finest plays, *General Confession.* You wrote this for the Davises' Canadian Crest? They asked for it?

RD: They asked for a play in which all three could appear. It is interesting how it had its beginning. Donald Davis said "I want to play a big romantic part before I have lost all my hair." I thought: "Now, what is a big romantic part? Certainly Casanova is a fascinating figure." I have always been interested in the *Memoirs of Casanova* which so many people talked about but so few people seem to read in entirety. The thing is that when you read them you become aware of an extraordinarily brilliant, interesting mind, and become aware too of something that Shaw talks about in connection with *Don Giovanni.* This man is a kind of intellectual seducer. He is doing it not because he is a physically ravenous lover; it is always a marvelous challenge. Every new girl is a fascinating problem. This intellectuality is spread over into many other realms. He was an extraordinary gambler, a great concocter of gambling systems and swindles and impostures. He was a man who was very well educated, and perfectly capable of talking with the most eminent men (Rousseau, Voltaire) in ways that commanded their respect and interest. He was a wonderful creature, and I thought a play about him and a play about why he was the way he was, and a play that would exploit the family resemblances of the three Davises, would be something extraordinary. And so I thought that if Barbara played as many of the women as you could get into such a play, if Donald played Casanova, and if Murray played Pal, the sort of doppelganger, the sort of adversary of the part of himself which is always seeking defeat—I felt that they would all have lots of opportunity to do their individual stuff, and yet they would be parts of a single personality. I felt quite thrown down when they decided, rather arbitrarily, not to put it on. Not because they didn't like it, but because they were greedy for the kind of distinction which they felt attached to the play Priestley offered them, *The Glass Cage.* He had written it before as *An Inspector Calls*, and he was grinding the same wheat again. They played it in London, and it was panned.

GR: *General Confession* never has been played?

RD: No. The CBC has looked at it and didn't want it; it would cost too much to cast. And I didn't want it played by an amateur group. It is not a play for an amateur group. I'll tell you, once again (several seasons later) the Davises thought of doing it. Michael Langham was going to direct it for them. And I was delighted because Michael Langham thought it was a great play, thought it had authentic stage magic, and wanted to do it. And again something went wrong.

GR: Langham would have done it well at the Crest. But he might have done it better at Stratford on the open stage?

RD: It would do very well at Stratford. But I am rather debarred from offering things at Stratford because I am one of their governors. This is a bad thing to be. It's a role I've been pushed into, which I don't fully like—that of being a sort of advisor and board member. It means nobody regards you as a creator at all.

GR: I hope there will come a time when we will see it.

RD: I'd love to see it because I think it would go well, because in the course of production it would be necessary to prune and reshape. But I think that as it is now it's a bit old-fashioned. There is nothing in it that is fashionable. But I think there is a lot in it which is perennially interesting.

GR: But if the fashions of the stage of the thirties and forties broke away from Shaw, Galsworthy, Wilde and others, in *General Confession* you moved off in your own direction also?

RD: To some extent. I think it would be fascinating to see them making the tableaus from the things around the stage. And getting on with the acting out of passages from his life, which would be quite sharply differentiated. The amusing one when he was young, the terribly romantic one when he was middle-aged, and the sour one when the girl is riding and beats him up.

GR: It has a much greater emotional range than your earlier plays.

RD: It is odd, you know, that that scene of the girl riding on Casanova's back and beating him around the stage was suggested by a picture which has fascinated me. It is a seventeenth-century print of Aristotle being ridden by a harlot, and she is naked except she has on what obviously is a very expensive fur wrap; I don't know what they called it, some fancy name like "Intellect subdued by Luxury" or some such baloney. It's a telling spectacle. It would have every middle-aged man biting his tongue. . . .

I thought it was the best play I had ever written. Depressing that nobody much liked it. But you know this is one thing which strikes me forcibly, which isn't easy to say for it sounds like whining, but I don't really think it is whining. So many people have told me how successful I have been; they think I have been a success because the successes are all they have seen. But the failures and disappointments they don't see. I had my share of these in the past; some of them were hard. I thought that *King Phoenix* was flubbed and clubbed down, and this play was never performed. I was sorry about those. It really looked as if I might strike twelve with *General Confession*. For Langham would have been a superb director for it with his command of the imaginative possibilities of the theatre.

GR: *Love and Libel* came along shortly after *General Confession*. Did Guthrie suggest that you do something together?

RD: No, he didn't. Quite different. It was the Theatre Guild in New York. I had a call from them saying they wanted to do a dramatization from the book, *Leaven of Malice*. They liked the book, and then they wanted a director for it, and they, not I, suggested Tyrone Guthrie. They were rather surprised to find that I knew him. They got in touch with him and made all the arrangements.

GR: You went to Ireland in the summer of 1960 to work with him? Wasn't he writing his autobiography that summer? Doesn't he mention in it that you read proof for it?

RD: He doesn't mention it at all, but I did. I even wrote a little of the book. After I read one long passage about men he had worked under and learned much from, I mentioned that he had overlooked one fine director; he agreed, and said you write it in.

GR: That must have been an interesting several weeks—it was several weeks?

RD: Three and a half weeks. I went over with a complete script, and he would have nothing to do with it; it all had to be rewritten. It was very difficult because I could never find out exactly what he wanted.

GR: Do you think he knew?

RD: No, I don't think he did. This is one of the problems that is involved in working with many theatre people. They don't know what they want, and they just keep nagging and badgering you until you come up with something they like. The idea that this is expensive in energy rarely occurs to them. This is the way they work; they perpetually try effects and discard them when they don't work. It is not the same when you are producing original material. Particularly for a person of my temperament, for I write rather slowly and deliberately, and I can't just fish up new notions in an instant.

GR: When you do write, you do have some general sense of where you want to come out? But you don't write according to a carefully articulated plan?

RD: The thing was that I was never as sure as the Theatre Guild that a play could be got out of *Leaven of Malice*. But I wasn't going to turn down such an opportunity. I was determined to give the best I could.

GR: But even more than with books, the writing of a theatre script is a gamble? There are so many things that can go wrong that are outside of the control of the writer or director?

RD: Yes. Then, you see, once we had got a script in rehearsal, he kept rejecting large portions of it. And not only Tony, whose judgment I have great respect for, but the actors wanted to get in on the revision. I can remember that inordinate old clown Dennis King storming at a rehearsal, saying I have got to have eight more sure laughs in this scene or I won't play the part. Now how do you provide eight sure laughs unless you are just going to write like vaudeville—if you can, which isn't easy.

GR: But what came out finally was an amusing play.

RD: What came out finally—and this had always been my comfort—was a play which played to crowded houses and an enthusiastic audience for a fortnight in Boston. And I think if Boston liked it, it can't have been all bad because I have an old-fashioned regard for Boston. The papers were kindness itself and the audiences loved it.

GR: It went to Detroit after Toronto, and before Boston?

RD: Yes. It went moderately there. It is a very tough town. I know that Gielgud once said that if aernhing would go in Detroit, you could play it in Central Africa and slay them. It is a tough, queer town. As for New York, you are the prey there to the Broadway system, prey to a lot of things that have no relation to the worth of the play itself. One of them was that we were playing in a huge theatre: no theatre for a small comedy at all, a theatre for musical comedies, like the O'Keefe. This is really tough. And for another we just happened to open on the night of the newspaper strike, so there were no notices. And when they did come out they weren't very good. And so it played four performances, three nights and a matinee.

GR: It did fairly well here in Toronto?

RD: Fair. It never played to full houses at the Royal Alex. As a comedy it was all right, I think, but I felt it had been produced out of its wits, and so did Mavor Moore. You know, things went up and down on strings, and things turned round. It was a kind of vaudeville show.

GR: Yes, when you think back on the performance, you think of some memorable scenes.

RD: There was one scene which I was very well pleased with, and thought it was marvelously well acted. That was the scene between Professor Vambrace and Norm Yarrow when Norm explains the Oedipus complex to the Classics professor. That excellent actor Laurence Harvey played the professor magnificently. He was terribly good—very moving because you felt the depths of the man's affront.

GR: The scene in the book where the professor attacks his daughter also is a very moving one. It is outrageous, but it creates more feeling for him than against him.

RD: And it's his own fault. Then the sad thing—and again in the play it was a very fine moment—when the professor realized that he had lost his daughter because of his own dreadful behavior. And Harvey did this well. Very satisfactory. Also the scene of the seduction of Mrs. Little was very well played. Libby Hall is a brilliant actor.

GR: And the scene with the three in the Cobblers' bed.

RD: It lost some things on the road which I valued. All the scenes of the dreams went. I liked the dreams better than anything. But it just went. It was better as a fantasy than when they tried to make it into a tricky, punchy comedy.

GR: Since you moved into the academic world in 1960, you have written *A Masque of Mr. Punch*. That was asked for by the Upper Canada boys. And for the Centennial you were invited to work with four others on a five act Centennial play.

RD: God, that was awful! It was a frightful hodge-podge. It was a crazy idea and we should never have got involved in it. It wasn't all bad; it was bad as a unity. The piece by Eric Nicol was very good of its kind; the piece by W. O. Mitchell was very good; the piece from the Maritimes was not good, and the piece from Quebec was disastrous. My piece went very well because it was full of children. As a unity the whole was a mess.

GR: Do you feel that you have done your playwriting or would you still like to do another three-acter?

RD: Well, I will give you the best reply I can: nobody wants me to write a play. Since the failure of *Love and Libel* I have been asked to do this Centennial play and the writing for the Spectacle which was rather special, and I don't pretend that I don't think my part in it was pretty good. But I never get asked for plays by groups who perform them, and I guess that they just think I am old-fashioned. Now if I were asked to write a play or if I very much wanted to write a play, I would do it. But I feel that I am out of fashion.

GR: Fashions change. And historically, are they not changing much more quickly now? Fashions become high instantaneously and are discarded as quickly.

RD: Yes, I think they are. What used to be vogues for particular types of plays which would last for thirty or forty years now seem to be run through very fast. I think we will see the end of the Absurd very soon; what will follow it I can't guess. When plays can be made out of what seems to me to be such undramatic material handled undramatically, you just have to wait to see if the theatre will change back again, or change forward into something more theatrical.

But you know when people make a big splash with a play about somebody having premature ejaculations, this seems to me to be kid stuff. Anybody who has had any sexual experience or ordinary gumption or a sense of humor isn't going to be conned by a play like that. Or when you excite an audience by the spectacle of people beating up a baby. This is just pandering to consciousness, because a baby isn't being beaten up in any big cause or for any reason other than shocking the audience. And I don't care about shocking people that way. I want to make them feel, to laugh, and cry. I don't want to startle them. You can only startle them once. It is like that wonderful passage in Peacock's novel where the man is showing his guests around the marvelous garden and he says "But you see the extraordinary surprise as you come around this bank of trees and behold!" And somebody says "Yes, but what happens when you come round it the second time?" A good play ought to be one you can see more than once with pleasure. These plays which depend upon revulsion can only do it to you once. I think there is more that is really shocking and sad in *General Confession* than there is in beating up a baby. The baby is a helpless agent; but when you see a man being brought face to face with himself, that is tough. And you find at the end you have settled for, well, before you chase any more girls you must have your nap, and what really is interesting is breakfast, I think that is amusing and also sobering.

GR: In the forties and fifties you thought of yourself as an artist primarily as a dramatist; or as a dramatist and novelist?

RD: I didn't make a distinction because so many of the people I admire have not made distinctions of that kind. But also I began to realize as I succeeded with one or two professionally produced plays that my temperament was not very well suited to being a playwright because I was sensitive, indeed, touchy, and a playwright has got to be a man of iron. The strain of getting a play to opening night and after is very, very great. Have you read *The See-Saw*? It is a very rough story. I kept a diary day to day all through the rehearsal and work on *Love and Libel*. It is rather the same story. The stress was great. You stop rehearsing about half-past five in the afternoon. There is a performance that night which you have to attend because you have to be there to see how things go. When you rehearse at ten the next morning you have got to have a new scene. Well, now, that means you've got to do it after you come back from the performance. A little of this and you get shredded. And unless you resort to things which I shrink from—you know, booze, and just running on your rims—I don't know how you can do it. Booze has never been any good to me; I don't write any better for a few drinks.

GR: After the give and take of talk during the evening, how do you go back to your room and shut all that out, to write? Do you find that after you have been with people, they are apt to go on talking in your mind?

RD: They go on with you. You can't just turn on your invention. Very often you find your invention won't work to order. And [looking in desk drawers for the diary] it is in this book. There are some parts of it which are: [reading]

Saturday, November 26 (in Boston): Deeply fatigued and when I try to work on some new bits so many keys of the hotel typewriter stick that I abandon the struggle. But I sort out the notes I made last night to take them to TG. Philip Langner comes and we work on them, with a new distribution of scenes. This evening we sold out completely for the first time. Langner thinks it will be a hit; I dare not allow myself an opinion.

Monday, November 28: Rehearsals at 11 and 2. Discussed what lay behind the park scene with Johnnie and Corinne, and later TG said he thought such discussion fruitless. An odd and rather shallow view I think, but perhaps not. Tonight some fuss at the theatre because the Langners, father and son, and Herbert were there, but no Tyrone Guthrie. Word came that he was ill. Stomach. But I think he now saves himself perhaps fearing for his heart. The upshot was that I took the full force of the Langners' displeasure afterwards because the play in three acts was ten minutes longer than in two; the length of an interval. Laurence Langner is always full of notions about cutting and has borne away the script to do some. God knows what he will suggest. What disgusts me is that after the second interval Philip Langner was like a courtier urging me to write a new play and let him have it at once, and afterwards he was barely civil. . . . I now know that we shall know no peace until after December 7, and if the decision is negative the Theatre Guild will know my name no more.

Tuesday, November 29: Last night disciplined gall; this morning dove's milk. The Guild people met TG and me in the downstairs foyer with the stink of disinfectant from the lavs and bullied sweetly about cuts. Was desperately depressed for the first time since this all began. For twenty years I have been a writer and never before have I been in a milieu where every consideration came before literary consideration. And the opinion of anybody—minor actor, money accountant or baggage man—weighed equally or more heavily than that of the author. My disgust is like a cap of fire bearing down on my head. Why would an author with any pride submit to the impertinences of theatre people?

You see, this goes on all the time. It really is rough stuff. I kept that diary because I was determined to know what I had really thought. And of course old King. What happened with him was that one time he demanded a new comic scene, he said the part wasn't long enough. So I wrote it for him. We rehearsed it very, very carefully, and it went very well. On the stage that night he forgot his first line, and just looked blank and walked off again, and left the actor who was on—it was Tony Van Bridge—to improvise something to get him into the next scene. Tony Guthrie was up in the balcony with me and dashed down backstage and found King in his dressing room sobbing and saying "Tony, I'm through. I'm through, old man; my memory's gone. It's the end; it's the end." Just like a big baby. And he had been flogging me unmercifully for the new scene. It is just madness. You have to be very strong, tough, to put up with that. When you are working on a novel, publishers are usually very courteous, and indeed friendly, and if they don't like something you have done, as a general thing it is put forward as an opinion which you can meet with counter-opinion or argument, but you're not just told that tomorrow morning at ten we've got to have a new scene and there must be eight guaranteed laughs in it or else presumably you are going to be driven out of town like a dog.

GR: These are the circumstances in which plays have been written since Shakespeare's time?

RD: Since Aristophanes. Temperament is rife, but mind you it is not all like that. Some of the actors are perfectly delightful. They are real artists. When they want something, they talk to you in the most courteous and understanding way about it, and you would do anything to meet them. I would have done anything at all to take care of Laurence Harvey and the woman who played Mrs. Bridgetower for they both had their ideas, they were firm, they knew what they could do and what they wanted to do. But they also felt that I had a word, too. With such people you can do almost anything. But when you get stars, and managers who are trembling because their money is in jeopardy, you have quite a different class of person. And you just have to face the absurdities of human beings. There was a fellow called Martinique who was the company manager for the Theatre Guild. Martinique was a little man who also was an interior decorator, and had an interior decorator's shop in New York. I think his wife handled the shop. Martinique almost drove me crazy because when we were in Boston he was always clapping me on the back and saying "Baby, we're in. I know it, I know it. I can tell the moment I go in that theatre we're in." The play had a bad first night in New York and Martinique was going around saying "The minute I set foot on Broadway I knew it was a turkey." It's funny, it's enough to drive you out of your wits. He was always coming up to me and saying "You realize what there is in it for you if this is a success? And it's going to be a success, baby. A hundred thousand to put it conservatively." Well, it wasn't a success. It wasn't a hundred thousand; it was nothing at all. That's the way it goes.

GR: Had it gone, would they have wanted another play?

RD: I suppose so. Things would have been very much easier with that other one, unless it had flopped, and then the fireworks would have gone up again. I often laugh inwardly when I am talking with students about playwrights of the Restoration who threw off a comedy to amuse themselves when they were not feeling up to serious things. God, if Congreve had ever had to work with the Theatre Guild!

GR: And at this time you were considering the invitation to be Master of a new Massey College?

RD: That came about very strangely. We came back from New York, feeling very down, and there seemed to be nothing much to look forward to. And I thought, what do I do now? And then about ten days later I had a phone call from Vincent Massey saying "Will you come to see me at the weekend? I want to talk to you about something." So I went down to Port Hope on the Saturday, and he popped this idea at me. It seemed to be what I ought to do. I have wondered subsequently at times whether it really was.

GR: That was December 1960, when you were visiting professor at Trinity?

RD: Yes. But really I haven't regretted it at all. And neither has Brenda. We have often said, "Well, sometimes it is pretty stressful. But would you like to be back in Peterborough, with the phone ringing and people saying 'Are you the fella on the *Examiner*? Well, can you tell me when Winston Churchill was born?'" You know, I had twenty years of it and I don't regret any of it, but that was enough. My father often said after you have had a certain amount of newspaper business you have seen everything that is in it. Massey

College on the other hand has been a beginning. In these first five years we somehow have got the thing not merely up and working but also financed. And now the next five years, if we can make it really put down roots. Because I have never forgotten the chilly reception which the idea had from a number of people on this campus.

GR: When you first thought of writing *Tempest-Tost* you thought of it in the form of a play, perhaps a farce, but then you worked it out as a narrative in order to give yourself more elbow room to create the effects on the reader you wished to produce?

RD: Yes, and then it became a narration also because I had at that time been reading about P. G. Wodehouse. His technique as a writer I think admirable, although I wouldn't want to write like him. There is no question that he is a master of getting on with the job and producing precisely the effects he wants to produce. I once read a very good article by, I think, George Orwell who said that Wodehouse's novels were in effect musical comedies without music. I thought that a very interesting idea, and thought it might be amusing to try something like that—a kind of play without theatre.

GR: That is the way *Tempest-Tost* opens. You introduce your characters by making them talk themselves alive, including Hector. But shortly after Hector is introduced, you used the flashback technique in a block of analytical narrative to show the forces which shaped him in his youth.

RD: I don't think the flashback in that block is done as deftly as it might have been. There is a similar narrative block on the city; that comes first, and there I was trying out a number of techniques. I was also fascinated with film, and marvelled at the way in which they can give you an atmosphere by showing you a great city, and then zooming into its particular parts. You can't watch the films without becoming aware of the marvels they can do in this narrative business, and without wishing to try something like it.

GR: You have portrayed Salterton as a character, a complex character, in *Tempest-Tost*.

RD: Yes, I hoped to show how its particular nature made certain human beings behave in a certain way.

GR: Leacock does something similar at the beginning of his *Sunshine Sketches of a Little Town,* and partly for similar reasons.

And the feeling he conveys about Mariposa is as ambivalent as the one you wished to convey about Salterton?

RD: Yes, but to go back to Hector. What I did about Hector perhaps was clumsily done, and ought to have been spread around a little more carefully, and introduced in smaller bites. I was trying to make it understandable how such a person as Hector came to be in such a place as Salterton, in which he was really a stranger, and it was his strangeness and his lack of understanding that he was a stranger in so many ways that was one of his troubles. He lived so tightly in his own little world. He created his world, partly in response to the world his parents created for him as a boy. Hector is very Canadian. He is the man who has risen above his beginnings which is a thing every Canadian is expected to do. It is absolutely vital to our country, and I don't think in precisely the same way as Americans do it. But we are very determined about it in a Scotch way. Everybody has to better himself.

GR: That was one of the dreams which brought so many of them here in the first place.

RD: I know, and it bites into you. This is the thing that I have to cope with in a way that will make you laugh. I have had to face the fact that I will not die richer than my father. And this is why by his standards and by many other people's standards, I will have failed. I will die, I hope, a very different person, and perhaps have a longer span in the future than his, and this must be accounted as gain. But this is not the real Canadian gain.

GR: But it ought to be. This is a land of many kinds of opportunity; it isn't necessary just to make money to "better" yourself. We do not always have to move up; we can move out from, aside from.

RD: Yes. But this aspiration upwards is the story of our country. And Hector is very much a Canadian. He bettered himself. He got ahead of his father, that poor, broken-down preacher, and that was his success. But it wasn't enough success in human terms. A whole side of his life was neglected, and when that side got him it just possessed him. This is what makes the suicide attempt at the end credible, I hope. Some readers thought I had gone too far in the hanging scene, but I have my own ideas about suicide. Often it is a cry for help. And many a suicide who fails deep down inside himself is aware that his action is a shriek for help.

GR: A desperate "Look at me; let me in."

RD: Hector's cry is "Look at me. Recognize the violence of my love. Look at my need," without much apprehension that this involves other people, and that the girl might have an equally strong need.

GR: You may have thought of *Tempest-Tost* in the beginning as a light farce, but this conclusion rounds it out as real comedy, human comedy.

RD: Well, I hope it did, and yet, you know I was startled when read that article by Hugo McPherson about it because he had seen so much in the book which certainly was not in my own mind when I wrote it. Now, I used to think that this was terrible nonsense on the part of the critic. I don't know now that I think that quite so intently. But it seems to me to be extremely dangerous to build upon what the writer has done an edifice of criticism of that kind. It never occurred to me that the characters in that play had much association with the characters in *The Tempest*. I mean the fact that Professor Vambrace was a kind of two-bit magician and that he had a captive daughter never really quite struck me. I have known many people who have had captive daughters.

GR: Why did you have the Salterton Little Theatre put on *The Tempest* rather than, say, *Twelfth Night*?

RD: Because *The Tempest* probably is my favorite play. I just delight in *The Tempest*. As evidence of that, I christened my first daughter Miranda, and it never occurred to me till long after that people might think I was casting myself as Prospero.

GR: Perhaps the reason why you like *The Tempest* so much is that deep down in those obscure regions of self you do yearn to be a kind of Prospero?

RD: Yes, yes, of course. This is basic to all my work. I very strongly believe, and not as a kind of fancy notion, that life has a strong mythic and fairy tale quality. And people don't recognize that they are living out myths or mythic patterns or archetypal situations. It all seems new to them. It is new to you when you are living it.

GR: But if the power of a writer is in that he deals with particulars rather than with abstractions, isn't it more effective if he starts with observation of particular human activity around him, and then perhaps glimpses some mythic pattern, which then he can use to help him pattern his work?

RD: Absolutely, and not strain too hard to define the myth, because you must look at people and see clearly what people are doing. But starting with myths is fashionable. In judging that Epstein Award at University College a few years ago, I picked up one of the novels submitted. The first page said: "The mythic pattern of this novel is as follows:" and then there was a chart which showed how everybody in the novel represented somebody in Greek mythology. Oh, sweet Jesus, this is just going to be awful, because the writer has taken her myth and strained her story over it as you might strain a drumhead over a drum. And when I read it, it was contorted and contrived in a sad way. Nothing moved naturally. The thing about myths, of course, is that they seem to us to move naturally and inevitably, however strange and extraordinary they may seem. They're really the way things are. After all, we are human beings, and not creatures of infinite possibilities. And you do live much as other people have done in the past.

GR: And so in *Tempest-Tost* you did try to touch deeper and more complex areas of feeling than one does in farce?

RD: I would like to think I did. For one thing, my feeling about Hector was very strong, because I knew the man who was the inspiration of Hector. He was a man who taught me, and I think he was like that, though of course that was not the whole of him. You can't pretend to know anyone wholly.

GR: He was a mathematics master, and a man who humiliated you persistently?

RD: Yes, he was, and he did.

GR: Yet in knowing that, it seems to me that you have handled him at the end tenderly, and with insight.

RD: Well, the tendency to make a clown of him was tempting, I can tell you.

GR: And you do at times. I did mention once that you showed compassion in handling Hector. You didn't agree with that word.

RD: Well, maybe not, but I think I understand better now what you meant. I always think compassion is a somewhat patronizing thing. People ought to be able to stand on their own feet, and if you feel compassionate for them you are taking a superior attitude, and I wouldn't want to do that.

GR: But you haven't stood above Hector; you have felt your way into him.

RD: Believe me, he and I were in a kind of struggle for a long time. I got to know him, and I don't think he got to know me. But I was a kind of challenge to him, and he never failed to meet a challenge. It was rough.

GR: There aren't many other characters in the book who are created as directly from one single real person?

RD: There are memories of a very large number of people, all mixed up, and all people that for one reason or another I was anxious to put down and some of them, I think, I was a little hard on. But one of them who appears a lot in the book, who meant a lot to me, and who I don't think has emerged attractively enough, is Valentine Rich, the Canadian woman who comes back from New York.

GR: I thought she did emerge well as the eye of the tempest.

RD: She is again the person I am so much concerned with—the Canadian artist, and she has had to go abroad to do her work, and she has come back, and she knows why she has to go abroad all over again.

GR: She also could be an Australian artist? There is something of Brenda in her?

RD: Yes, quite true, and I felt that her relation with her grandfather was very interesting.

GR: That is an effective touch at the end of the first chapter when you have her reading the letters. It establishes her depth of feeling strongly.

RD: Well, I hoped it would. I hoped it would give humanity to the character who appears otherwise as *the* Canadian artist.

GR: The Canadian artist will turn up in other characters in your other books. This suggests to me that all the way along, throughout your writing, you have been writing largely out of your own feeling, your own problems, and not following current literary fashions?

RD: Well, that is absolutely inevitable for me. I can't make up things. People think sometimes that you have made up stories. You don't make up stories. If you make up stories you become the kind of writer who is in every way admirable and respectable artistically but you are sort of like Jack London or someone.

GR: Or like Mark Twain, at one level of his work; he would get an idea and it would explode in him, and he would get all tied up in it. But he knew at times that his best work came when he was recalling and reshaping his own felt experience.

RD: I know, and some of the finest Mark Twain stories, like "The Jumping Frog" have the real feel of experience.

GR: I think that is what may have gone wrong with the closing chapters of Huck Finn.

RD: That is what may be wrong in *Pudd'nhead Wilson*. He had a good idea, but it never acquired that firmness of flesh, that vivid reality, that Huck Finn has.

GR: What was the germ from which *Leaven of Malice* grew?

RD: It was a Peterborough incident. We (the *Examiner*) got into a lot of trouble at one time. People were always trying to put in false engagement notices. And one just slipped by. Now that was the only thing that had any relation to the book. Because the people who did it were uneducated people, who had a crude notion of a practical joke. They were in a farm community, and they hurt and humiliated some people. I was very much impressed with the depth of their humiliation and the miserable situation it put them in. And that is what it was, and the way it went.

GR: I thought it was very effective of you to create a newspaper man as one of your centers of emotional and intellectual response. He was not intended as a picture of yourself, I assume, but he gains from being able to use your own newspaper experience.

RD: I wanted to put in a book a newspaper man who was like a newspaper man. People assume that newspaper men are entirely external people, who rush around up to their necks in violent incidents. Many of them, particulary the ones who get responsible positions, are haunted people, and are terribly aware of their communities, of balances, of inter-relationships in their communities. And I thought that something of that would be interesting and instructive, because I have all kinds of letters which have given me the keenest pleasure, especially from people in the States who say that it is really the only novel they have read of newspaper life that has the real essence of newspaper life in it. It isn't fantastically exciting; it is really much more like the theatre than like anything else. Every day at a particular time which must not vary by more than a minute or two the curtain has to go up and the product has to be revealed. And this is far more rigid than people suppose who think that they are always running around, stopping the press. It costs an awful lot of money to stop the press, and you don't do it. And this sense of newspaper stringency I thought was something that would be of interest. And also the notion that editors spend all of their time worrying about whether governments are going to fall. That's not their business. But they certainly have to worry about whether somebody within a mile of their newspaper office has been wronged, or ground down. And you get to feel this way very, very strongly.

GR: I thought a newspaper man, a good man, was privileged in his community, much as a priest or minister or a doctor are, and comes to know much about his fellow townsmen that ordinary people do not.

RD: If he is any good. If he is not just a coarse ruffian. I am afraid that the tendency nowadays when the newspapers are becoming increasingly very big business, is to have these toughs in charge. They really are not awfully tough, but their prime aim is business, and the old domination of the writer and the editor is passing.

GR: And the chances are that they come into the community from outside, and then go on their way outside again.

RD: One of the things that was really remarkable about Ralph Hancox (on the *Examiner*) was that he made himself deeply involved in the Peterborough community. Of course, it was the fact that he was a man of this quality that led him right out again because he was just so good that a lot of people wanted him. I think it is made plain in *Leaven of Malice* that the reason why Ridley, who is a very good man, stays is because he gets a slice of the profits, and this is what would keep him there. Yet he has a sense of isolation in the university community. He was in the community but not of it. He is a lonely man.

GR: There are different levels of feeling in *Tempest-Tost* and *Leaven of Malice*. They are comedies, but sometimes the comedy is close to being satirical. But they are not satires; it seems to me that satire is a useful term to describe the tone and intention of a whole work, not just a tone which crops out at certain places.

RD: I'm delighted to hear you say that because people are always plaguing me with being a satirist. But I don't honestly mean to be. If it comes out that way, I cannot help it. But I don't really mean it.

GR: Yes, if it does come out, there are other tones which come out to contradict it or contain it. You are really concerned with presenting the human comedy as it is, not trying to savage some people or attitudes?

RD: Well, I hope so. But you know there is something else about *Leaven of Malice* that a lot of people were worried by. That was the scene of the Morphews. People said "Oh, you were so cruel to these people; you depicted them as ignorant and stupid. . . ." But you know, I really cannot delude myself. I think it is false democracy to suppose that uneducated people, and particularly uneducated people of coarse sensibilities, often because their sensibilities have been made coarser because they never have had the opportunity to possess any other kind of sensibility, aren't funny. They *are* funny. Just as people that accept this are funny. And why you shouldn't say so, I cannot understand. I think this is again false democracy when you pretend that when somebody is not very well used in life they are more marvelous than if they had not been pushed around by Fate. You must try to see it as it is. And you see there are so many things in that book which are drawn from experience. I remember very vividly the man who came out from Ireland who had been an actor and who wanted to teach elocution and singing. He hooked into one family in Kingston and milked them for an awful lot of their savings. He encouraged the foolish man of the house that he had a fine voice, encouraged the wife to think that she had undiscovered talents, and just conned them by flattering them and sort of massaging their vanity. I remember the awful concert that he gave in a church hall where these poor souls performed in public, and I went because I was very interested in the situation, and it was a grievous thing. They and their friends were happy and pleased, but I couldn't ever get beyond the feeling that they had just been taken in by an ugly, cynical beast. And it was their ignorance and unsophistication, and his lower class, vicious opportunism. I think these are things you have to face. People are not saints just because they haven't got much money or education, and if they are the way they are, that's the way you have to show them, the way you see them.

GR: Throughout your books and plays you create an oppressive sense of the force of ignorance, of meanness of spirit, of evil.

RD: There is evil. And another thing there is I know that gives great offence. For instance I had quite an argument with a newspaper woman in Boston, who hated those scenes in the play *Love and Libel.* There is evil, and there is class. There is no use trying to kid yourself that the people who haven't had education in some of the broader aspects of life are the same kind of people who have. They are not, and they are not going to behave in the same way. They may be people of quite exceptional abilities; this does happen. The world and Canada certainly is full of people who have risen above an underprivileged background and rotten situations, and who have made something remarkable of themselves. They've done it. But there are those who haven't done it, and they are not the same kind of people. There's no use kidding yourself they are. And it isn't that silly, stupid notion of inborn class and privilege; it's economic. If you gave them a better deal they might be fools but they would be fools on a larger stage. As it is they are fools on a petty stage.

GR: The people like the Morphews who have had no experience of the broader aspects of life and who have enormous energy and zeal can corrupt or inhibit many others.

RD: Yes, inhibit the real aspiration in others, and the thing seems to me to be really of our continent, certainly of this country.

GR: In reading *A Mixture of Frailties* again I encountered something that is puzzling unless you have read *Leaven of Malice.* That is, the opening chapters are much closer to the world of *Leaven of Malice.* But once you get Monica out of that world, the novel moves into another world and becomes another kind of fiction.

RD: I am always conscious when I have finished a book that I have muddled things. I think I muddled that. But you know when you are in the thick of things it is hard to see your way clear. And what I really wanted to do was to put the world of Salterton into perspective and compare it to another world which has very different values, with a notion of just talking about how Canadians regard the arts. Still so much of it is platitudes: so many secondary things are more important than primary; talent is not as important as being a nice person or having respectability, or being differential to your betters when your betters are some kind of provincial lawyer or people who control the money. And it was an attempt to explore in some sense the awful provinciality which still prevails in Canada about the arts.

GR: But it goes on to become an exploration of a much deeper theme than Canadian provinciality about the arts. For instance, you show Ma in her provincial mileau at the beginning, from the outside, and she is funny. But later on when Ma is dying and Monica responds to her frustration you are working at a much deeper, inner level.

RD: This is something personal. Ma Gall is in no sense a portrait of my mother, but she had many qualities like my mother and I am very strongly aware that my mother's thwarted imagination and thwarted artistry is something which I have inherited and I must not allow to be thwarted. Circumstances made it impossible for her to exercise her ability as she might have done. You see, I think, I forget exactly what Ma says, but Monica realizes that Ma always had imagination and that Ma never had much of a chance to do anything with it except these awful rowdy performances where everybody ate themselves sick.

GR: So this is one side of the major theme of the book, which I hope I am right in assuming is the education of an artist?

RD: Yes, and with a twist, because the artist is not really a very big artist, not a world-shaking artist like Boris Christoff. It is about a girl who is going to be a pretty good singer. It is an attempt to explore how terribly difficult it is just to be as good as you can be, to fulfil your potential. One of the things that is impressing me increasingly is how hard it is even to be second-rate. I hear students, you know, brushing aside writers and artists of other kinds, and my heart sinks because I think they have no conception of how tough it is to be just as good as that. They brush aside somebody like Oscar Wilde as essentially a second-rate mind, a beta-class mind. How hard to have a beta-class mind like Wilde! They don't understand how tough.

GR: Yet we expect them to comprehend the quality of a first-class mind.

RD: I suppose so, but I fear that they are going to go around teaching in universities and saying "Wilde, of course, is essentially a beta class mind." Who are they to judge anything? Why, some of them have epsilon-class minds.

GR: What you are particularizing in *A Mixture* in flesh and blood people is what you have called elsewhere "the conscience of the artist," the development of that conscience. Along with her technical training, you show that she must become aware of the broader modes of experience, and that above all she must come to some understanding of herself before she is freed to achieve her potential.

RD: Yes, because if artists don't, they are going to come a cropper in middle age. For you must have some self-knowledge by middle age or you can't get past that barrier and you notice this time and time again. This was put to me very forcibly once by a first-class ballet choreographer who said: "Do you know, people say that our dancers go off at a certain age; they don't always do it; they may go on dancing for a long time after what is, for a ballet dancer, middle age (it is about the same age as it is for a boxer), but if they have really understood what they are doing they can teach, become choreographers, do all sorts of remarkable and fascinating things which they haven't done." This is true. If they don't understand, they sort of wither up and they get like old bullfighters, who are a sort of shrivelled class of gnomes whom you see around in Spain. They just put all their eggs in the basket of youth.

GR: Essentially they are energetic technicians.

RD: They have been technicians, and they have thought that what they had was all, and would carry them through. But it won't. They must always be changing. They have lost; they have fallen behind in the procession of life. They have felt they were younger than they really were, and paradoxically if they would only keep up with their age they would always be young in the sense that they would always have energy and inventiveness and something fascinating to do. But if you just cling to what you can do when you are young, well, you know the poetic development of many poets—they just seem to fizzle out by middle-age. They perhaps have been lyricists; they have sung like birds.

GR: But most birds become silent in August.

RD: Yes, well, writers often become silent in August. What Monica has to do is to cast aside just about everything which she thought was the framework of life, and get down to pretty basic facts. And this is I think what everybody has to do if they do not want to find themselves suddenly pathetic in middle age. And it is sad because you can keep up a front, keep up a pretence.

GR: Especially to yourself.

RD: Yes, but I feel, you know, this is what happened to Leacock. He started his career quite late, and he never tried to cross that bridge.

GR: Some of the sketches in his first book were written much earlier, but after the first three or four books there are very few gleams of anything new, or perhaps as good as the earlier work.

RD: And that book about *How to Write* with its chapters on how to write humour are pathetic for a man of his abilities.

GR: But at his best Leacock is a wonderful writer, in the flow of his language, his ease of movement, his timing, his tone. It all seems so natural, and yet of course he must have had to work hard to achieve such grace.

RD: I wonder if that is not owing to his classical education which he mocked so much.

GR: And yet you find the same grace and naturalness in Mark Twain and he did not have a classical education.

RD: No, he didn't, but of course I don't think that Leacock was a figure nearly as important as Mark Twain. Mark Twain was a great natural and that flow of language that he has is really classic because it is so compressed and clear, and really beautiful; even when it seems extravagant, it is never just wordy. But when he started to "write" he was really in trouble. There are things in a book which I read about thirty times when I was a boy—*Innocents Abroad*—which seem written, just written out of Baedeker. At his best he seems to have written as he spoke.

GR: You have that strength of writing as you speak often in your own work. But have a number of styles, and I think your range of styles has grown over the years. Are you conscious of that?

RD: I try always to simplify. My tendency in the beginning was to use style as a disguise. I put up a smart-alec front, of the educated fellow who was full of Oxford jokes that other people might or might not get. But you have to get over that.

GR: It seems to me that compared with *Tempest-Tost, A Mixture of Frailties* is much simpler in prose, and is more telling.

RD: Yes it is simpler; I worked hard for it. I have had to learn anything I have learned with terrible difficulty, because I have a passion for the baroque and the ornamented and the sort of tizzied up.

GR: And yet you wrote day after day editorials for the *Examiner* in which you had to suppress gaudy writing.

RD: I did it consciously, but you know I have had to go through books I have written and strike out all the smart-alec, little Oxford cracks, and it hurts because I prize those; I like those best, and I do know they are no damned good.

GR: Then you write slowly?

RD: Yes, quite slowly. I write and then before I write again the next day, I revise and the revision is very slow and sort of tiresome. Because you can't get continuity unless you do. But it is slow, and I find it very exhausting. As a writer I haven't really got a lot of disciplined energy, and I find that when five separate pages are done I feel beat.

GR: Yes, but when you look at the line of your published books— and they are only a third or so of what you have written over these thirty years, you obviously are a very hardworking writer.

RD: Well, I do work hard at it, but I don't feel that this ought to show. It is not proper to make a parade of your industry. It is vulgar, and yet, you know, when you are talking to rather simple-minded people you wonder sometimes if you shouldn't do so, because I know when I was talking with some students at York University recently and they began to question me, they seemed to think that it would all be very easily done. They asked if I worked hard at it, and I answered "Oh, not any harder than I have to" or something like that, but they seem to think that unless you make a big show of industry and blow about how hard you work. . . . Where do they get these crass ideas?

GR: Well it's fashionable to blame the Protestant ethic. Luther and Knox would be surprised how many Protestants there are in North America nowadays.

RD: And some students have very little notion of the art which conceals art, and I feel that this is strange in students, but I think it is very proper to know how it is done. It is part of the conjuror business.

GR: You do feel that art is a kind of magic.

RD: Yes, if they knew how it was done it would take away a lot of their pleasure, and a lot of your pleasure in doing it, because who wants to stand over the stove and see the eggs being broken?

GR: Or the cook sweat into the soup. May I ask some questions about how you write? Do you find in writing that your first problem is not that of making it clear to the reader, but in writing to make it clear to yourself?

RD: Well, you have to do that before you start, if you can. You have to know what you are going to say. One of the things in writing editorials is that you have to recognize that you can't say all there is to say on the subject. You really can only make a point or two. Because if you try to say all there is to say you are going to write an unreadable editorial.

GR: But in rewriting, you do discover some things you hadn't imagined in your first draft?

RD: Yes, and then you must emphasize it or play it down to give balance to the whole.

GR: That means that when you are well into a book you often have to go back and cut and reshape?

RD: Yes, there is a good deal of that, although I do a lot of that mentally. I fight it around in my head, and that's what I have been doing with this book I want to start writing in the autumn. For quite a long time I have been trying to get the shape and the tone right.

GR: Tone is such a difficult thing for the writer; it is one of the elements the critics so rarely talk about.

RD: Yes, and yet it's enormously important. The tone of a book you ought to get in the first few pages.—I shouldn't say "really ought to" do anything. What I do is to try to write a book so that when people pick it up in a bookshop or library, and look at the first page they'll wonder what's coming, and I feel this is the way it ought to be. This is the story-teller in the market place. If you can't get the reader nailed right at the beginning. . . .

GR: "Call me Ishmael."

RD: Yes, indeed. That is why I started *Leaven of Malice* with the announcement. People are going to be curious about what will follow.

GR: Why did you start *Tempest-Tost* with Freddy's and Tom's conversation? It is an effective beginning.

RD: Yes, I think it is. She is an effective character. The reader doesn't know who Freddy is until he reads on and puts Freddy together for himself, one little surprise after another. It is funny how hard it is to get away with that with the publisher. Immediately I began to read the manuscript after I got it back from the publisher I found the note "Is Freddy male or female?". The editor couldn't wait. It is one of the things you want to find out. If Freddy is really a boy, why does he talk like a girl? And if she is not a boy, why does she not talk like an ordinary girl? And in *Leaven of Malice* when Ridley at the breakfast table first thinks of "Constant Reader," there was a note in the margin of the manuscript: "Who is 'Constant Reader'? Explain." Well, you don't want to explain. That's what you want to find out. Keeping the publisher out of your book is quite a trick. But actually it is the history of my own development because I have been conscious all my life and only comparative recently have I recognized that a lot of people do not share this consciousness that life is a sort of thing that you have been given, that you are expected to make something out of. Just to slide along in it would be base.

GR: Well, it would be like writing the same thing over and over again. The artist has to shape the whole thing, not just present scattered moments. I suppose this goes back to the notion that living is perhaps the most difficult of all the arts.

RD: Yes, and living is like writing a book. You have to be sure that you don't have just a mess when you finish—so far as you can manage it. You can't control it fully, of course.

GR: I often find a peculiar combination in your books of telling a lot—more than most Canadian writers have, and also a reticence— saying much less than some younger Canadian writers now do.

RD: Yes, that might well be. There are certain things which I don't feel are proper in a novel written by me. They may be proper in novels written by other people. This business in *A Mixture of Frailties* about how the young people are supposed to have a son and then they will get the money: Well, I can imagine many novelists would have a number of bedroom scenes where she wept because he was rough, or beat her up because she wouldn't sleep with him, or they wore themselves out. All this seems to be not for me. I am very old fashioned about sex, and I think that sex in a book has to have a real meaning, and not be just lugged in, for kicks. It is too serious, too private, to be just used as a sort of Tabasco sauce.

GR: I think that is one the reasons why *General Confession* is one of the richest plays or fictions you have written. You deal there with

sex as it permeates thought and feeling, as if it had consequences in
the relations between actual people.

RD: Sex is part of life, an enormously important part, but it is not,
I think, what a lot of people seem to imagine it to be. It is not an
isolated area, and it is only an aspect of love in the much larger
sense, the relationship between people. And not necessarily people of
different sexes, or anything like that, but just the manifestation of our
loneliness. This desire somehow to make contact with other living
creatures: that is one way of putting it. It is not the only way, and it
may not be the most important way.

GR: Do you feel that this making contact is fundamentally what
the artist is trying to do; is what drives him primarily?

RD: Yes, this is why the writer has to be straight with himself,
which is extremely difficult. One of the functions of the artist is the
questing inside himself; it is toward self-discovery. But then he is not
doing this just for self-satisfaction, but eventually to be able to get
over the gulf to other people. This is why my preoccupation with the
problem of middle life is great now, because it is the time when you
realize that the sexual side of life is a passing thing; it is no longer the
all-absorbing thing it might have been. It may seem repetitious. And I
feel that this should trigger off an infinitely richer relationship with
other people. By that time you should have got over the embarrassment and the foolishness that makes you stupidly reticent in early
years. You ought to be able to open up, to level with people, because
you have conquered certain of the unimportant things of life. This is
when you ought to glow with relationships.

GR: But after all, reticence in living is like the artist's process of
selectivity in deciding to leave this out, to have this in, in his book. It
is a way of emphasizing, or pointing-up?

RD: The writer who tells all, and only all, over and over again,
finally reduces everything to a stuck juke-box sound, and does not
communicate much. And inevitably he is trying to make a show of it.
This is, I think, a thing you cannot do. You always have to go round.
This is one of the most thrilling moments in drama for me in *Peer
Gynt* when Peer Gynt encounters that huge, cloudy muddle, the
Great Boyg and he wonders how he is going to get through it, and a
voice says to him "Go round about, Peer." He finds he can go round

but he cannot go through it. And I feel this is terribly important in art. You don't just charge right down the middle, wading through blood and guts. You must go round about and you will arrive there with a much greater understanding of the way things are.

GR: It becomes a communion rather than an assaulting.

RD: What you often see in the new plays today is not a communing, it is an assaulting. The writer does not want to communicate with you; he wants to assault you. It's the old nineteenth-century popular melodrama writ large. Often I think the Victorians were more skillful; they had a more human relationship with their audience.

RD: It is made clear at the end of *A Mixture* that Monica is going to have perhaps a very interesting and even a distinguished career, but she is going to have it essentially as the wife of a much more knowledgeable and artistically astute person. She perhaps is the one who will stand forward on the platform and reap in the applause, but essentially she is going to lean very heavily on her husband. That's the kind of girl she is; there is nothing in the world wrong with it, but it's different from what she dreamed when she was going on the ship to England, and she thought of herself as La Gallo, and self sufficient and the whole world's centre. You know a whole lot of artists are like this. You take Joan Sutherland who is probably one of the most famous singers in the world today, but without Richard Bonynge she would be up a tree, because he provides the sort of background, the firm post against which she leans.

GR: This is true in most of the arts? The artist who cultivates his alienation is rarely the artist who works fruitfully over a large span of years?

RD: It is true. I have had the opportunity for observing at fairly close hand occasions where it was the other way, and very splendid the other one can be. One of the most notable is or was till fairly recently Dame Sybil Thorndike who is or was one of the greatest of living actresses; without her husband Lewis Casson she herself would be the first to tell you that she would be nothing at all, because the support, affection, the whole thing which he provides is a very large part of this public figure. Because (as she again would be the first person to tell you) he has more brains than she has and a kind of infallible taste and so she is a great actress with a marvelous intellect and fine critic working with her.

GR: Writers sometimes have had the same kind of supporting and shaping forces in their publishers—Maxwell Perkins of Scribner's for example.

RD: Yes, so it is with a lot of writers, far more than romantically minded people are prepared to admit. You get very remarkable wives.

GR: You have a very remarkable wife.

RD: I depend upon her absolutely. She reads everything I write. I depend upon her advice because without being academically trained for it, she is remarkably good for putting her finger on what is wrong. And one of the things that I have paid great attention to is that she is always cautioning one against the inflated, and grandiose, and the sort of heaven-storming thing which possesses you. You want to bust yourself writing a great thing. And she says "You mustn't be life-workical and masterpiecical; you have got to write it straight." Good advice, because the minute you get lifeworkical or masterpiecical you probably get false and stupid. I have been reading with great interest that life which has just come out in English by Troyat of Tolstoy. The way Tolstoy leaned on his wife was fantastic. I don't think, because he was the kind of man he was, he was able to recognize how much it meant to him. But without her I don't think he would have been anything like the same writer.

GR: Did she die before him?

RD: No. She outlived him. He sort of passed her off when he went mad.

GR: You mentioned how you conceived of Domdaniel and his function at the end of *A Mixture*. You didn't think of him as Prospero?

RD: No, I don't think of him as Prospero. I thought of him as Sir Adrian Bolt. I know a little of Sir Adrian Bolt and I know much better people who know him well. I have the greatest respect for him. Because he is just that kind of man. He is an absolutely marvelous orchestral conductor and musical first-class person without ever becoming a kind of showy ass, something like Leonard Bernstein has. I never thought of him as Prospero.

GR: Going back to our talk about myth. You have said that you do like to start with your own experience, with people you have known, with places, situations, actions you have known; out of them you can work a transformation. On the other hand when you were talking about myth you said it informed a great deal of your work. I didn't ask you then what you meant by myth.

RD: This is a word which in a way I distrust because when I talk about myth I really mean patterns, archetypes, and very often when people talk about myths they only mean classic myths. It seems to me that in a great deal of writing and in a great deal of life what you find is not the patterns you discover in classic myth, but the patterns you discover in fairy tales, and fairy tale is of our own sort of people, Celtic, Teutonic, northern people. You know you meet the lucky third son, and meet the step-daughter who marries the prince, and you meet the princess who doesn't have enough sense to see that a frog is really a very fine fellow, and all that kind of thing. And it is in this curious fairy tale world, the world of the northern forests rather than in the Greek or Hebrew, which don't seem to me to be tied in with our way of feeling as intimately.

GR: This is a curious thing about some academic myth critics; they never get far out of their Garden of Eden, or one or two other myths.

RD: I know; they can never get it through their skulls that on this continent it is really quite different, and the application of Greek myths to modern North America sometimes has to be stretched very far, but these northern things often are really not far under the surface.

GR: In all of your books, and increasingly in the later ones, certain woman figures recur. You have at least three kinds of women in *A Mixture of Frailties*. Has this any connection with Robert Graves' notion about the White Goddess?

RD: Not consciously. I am interested in the idea of the White Goddess. But I think that Graves has codified it in a way which anybody would be crazy to use. You let a thing like that take possession of your mind, and immediately you begin to work falsely. But it really is true that the young, desired, adored girl, and the fulfilled woman with a lover or many lovers, just full of a kind of magic and what is in really first-rate women a kind of solid intelligence; and the old witch, hag, layer-out of the dead—my God, you only have to go to a few cocktail parties and there are witches and hags all over the place. The trouble is they haven't the dignity and zip of a witch or hag; they just have the malignance and bitchiness. You get a figure which Graves seems to leave out: the noble old woman, the splendid kind of life-enhancing person who is like the great old men, the patriarchs.

GR: Yes, for this too goes throughout your work: the value you place on wisdom, the wisdom of experience and high character. In *A Mixture* there are few real fathers apart from Domdaniel, who is a kind of surrogate father.

RD: The girl's father is a flop, and I think without my having contrived or arranged it that way she is looking for a father. She finds a father in art.

GR: Rather than a father in bed, as some novelists would have arranged it.

RD: It was indicated that Domdaniel has been married before, but the attraction isn't strongly sexual. That isn't the main point about it. To me it is so plain, and I get so vexed when people talk as they do so often now as though sex is the only thing that ever mattered. To a lot of people it is secondary, or tertiary, or even less than that. It's there, it's interesting, it's important, and necessary, but it isn't the whole thing. It cannot be or else we would be just chasing one another around like monkeys. It's such kid stuff.

GR: But the mothers are more important in your work? First of all is the dead hand mother. But in *A Mixture* most of the other major figures have a mother or a mother-wife. Persis, of course, has a father, but Giles' mother fades out his step-father.

RD: Yes, that was precisely the case with Peter Warlock. The step-father was a delightful fellow, but he admitted that it was not in his character or his ability to have any influence on his stepson.

GR: The mother's portrait is effective.

RD: It is that woman. It's that woman as well as I could catch her. She was just a featherhead. And she was like a hen that had hatched out an eagle. She would say "I never knew what ailed Phil. I never knew why he wasn't happy. I did everything I could." She just did too much.

GR: Returning to the dead hand. The dead hand isn't only manifested in Mrs. Bridgetower. It's also in Ma, thwarted as she is. You also show the force of the dead hand at work in England and in Wales in the book.

RD: Yes, and it was in my own family. The ruin of my grandfather was a promise he was made to make to his mother on her death bed. He was a very clever young Welshman. He was the first generation of his family really to be English speaking. He sat for a Cambridge scholarship examination and came second in the whole of England and Wales. He was going to Cambridge and he would have had, I think, a very good career, probably in some branch of the Civil Service, because that was the kind of thing he leaned towards. That summer his mother died, and she called him to her bedside and said "Walter, you must promise me never to leave your father. He needs you so much." In those days you had to bear a great disappointment. And Walter promised and Walter was a gone goose from that day. Walter just gave up what might have been a really good life, and tied himself down to things he had to because of this. He could never go back on it. A promise was a promise. If it killed you it was still a promise.

GR: Incidentally does he or someone like him figure in *A Jig for a Gypsy?*

RD: Yes, he is the girl's father, Richard Roberts, because he used to have doubts sometimes about the wonders of the underdog. He was the first Liberal to be elected in that constituency.

GR: The dead hand is not just in individuals; you also show it in your communities. In London, for instance, you picture Mrs. Merry with her lack of imagination, her clinging to certain forms, her self-enclosing ignorance.

RD: And all this awful clinging to a trivial aspect of the past. And never much attempt to find out what is vital about the past, and to renew it, but to cling to nonsense like Mrs. Bridgetower's at-home days. And old Miss Puss who loves to suck around bishops not because a bishop is a spiritual leader, but because you call him "Mi Lud."

GR: Rob, your work compared to that of Morley Callaghan or of Hugh MacClennan is much fuller of a vital past than theirs. The pasts are different. In Morley Callaghan's work it is mostly now, here and now, and a historically undifferentiated sense of man. MacClennan's past extends back to the fathers but not really beyond that in time, and not beyond Cape Breton in place. Your books teem with people, anecdotes, information, feelings out of the past, in Ontario and in Wales and England. Your sense of Victorian life is particularly vivid.

RD: Yes, I feel this has something to do—perhaps without exaggerating it foolishly—something to do with a Welsh heritage. The Welsh are great ones for possessing and continuing the past. I was just reading a few days ago an article by some Americans who had been travelling in Wales last year and who had been startled while travelling over a road and said "This is a very fine road." Their driver who was a Welshman—this was in mountain country—said "Yes, a fine road. They designed it; we built it, and you know they never paid us for it." They said "Well, who are 'they'?" "The Romans." This is not exaggerated. They still hang on onto old grievances, old feelings; they hang onto a lot of old things too. You know that in the area where my father lived, which I know well, they always refer to Powys Castle as the "new castle." Why the "new" castle? because the old castle was about twenty miles away at a place where there hadn't been a castle for 800 years. But they had moved down from there to a new castle, and it is still the "new castle." This is not self conscious. It is as though you possessed all the past and you have a fairly happy consciousness that the future is going to possess you too. You just don't live once, a rotten eighty years. I never conceive why people want to be modern all the time. Being modern really means only now. There is only one instant of time.

GR: In our world the sense of "now" is a great force which can be manipulated to sell people things. This more comprehensive sense of time must also be a sharing of a communal sense by the individual, being one with the past and the future, not just an alienated "me."

RD: The family sense, too. You are an extension of a family, and not the other way around.

GR: Do you see anything parallel to this in your *Leaven of Malice* and *A Mixture of Frailties*; where the value of the necessity of finding yourself in art, not finding art in yourself; being able thus to give, to obliterate for the moment the pulsating self?

RD: Yes: get with something really important. Something bigger than a trivial personal concern. Something which will feed you and if you yourself can feed, if you are very lucky, and be something more than the cheaply and fleetingly personal.

GR: So you think that your feeling about the nature of art may have been shaped somewhat by your Welsh background as transmitted by your family?

RD: I think so, although I wouldn't want to exaggerate it because it sounds as if you are playing the mystical Celt, which is a cheap impersonation. But there is something real, too, in all this.

GR: Does this link up with Jung's notion of art? You have been very much attracted to Jung's writing, much more so than to that of Freud.

RD: Yes, much more than that of Freud. And what Jung seems to feel about art is that it is the job of the artist, without being a job in the sense that you can set to work and do it at will, is to dig into a deep kind of consciousness which is shared by a great number of people, and to find in it things which are of much more than personal importance, or individual importance, and to bring it out and make it live or make it vivid to other people. And this is really what art is about.

GR: What Frost meant when he said it makes him remember that which he didn't know he knew. How does this relate to the way you hope readers will respond when they read a book like *A Mixture of Frailties*? You do write so that the reader will be engrossed line by line as the action happens, but do you also hope that they will respond at a deeper level of understanding—unconscious perhaps—as they approach the last page, and beyond the last page?

RD: I don't honestly know. I just know that some people whose work as artists, people whom I respect, liked the book very much; one of them is Lois Marshall who said that she had never read a book about a singer that she thought was so true. I find this immensely encouraging. But there are many other readers I know who did not think about it for five minutes but who enjoyed it as a story.

GR: And yet there is so much there, in the larger shape and flow of it that is an inside story of an artist. In each of your fictions you have exploited a certain area of human experience from the inside out—have tried to tell the truth about it as it really is; in *Tempest-Tost* it was the experience of putting on a good amateur production; in *Leaven of Malice* it was the truth about being a good newspaper editor; in *A Mixture*, the truth about becoming a singer. You have provided a level of "how to do" interest, as Melville gave ballast to *Moby-Dick* by the level of how men whaled.

RD: Yes, well, I hope that this is so, and you see it is also because of one of my most firmly maintained ideas which is not a very profound one, but is one a lot of people never seem to consider, and that is the truth about something is at least, in part, going to be the exact opposite of that which appears to be the case. This is very often the truth about an individual or about an adventure like putting on a play. And so often what is interesting in putting on a play is not the total result, which may be rather crummy, but it is the fascinating relationships of the people who are doing it.

GR: Our interest in art lies largely in the process than in the result? The going, not so much in the getting there? This curiously is contrary to the whole museum notion of art, to the notion underneath the survey course in literature. Some students have assured me they have taken *Moby-Dick* before; but you haven't taken *Moby-Dick* or any other book until it has taken you.

RD: Yes. This is what, for instance, you become aware of at Stratford, where the plays that are presented are among the greatest we have and yet the goings-on of getting them on the stage are of the utmost fascination. The excitement of art is in the doing, the becoming. . . . Perhaps I can hope that readers to a more modest extent will respond to my writings as I do to Jung's. I find Jung's immensely stimulating, not in a galvanizing kind of way, but an expanding way. It makes the work much larger, more alive, more fascinating, and he does it, not by inventing, but by exploring and revealing.

GR: When Freud on the other hand starts with conjectured answers and then demonstrates.

RD: He is so reductive. You have a great tragedy by Sophocles, *Oedipus Rex*. Well, we all know what that is; it is something children have properly before they are a year old, and that's that. That is a sweet way to approach life. It is reductive. It is fascinating.

GR: But it isn't the fascination that is created by an opening up. Is this what is at the heart of what you meant when you have the Dean preach on education almost at the end of *A Mixture?* Education is the responsiveness to the opening up process life offers?

RD: I really meant quite a lot by that passage. It is the one and only sermon which is preached as part of the Bridgetower bequest. There are people who see things because they have marvelous revelations that are sort of gifts to them; then there are people who see things because they study and get wise; and then there are just wonderfully saintly people who get it because they've got it.

GR: That is Monica. But she works hard too.

RD: She works hard, but she gets it because she is just a marvelous sort of girl. She is marvelous because she is simple, she is not all complicated and tricksy. You see that kind of girl in Persis Kinwellmarshe. Persis is just really a lay; Monica is someone in whom you can repose.

GR: There was a model for Persis, as there was for many of the Tite Street characters?

RD: Yes, she was an Admiral's daughter, too. She was a most beautiful girl, but my God, five minutes' conversation with her would drive you out of your mind. She had a most conventional kind of English mind, but she was a lustful girl. This is where her talent lay.

GR: And yet, would you say that one of the qualities of your Salterton is a particular kind of innocence. There are corrupting forces in Salterton people, but there is also a force of innocence in some of them. Or is their innocence just unawareness? I assume, of course, that Salterton is like Leacock's Mariposa, a very particular Ontario town, but also quite representative of many Ontario and northeastern North American towns as they were before the last War. Domdaniel tells Monica that everybody is in some way provincial. Henry Adams and others have made the same observation.

RD: And you know in Salterton it is like in Canada. We are so innocent in such a lot of ways. We think we're a terrible lot of fellows, but we're not.

GR: Innocents at home, but innocents abroad, too, for you run into the oddest kind of provinciality in the most sophisticated non-provincial people.

RD: Yes, I think possibly the final sophistication is the recovery of innocence. Where you really get where you take things rather simply. You can't have the innocence of peasants; you are not a peasant; you can't be one of them. But you have to work awfully hard to recover that with a few additional hot licks, by getting smart, wise. I think the final gift of sophistication would be a kind of innocent, clean view of things—which doesn't mean a simple, dumb view.

GR: Innocence then is an aspect of integrity? By integrity I mean unity or inner harmony, all things coming together.

RD: Yes, integration. You're one. You're of a piece.

GR: Jung and Emerson aren't very far apart in that belief.

RD: Yes, as Jung once said when he had an interview with a young American journalist, who said "Dr. Jung, we have been talking for nearly two hours and it seems to me that you haven't said a thing that didn't seem to me to be plain common sense." He was rather disappointed, but Jung went off into fits of laughter at the notion that this young man's idea that really great thoughts would be quite unlike common sense.

GR: In *A Mixture* you were not only concerned with presenting the education of an artist, but also the necessary part of that education, the growing up of a person. In reading it recently again, I was impressed with how economically you make each character or action contribute to our illumination of Monica's growth—much as James did with Isabel in his *Portrait of a Lady*. The McCorkills are not only there because they are comic, but primarily because they cause Monica to become more aware of herself?

RD: Yes; the London suburbs are full of McCorkills. They come at a point in Monica's life when she is breaking away and they help her to the sudden realization of some of the limits of Salterton views. She is dismayed by their desire to maintain a kind of Canadian provincialism in the face of a different kind of experience. They represent another form of the dead hand. You can't eat meat from cows who have eaten dirty grass.

GR: The dead hand also is in Ma's armouring Monica with toothpaste and other things you can't expect to get in England.

RD: I remember when first I went to Oxford my mother loaded me up with more junk of that kind that you could possibly use.

GR: It's a way of extending the hold of home.

RD: Yes, making sure you don't use any heathen toothpaste. You're going to be as much of not being away as is compatible with being somewhere else.

GR: The bathroom scene shows that Canadian toothpaste isn't an infallible protection. You both buy the sensational use of sex and, at the same time, relate it to other levels of experience.

RD: You know a lot of people were shocked by that. I had a lot of letters.

GR: Were readers shocked because of the unconventional way in which you depicted it?

RD: But it is the way these things do happen.

GR: Excepting there are very few bathrooms like that.

RD: Well, there was one in that house. One of the things that interested and pleased me very much was that Scott Young said that the seduction scene and the one in *Leaven of Malice* were the best he had read in any book because he said that is how it happens. It is not romantic; there are no silk sheets. It's in boarding house beds, maybe a child next door. There is an awful lot of flannelet pajamas. This is how these things happen. It is only in opera that you get seduced in a place the size of the Varsity Arena. But that scene was a happy invention, I think, because of Monica's innocence. It is also rather sad. They are sad people because they are lonely, and it is rotten for them. But there it is.

GR: A lot of sexual experience may come from loneliness—a way of escaping from one's self, not from simple lust?

RD: Yes, lust is rarer than people may suppose, just that snorting kind of passion. This is a thing that fascinates me about Jung. He puts sex in its place. It's a big place, but not the top place. He keeps pointing out because of his studies of primitives that in real primitive civilizations they had to do dances and have special times to work themselves up before they had a really big go of sex. It wasn't something that everybody was thinking about all the time. A lot of the time they just sat around and whittled sticks.

GR: Perhaps that is still true of our society; we put on a lot of special shows to work ourselves up, and we also have found what the primitives didn't know, how we can make an enormous amount of money out of working ourselves up.

RD: But there is also the implication that if you are under a figure of age and aren't always aching to get somebody into bed, maybe you are not up to par. It's absurd. It's like expecting your clock to be striking all the time.

GR: I thought this came out in Giles. He is lusty often but it is fused and subordinated to his music.

RD: His real energy goes into the music.

GR: How did you get the initials of the names of the three Magi to match the names of Molloy, Benedict and Giles?

RD: Well, I didn't.

GR: But they do. Couldn't a symbolic critic see you contriving parallels?

RD: Maybe they are, but I certainly had no conscious awareness of making them match. I hadn't the faintest notion they did. I chose the names of my characters long before I wrote the sermon scene. I do write my books from start to finish. I don't juggle them around. And so there was no contrivance about that. This may be what old Jung calls synchronicity. He has a fascinating essay on synchronicity which he calls an accusal principle in life. He points out that consciousness is very, very rarely even as coincidental as it looks. It is a kind of what Dickens called a kind of universal dovetailedness. When you hit on a really interesting coincidence, there must be an extraordinary chain of psychic causality behind it. And there might have been something of this kind in what you say, but I certainly had no consciousness of it, and indeed, until you mentioned it this moment, I was unaware of it. You had better point it out in your book; it would make me look a lot smarter than I was.

GR: Yes, and as critic I would have one-upped you, and made me look smarter than I would want to be. But I won't. The ending of that book is very effective. It is a true comic dance of the spirit. The emotional effect on the reader is that all things are coming together, and all things are opening out wonderfully.

RD: It's the finale. It's an opening up like the end of a piece of music where you have to get everything worked up so it just has to come to an end. That's the end. That's the end.

GR: Do you think this complexity of fusing comedy doesn't touch our feeling more profoundly than tragedy?

RD: I have thought so for a very long time. It is silly to be dogmatic about this, but it does seem to me that it is a great deal simpler to fake tragedy than comedy, because I have just finished a study of a period of English drama from 1750 to 1880 when for a long time they were trying to fake both. The faked tragedies you can go through and identify everything that is supposed to make a tragedy, but they are still no good. But the comedies, you know they are flat from the moment you start. You just know they are not going anywhere. Comedy relies so much on what G. K. Chesterton says in one of his very finest passages "the mysticism of happiness." This is something I am very much concerned with.

GR: Is that another way of describing the upswelling of wonder, the suffusion of the sense of well-being, the coming together, the expanding, the unfolding?

RD: Yes, a kind of marvelous sense of the glory, splendor, gorgeousness of life.

GR: Do many comedies help gain this effect in the audience by some kind of hands-all-round dance as the curtain comes down?

RD: Yes. Just last week we were down at Stratford to see *A Midsummer Night's Dream*. At the end of that you are just left breathless, the miracle of splendour.

GR: You aimed at producing this kind of excitement at the end of *Eros* and *A Jig*. In a play of course you are in the hands of your director and actors, but you do provide the script and the initial suggestions. You get this in a modified form at the end of your fictions. At the end of *A Mixture* Cobbler whoops it all together and up on the great organ, making a many-levelled joke of it all.

RD: There again is something that I didn't contrive, but which I realized later on. The birth of a child is always a kind of miraculous reaffirmation of life. It is not only the birth of a child for Solomon and Veronica but it is the birth of something new and splendid in Monica's life; she has at last really got her feet on solid ground. And everybody has got something. There is a moment in it which I do rather like, because I think it is really funny; that is where Monica is looking at the Bridgetower child; "Well, there goes the stack." But she has to come through and be decent, and behave as a first-class artist, and say something nice, show herself pleased, and do it with sincerity. This is really very fine.

GR: In an earlier scene where Monica says no to Veronica's request you present the conflict within her so the reader sympathizes with her complexity of feeling.

RD: Yes, she is torn; but she has to deliver the goods to that man.

GR: But you do stack the cards emotionally against Giles, so although you respond to his death with some complexity of feeling, you do feel the musician in him was greater than his other roles.

RD: A lot of people have said to me that they thought it was incomprehensible that she should find him dead and run away. But I don't know. It seems to me that many people would be quite capable of running away. And Monica is one of them.

GR: This candidness underscores the realism of your comedy. After all, in *Tempest-Tost* sometimes people did things because what they did was funny, not because they were people; but in *A Mixture* people never do anything just to provide comic effect.

RD: In *Tempest-Tost* several scenes were lugged in.

GR: The description of Mrs. Forrester's House Beautiful? Do you remember the House Beautiful passage in Huck Finn: Huck's description of the Graingerford house? Here you do it in the opposite way. You went through it rather than around it. Mark Twain went around it by having Huck describe it from his own viewpoint without being aware that his description is funny. You go after Mrs. Forrester for her taste, you savage her without relenting, and so the reader is apt to take sides with her as underdog, because you are bullying her.

RD: I know; later I was bothered by it. But it was something I couldn't let alone. I think it is a pity for people to diminish themselves.

GR: Or even more so, to diminish other people? Such people smother the play of imagination in themselves, and in others around them? Without money imagination is apt to shrivel, is atrophied?

RD: Yes. Poverty is cruel in so many ways. It closes people in. There is no flowering. It was interesting to read where that worldly man Somerset Maugham had said that he had read so much about poverty and art going together, but he had seen so many careers blasted by inescapable poverty, and he had seen so many people become larger, more charitable, more decent because they could afford it. And this is the economic force. Having to be worried always by the lack of money is terribly hard on people.

Prof. Robertson Davies:
Courteous Conservative

The Toronto Telegram/1970

From *The Toronto Telegram*, 26 September 1970, p. 23. Re-printed by permission of York University Archives. All rights reserved.

Prof. Robertson Davies is a master at the University of Toronto's Massey College for graduate students and senior scholars.

He was born in Thamesville 57 years ago, is married and has three daughters.

Prof. Davies was at one time publisher of the *Peter-borough Examiner* and is now vice-president of the *Kingston Whig-Standard.*

He has written more than 20 books, including novels, essays, plays and literary and dramatic critiques. His latest novel, *Fifth Business,* will be published next month.

Is there a job or profession you would prefer over any other?

I like my own work, which is primarily that of an author, because it suits my temperament. I am an observant, reflective and also an emotional sort of person; I chew over all that happens to me and to people around me, and try to discover what lies beneath the surface of experience. I also like my work as an academic administrator because I enjoy organization and business, and I like being a professor because I like teaching, and meeting students.

Why do you live in Toronto? Would you move elsewhere if you could do the same work there?

I could easily do my work elsewhere than in Toronto, and I like traveling, but Canada is my home, and Toronto is the place in Canada where I can do most effectively the things I like doing.

What worries you most about life today?

I am worried about what appears to me as the de-humanizing of life—the elevation of bureaucracies and machines and systems at the cost of human and spiritual values. So far as it can be, I think life should be intensely personal in feeling, and that every personality should have a chance to develop to the farthest limit that is compatible with a reasonably orderly society. The impulse of much modern science is toward impersonality, and the decline of religion emphasizes this trend, as does the age-old desire of mankind to achieve his ends quickly without having given proper attention to the means whereby he will do so. It is not Ends.

Is there anything that makes you angry about your everyday life? The people you meet? Bureaucracy? What about petty things that are major annoyances to you although other people scarcely notice them?

I do not waste much time in anger. But I am both amused and saddened by the readiness with which people throw themselves into efforts to improve others—the Africans, the Vietnamese, the colored peoples—without having considered what is wrong with themselves. And I am depressed by the readiness with which people attribute to the Russians, or the Chinese, the evil passions and tendencies that make them dangerous themselves, without any awareness of what they are doing.

How do you spend your spare time? What do you read?

I am a walker, a concertgoer, a theatregoer and a reader. I read new novels, Victorian novels, old and new plays, and a great deal of psychology and mythology, with poetry as a special treat. I do not like parties at which it is impossible to talk to everybody. I am extremely fond of solitude.

What's your idea of a perfect holiday? Have you ever taken it?

I should like to spend Christmas in Copenhagen, because I think beautiful cities look their best in autumn and winter. I hope to do so one of these Christmases.

What satisfies you most about your life? What do you like to spend your money on?

I like the pattern of daily life, and I suppose I lead a very orderly life. People tell me that I get a lot of work done, and I could not do that without a pattern. Missing meals, sitting up late and an atmosphere of tension are ruinous to my work. I like spending money on my collection of books, letters, pictures and objects that relate to the history of the theatre, but I cannot escape a sense of guilt about spending for purely personal gratification. I was brought up to think that it was wrong.

Do you consider yourself a rebel in any way?

Because I believe that life should be very personal I am a rebel against virtually all accepted ideas, but I am perfectly happy to observe harmless conventions that make life smooth, like good manners, orderly behavior and courtesy in controversy.

What do you consider your main weaknesses?

In my experience people are the worst possible judges of their own weaknesses, and therefore I had better not try to describe them.

Who do you admire most (living or dead) and why? Who do you dislike most and why?

I admire countless people, but from their multitude I shall name only Johann Wolfgang von Goethe, Carl Gustav Jung, and Thomas Mann. The people I dislike are, not surprisingly, the people they disliked—the people of rigid ideas; of flat, obvious, superficial mind; the people who often possess well-fattened intellects, but under-nourished and rickety spirits; the people whose ideal of life is static, rather than free and growing.

What about your children? Are they rebels? What do you think about their future?

My children are most certainly rebels, but they do not express their rebellion in foolish trouble-making. Their rebellion is against the forces of death, of rigidity of mind, of the subjection of people to systems. Such rebellion is too deep and too constant to express itself in picketing, marching, sitting-in or freaking out; it is the serious, unresting protest of serious people. It is 24-hours-a-day rebellion, not intermittent, showy, status-seeking public uproar. It is rebellion as a way of life.

College Master Looks at His World: Author Davies Finds Youth Little Changed

John Cunningham/1971

From the *Montreal Gazette,* 23 March 1971, p. 7. © *The Canadian Press.* Reprinted by permission.

Author Robertson Davies, master since 1962 of the many-faceted activities of Massey College of the University of Toronto thinks—among other things—that today's youth really isn't much changed from the youth of any other era.

Mr. Davies is the author of the novel *Fifth Business,* a best-seller in the United States as well as Canada. He is a man of thought and ideas and of appraisal. And, at 57, in an interview, he pondered such issues as women's liberation, abortion, religion, education, sex in entertainment, and youth. He showed himself to be a man of both tolerance and strong principles.

A concise sampling of his views goes like this:

Women's liberation: "I didn't know women were anything but free."

Abortion: "A sharp psychological wrench on the woman who has it."

Religion: "A man who recognizes no God is probably placing an inordinate value on himself."

Education: "It is time we took a long appraisal of mass education."

Sex in entertainment: "I'm too old to think naked people having sexual relations is a great thrill . . . unless it has charm, humor or romance."

On youth of today: "It's very much as it has always been."

Mr. Davies, author of 21 books, said he finds it difficult to formulate a definite opinion on the women's liberation movement because "I never hear any reasonable statements of the aims of the movement."

He described demands for equal pay for equal work as "a reasonable aim," but said abortion on demand was another matter.

"If you polled the women who want it you would probably find they are opposed to capital punishment. If it is not wrong to terminate a life at the end of two months why is it wrong to terminate it at age 40?

"If women would declare themselves on capital punishment we'd know better how to estimate their opinion on abortion."

Mr. Davies said he was not "declaring myself opposed to abortion in all cases."

"I just want to know why it's all right to kill a fetus and not a murderer. If we are permitted to terminate life, as a means of convenience, of those who have no defence, why not those who are destructive to society?

"I don't ask for an elaborate plan to get rid of nuisances—just some nuisances."

Mr. Davies said his views on abortion are tied with his religious views, which follow those of the noted psychologist C. G. Jung.

Like Jung, Mr. Davies said, he is religious "on philosophical grounds."

"I not only accept his views on religion but I've found them to be true in practice, which is something else.

"It's impossible to express his ideas in concise and brief forms. He makes it pretty clear that a man who recognizes no God is probably placing an inordinate value on himself. He will inevitably be disappointed with that God, and he's in trouble."

Speaking on education, Mr. Davies said: "I think we should see whether we are wise trying to educate everybody to a high standard the way we are trying to do now."

"There has to be a high level of education so everybody is literate, but whether university or high school education is necessary for everybody is open to question . . ."

Mr. Davies has little use for sex scenes in movies and plays unless they are done "with subtlety and charm."

He described the scripts of *Oh! Calcutta!* as "like something done on stunt night at a military camp."

"I am getting so old I like to have things both funny and dirty if I'm going to look at them."

Mr. Davies, who has active contact with modern youth in his

college work, reiterated that young people today are much the same as they have always been. But, "as one of my friends said to me recently, they are making a lot more fuss about it."

"There is some revolt, but a great deal of it is revolt with good reason.

"A whole generation has grown up which has never known anything but peace. It's a question of whether peace is a natural state. If man doesn't have a war he'll invent one. Youth hasn't seen what war is like, and they are bored."

Described by one critic as "one of the most colorful men in the Canadian literary world today," Mr. Davies is a former editor of the Peterborough *Examiner.* He has also served as literary editor of *Saturday Night.* In 1955 he won a Leacock humor award.

He attended schools in Renfrew and Kingston, Ont., and Upper Canada College and Queen's University. He later obtained a B. Litt. from Oxford University.

Mr. Davies, who said his work day now varies from six to 12 hours, described his position at Massey College in the words of his colleague Marshall McLuhan: "You don't have a job—you have a role."

Because of the pressures created by this role, he does most of his writing from April to October.

"The rest of the time I don't get a chance."

But he doesn't begrudge the time not spent writing.

"It gives you a chance to think what you are going to write and criticize it."

He described the college environment as "an apartment without walls" and a good place in which to develop relationships useful in his writing.

"I like to live in the midst of people and in a real world. I don't know where people get the idea a university is an ivory tower. It's amazing what a complex sub-culture it is."

Mr. Davies said he scoffs at critics who say his fictional characters are unusual and unreal.

"I meet a lot of people who are like people in the books.

"This notion that we Canadians are square, dull people is absolutely ridiculous. There are more stories running around to get written than will ever get written."

Mr. Davies feels that no general opinion covers Canadian writers.

"They pretty much have to be regional writers. No writer writes about all of Canada. He isn't going to write about the whole country unless he's a political commentator. There is no single Canadian writer."

The Merlin of Massey College:
Books In Canada Talks with Robertson Davies
Douglas Marshall/1971

From *Books In Canada*, May 1971, pp. 4, 28. Reprinted by permission of Douglas Marshall.

One can't help envying Robertson Davies. There he sits at 57, a man in his prime and of his time, part Merlin ("The artist is a magician in that he makes something out of nothing") and part hard-headed word merchant ("Writers can't live on the smell of flowers; not only should they get money, but they should get as much money as they or their agents can secure"). He plays the slightly theatrical Master of Massey College and the common marketplace story-teller with equal relish. He basks simultaneously in the creature comforts of recreated Oxbridge and the less material comforts of literary fame. As he toys harmlessly with his mandarin paperknife, the points he makes cut ruthlessly through to the heart of what's wrong with Canadian writing. He has the assurance of the man who practises as well as teaches and practises as well as anybody else in the country. He has the best of both worlds and words.

Behind him are 20 years as a newspaperman, 10 years as a professor of English at the University of Toronto, four novels and 15 other assorted works of fiction, drama and criticism. His latest novel, *Fifth Business,* (Macmillan, $6.95) is a very good book indeed. It is about magic and Original Sin and rural Ontario and several other well-juggled themes and it earned international praise on a scale that can only be described as lavish. The Paris edition of the New York *Herald-Tribune* called it "one of the best novels of this or any other year." The New York *Times* observed that Davies' work "deserves to be better known" and even a few Canadian critics confessed themselves impressed.

Gordon Sinclair, for instance, made a rare voyage of discovery into literature and returned to announce that *Fifth Business* was "perhaps the great Canadian novel." (Sinclair was undoubtedly also impressed by the fact that *Fifth Business* is big business by Canadian terms;

more than 15,000 copies had been sold in the United States and Canada by April, the paperback rights went for $29,000 and there have been three nibbles from film companies.)

The trouble is, we seem to have discovered not just one great Canadian novelist but half a dozen of them—all in the same man. Reviewers variously describe Davies as another Dickens, another Thomas Mann, another Evelyn Waugh, another John Fowles, another Henry James and another C. P. Snow. While one Robertson Davies is mildly flattered, another of him is furious:

"Of course, everybody with a strong narrative style is compared with Dickens and I'm grateful to be compared with Thomas Mann. But I wish to God I didn't always have to be somebody else. I think by this time I'm really old enough to be me and if the critics don't know who I am, they might as well say so. We no longer have that absurd business in music where every girl who can sing is called the Canadian Callas. Why should we still have it in literature? It's awfully offensive to be a two-bit or road-company something else. It's very Canadian, this notion that we have no reality except in relation to some other standard."

One of the other problems that has always plagued the Canadian book world, Davies says, is that it's so small. Publishers double as novelists and novelists as critics: "This is a very bad practice because there's always a certain amount of infighting. If we're going to establish anything serious, people have to start declaring themselves as either writers or publishers. They can't wear too many hats.

"Finally, Canadian criticism must stop being so dismissive. We're too quick to decide whether somebody's any good or not. We take the attitude that a writer is through forever if he misses once. If every Canadian novelist had some sort of cutoff applied to him when he happened to write a book that wasn't quite as good as the previous one, there wouldn't be many of us left."

Better standards of criticism, however, are relatively easy to achieve compared with what Davies really wants for Canadian writers: "What I want I'm not going to get. That is, more *readers* in Canada, more people who actually buy books and are interested in them.

"A while ago I met a woman at a party who was wearing what my wife told me was the most superb mink coat that she'd ever seen in her life. This woman said, 'Oh Mr. Davies, I'm so looking forward to

reading your book but you know the list in my library is so long that I
don't know when I'm going to get it.' You run into that all over the
place. I was told by a Canadian publisher that Canadians hate to buy
fiction. They will sometimes lay out money on a good solid book that
they think has a lot of value but they won't buy novels. And yet, what
does a novel cost them? It costs them between $5 and $6.50. They'll
go to a restaurant and eat that before they've begun to pay for their
booze. *But they will not buy books* and I don't know what in the
world can *ever* persuade them to do so."

Predictably, Davies has even less use for librarians. "We hear so
much propaganda," he snorts, "an enormous amount of it from
librarians, about the marvels of our library system. But nobody seems
to face the fact that our library system *chokes* authors." He fervently
believes libraries should develop a system for paying royalties to
authors (such a system, long advocated by A. P. Herbert, is now
being considered by the British parliament) and dismisses suggestions
that it would be too costly and complex to administrate:

"I don't see that it's really beyond the whim of man to devise.
Admittedly, it's difficult. And it's a nuisance to librarians, who regard
themselves as in a class with clergy and YMCA secretaries as public
benefactors. Why shouldn't they do a little bookkeeping? *They* don't
work for nothing. Their anxiety to get books into the hands of the
public is not so great that they do it cheaply."

Davies is also extremely annoyed by the modern tendency of
educational institutions to *Xerox* any books they want. "The fact is,"
he says, "however much people want to write, they are not going to
do it if they're put in an inferior and disadvantaged position. Nobody
expects painters to give their stuff away or allow anybody to
reproduce it. And musicians have taken a rigid and hardnosed
attitude to copyright regulations. But it's still thought that authors are
simple, unworldly fellows who are just delighted if somebody will
read their work and never think of getting paid for it.

"I think of the author as somebody who goes into the marketplace
and puts down his rug and says, 'I will tell you a story' and then he
passes the hat. And when he's taken up his collection, he tells his
story and just before the denouement he passes the hat again. If it's
worth anything, fine."

Robertson Davies is about to go into the marketplace and put down his rug again. He is at work on his fifth novel. As usual, he is writing on a typewriter ("You can see quite clearly what you've said in cold and impersonal print; I think it was J. B. Priestley who pointed out that there is nothing easier than to fall in love with all those pretty pages of calligraphy"). He will polish up his story with three very extensive revisions before he hands it to his publisher. And then it will be time to pass the hat.

Judging by *Fifth Business*, it will be a good story. It might even be so good that a few more Canadian readers will be tempted to pay money for it. But if you're one of those people who still feels that Canadian authors are simple, unworldly fellows who should be happy just to have their works in a library, don't go up to Robertson Davies at a party and tell him. The Merlin of Massey College is beginning to lose patience with petty-minded mortals. Remember, he can always wave his wand and whisk you into his next story, meanness and all.

Robertson Davies: The Bizarre and Passionate Life of the Canadian People

Silver Donald Cameron/1971

From *Conversations with Canadian Novelists* by Donald Cameron. Toronto: Macmillan of Canada, 1973, pp. 30-46. © Paper Tiger Enterprises, Ltd. Reprinted by permission.

Walking into the porter's lodge of Massey College in the University of Toronto, I was frightened. Robertson Davies, the Master of Massey College, is not only a sensitive and urbane novelist, but also an accomplished playwright, an exceptional journalist, a penetrating critic, a professional actor, a scholar, and an astringent wit. "Mr. Davies," A.J.M. Smith once wrote, "brings the virtues of urbanity, sophistication, good humour, and a certain consciousness of superiority to bear on books, food, wine and social behaviour." I greatly admired Davies' 1957 essay on Stephen Leacock, but I felt his Leacock anthology, *Feast of Stephen,* was a waste of time; Davies in turn considered my *Faces of Leacock* altogether too earnestly academic; and both of us had published these opinions. I knew, too, that Davies was at the top of his powers: at fifty-eight, he had just published *Fifth Business,* by any standard the best novel he had ever written. I expected an ironic and uncomfortable afternoon.

Inside Davies' study—a room so elegantly comfortable can hardly be called an office—I encountered someone considerably more rumpled, more round, and more quiet than the tall, suave, saturnine figure I had prepared for. I began asking questions suited to the man I thought he was, and got disconcerting answers. Was he a connoisseur of wine and cheese? No, he didn't know much about wine and didn't greatly enjoy cheese. Didn't the Salterton novels assume the reader and author agreed on the primary importance of social reality? No: consider the use of sermons, music, fantasy.

Confused, I resorted to the basic principle of good interviewing: when in doubt, shut your mouth and really *listen.* I heard Davies saying that he was very different from

73

his public image, and as I reshaped my view of him I found
myself experiencing a deeply personal, almost confessional conversation.

Cameron: As I read them, the Salterton novels show a very strong
feeling for the Western cultural tradition, and specifically the English
tradition.

Davies: Well, I am interested in a lot of cultural traditions, as many
as I can experience, really, but what is apparent in the Salterton
novels is a Canadian cultural tradition which I don't think gets the
kind of attention in Canadian fiction that it might expect: a sort of
delayed cultural tradition. About the period that I was working on the
Salterton novels, just after the 1945 war, there were still people living
in places like Salterton whose tradition was directly Edwardian, and
who saw nothing wrong with that. They weren't even conscious that
their ideas were not contemporary. I remember driving with my wife
from Peterborough to Cobourg to see a production of Chekhov's
The Cherry Orchard, and in that very beautiful little theatre was an
audience which contained a considerable number of people in
evening dress, which I thought was very curious. They had come
from that district, and they felt that that was the way that they ought
to dress for a theatrical production. After the first act I wandered
around in the corridors listening to the people talk, and they were
talking about the play as if it were a brand-new play—because it *was*
a brand-new play to most of them, and yet they were people of some
education, of a very considerable amount of tradition; they had the
kind of dress clothes that suggested that they were well accustomed
to wearing them and had indeed been wearing them for a very long
time. Suddenly it broke in upon me: these people don't know that
the play is about *them*—and yet there it was. I knew who some of
them were: they were descendants of people who'd come to this
country in the middle of the nineteenth century or earlier; they had
homes in which they used silver which their families had brought with
them, they had pictures of Great-grandfather in his Bengal uniform,
they had connections with England, cousins that they wrote to, and
they still hadn't grasped the fact that an entirely new Canada had

come into being, and that their sort of person was really almost
dinosaur-like in its failure to fit into the modern scene. You could see
what happened in *The Cherry Orchard* happening around there,
because all kinds of places were having to be bought up, and people
didn't quite know why, but somehow the money had run out.
Canada is full of these people, and very rarely do they get written
about, but I write about them, and they're *real*. I could lead you out
on a walk within a mile of where we sit which would uncover a great
many of them. This is something in Canada which people on the
whole don't recognize: we've got a fantastic sort of fossilized past
here. We always talk about ourselves as a country with a great future,
but we never talk about ourselves as a country with a sort of living
past.

Cameron: Don't those novels show a fairly strong current of
sympathy for some aspects of that tradition?

Davies: It is sympathy for the people—not, I think, the tradition—
because they *are* people. They're not caricatures, they're not oddities,
they're not cardboard. They bleed when you stick them and they
weep when they are miserable, and their sorrows and their distresses
are made sometimes more poignant by the fact that they don't know
why things are happening to them.

Cameron: The shape of the novels themselves is rather in the
tradition of English domestic comedy, like Jane Austen or Henry
James, in a way.

Davies: No. No, I've never read a novel by Henry James in my
life, and I don't like Jane Austen. I agree with Max Beerbohm that
the novels of Jane Austen are a marionette opera. I have no use for
them whatever.

Cameron: I'm becoming convinced I've misread you—but I
thought there was an assumption in the Salterton novels of a kind of
accepted social reality.

Davies: The people in the novels agree that there is a certain kind
of reality; I don't think that should be taken as the *author's* opinion.
In *A Mixture of Frailties* there are things which a lot of people who'd
liked the previous two novels disliked very much indeed, because it
suggested that I and they had not agreed upon a kind of little
provincial city which they could be cozy about. *They* may have
reached some such idea—but *I* never did.

Cameron: You must have surprised them even more with *Fifth Business.*

Davies: Yes, and I hope to go on surprising them.

Cameron: Are you working on a novel now?

Davies: Yes, and a great many people, I think, will find it uncongenial. Some people wrote to me and said that they liked *Fifth Business,* but it wasn't as funny as the other books. I'm grateful that they found the other books funny, but I am a little dismayed that they thought that funny was *all* they were. I think it is the writer's duty to be as amusing as he can manage, but not to sacrifice everything to that. That was what happened to Leacock: he eventually got so that he'd rather be funny than honest or sensible or intelligent, and that's bad.

Cameron: Isn't it true that the comedy of the Salterton novels is a rather anguished comedy, too? That the reader is invited to feel for the character who is the butt of the comedy, as well as laughing at him?

Davies: Yes, he is the victim as well as the sort of originator. One of the things I was interested in doing when I wrote those novels was to try and find out whether such novels about Canada were possible, because I don't know of any others that deal with Canadian situations in quite that way—and yet they *are* Canadian. Many people said, Oh, I was trying to write as if Canada were England or as if I were an Englishman—but I'm *not* an Englishman, and Canada is *not* England, and English people found the books quite peculiar.

Cameron: The play you mentioned in Cobourg was Russian. I've talked to novelists who've said that if some things that go on in Canada were written about accurately, the only parallel would be in Russian literature.

Davies: Exactly; I agree a hundred per cent. In fact sometimes I get irritated with people who complain that Canada has no drama. The two great Canadian dramatists are Chekhov and Ibsen. The Ibsen and Chekhov situations can be paralleled in Canada twenty times over—the same sort of rather uncomprehending clinging to the past on the part of a certain group of people, and the same sort of self-satisfied littleness of mind that you get savagely dealt with in so many of the Ibsen plays. What do the trolls tell Peer Gynt is their philosophy? Troll, to thyself be self-sufficient: now that's *Canadian.*

We make modest faces sometimes to the rest of the world, but the
hopeless self-satisfaction of a large number of Canadians is a marvel
to behold.

Cameron: I sense a good deal of Freudianism in your thinking. Is
Freud someone you've read seriously and thought about a lot?

Davies: Yes, I have, as a matter of fact. I am, I guess, one of the
very few people I know who has read Freud's collected works from
end to end. Freud was an enormous enthusiasm of mine before I was
forty; after forty I came to examine the works of his great colleague
Carl Gustav Jung, and I have been, over many years, reading and rereading and reading again the collected works of C. G. Jung.

Cameron: What gave you that serious an interest in psychoanalytic thought in the first place?

Davies: Well, I had been interested in the notion that this line of
thought existed even when I was a schoolboy; when I went to
Queen's University there was a remarkable professor of psychology
there, Dr. George Humphrey, a notable man who later on became
Professor of Psychology at Oxford and wrote a great book on the
theory of learning. Humphrey talked a great deal about Freud, about
whom he knew a lot, and so I was led to read some Freud. One of
the things that enchanted me was that Freud was saying explicitly
things which I had vaguely apprehended as possibilities. This whetted
my appetite enormously, so on I went. Later on I discovered the
same thing in Jung: he had had the intellect and the ability to go into
very deeply, and to talk about superbly, things which I had dimly
apprehended, and so I was eager to follow.

Cameron: Was there something that you became unsatisfied with
in Freud?

Davies: Yes, there was. It was Freud's reductive train of thought,
which is very welcome to the young mind but becomes, I find, less
welcome to the older mind. Freud didn't indulge in this kind of thing,
but a great many of his disciples do: you're afraid of thunder because
when you were little you heard your father fart and then he spanked
you, or something of that sort. Well, this seems to me unworthy of
the human race. It's not the kind of cheap wares in which Freud
dealt, but it's a thing that people have rather developed from his line
of thinking, and much of his thought *is* violently reductive—the
tendency to feel that the sexual etiology of neurosis explains

everything, and that sort of thing. As Jung pointed out, a surprising number of people seemed to turn up in Jung's consulting room with manifest neuroses which were not primarily related to any sort of sexual hangup. As Jung also pointed out, Freud was an extraordinarily brilliant and very, very successful young man—the darling of his doting mother—who had always lived a city life. Jung had led much more the kind of childhood I myself had had—going to country schools, living with country children, knowing country things, being quite accustomed to animals and the sort of rough and rather sexually oriented—but in an ordinary, daily way—life of the country person.

Cameron: Robert Kroetsch, who lives in the States, feels that Freudianism had great success there because it really appeals to something in American experience, in American ideology: the stress between the good guy and the bad guy, the id and the ego, a kind of Manichean view of the psyche.

Davies: That's extremely interesting.

Cameron: And he felt that Canada was a much more Jungian society.

Davies: Ooooh, this is music to my soul! I think we're a much softer-focussed country. In the intellectual life of the United States, there seems to be such a very, very strong Jewish strain—I would not for an instant suggest that that was a bad thing, but it is an intensely *conditioning* thing. This intellectual ferocity and sort of black/white quality is very strong there. We're fuzzier, but I think we're more humane, and that's what I think about Jung, too.

Cameron: Kroetsch thinks that instead of seeing polar oppositions all the time, we tend to see two sides of a conflict as aspects of the same thing.

Davies: Yes, and tending to run into one another. You know, we had a very extraordinary evidence of that, in something which I think of as enormously important and significant about Canada: in the character of Mackenzie King, who was our Prime Minister for longer than any other man in any British country in the world. Mackenzie King seemed to be the quintessence of dullness. When you read in his diary that when he met Barbara Ann Scott, the skater, it seemed that he was expected to kiss her, and he "acquiesced"—a duller, more pedantic, dreary man you could scarcely think to find. But what

was he in reality? A man who communed with the portrait of his
dead mother to get political advice; a man who never set the date of
a general election without consulting Nan Skinner, the Kingston
fortune-teller; a man who could—and I know this from my father,
who knew Mr. King quite well—burst into the most highly coloured
and inflammatory kind of blasphemous, evil language when he was
discussing certain topics; a man who wooed and sort of managed to
keep peace with Québec, but who could talk about French
Canadians in a way that would take the paint off a barn door—this
was Mackenzie King, this was the opposites running into one another,
and this is very Canadian. We now blackmouth him and pretend that
we knew about him all the time, but he got elected over and over
again; he knew this country marvellously, because he was essentially
one of us. We're great withholders, Canadians. This is the sort of
thing that my Australian-born wife has pointed out to me. Accept the
bland, quiet, rather dull Canadian for what he seems to be: it's just
like putting your hand into a circular saw, he'll have the hand before
you know what's happened. I think this is very characteristic of our
country, and when we really come to ourselves, we're going to be a
very formidable people. We're going to be as formidable, I would
say, as the Norwegians, or the Swedes, who are very formidable
nations indeed; perhaps as formidable as the Russians. I was asked in
connection with *Fifth Business* to say what I was trying to do, and I
said that I was trying to record the bizarre and passionate life of the
Canadian people. Well, I was dropped on by some Canadian critics
who said, There I was again, trying to make an effect and talking silly
so that people would look at me and think what a fancy fellow I was.
They were the ones who didn't see what it was. I was speaking the
exact truth, but they didn't see it. They *will not* see it.

Cameron: As you spoke, I thought, This is the theme of *Fifth
Business,* the contrast between—

Davies: —the appearance and the reality, the grey schoolmaster
and the man who was burning like an oil gusher inside.

Cameron: Yes, and at a place much like Upper Canada College,
which many people consider the epitome of all that is dull and
Edwardian.

Davies: You see, they don't know anything about it. I went to
Upper Canada College, and I know what a tempest of passion can go

on in there. I'm not saying it's individual to that college; it would be
so in any school in Canada, I would think, if you just look. Some
very rum things indeed go on in them. Every once in a while a
teacher commits suicide, and everyone says, "Poor old Joe, you
wouldn't have thought it of him, would you? He seemed to be the
most level-headed fellow there ever was." But if you knew old Joe,
you knew old Joe had been nutty as a fruit cake for years. I went to a
collegiate institute for a while where there was a mathematics teacher
who used to break down in the class sometimes; he would burst into
tears and say, "Children, I don't want to die of cancer, I don't want to
die of cancer." He eventually did—he wasn't doing it at that
moment—but we just thought, well, that's the way old Scotty is. The
goddamndest things go in schools.

Cameron: How on earth did you get that astonishing report of the
experience of a foot soldier in the First World War? You were all of
one year old when the war broke out.

Davies: I wish I could give you some helpful and illuminating
answer, but I can't. I just remember when I was a very little boy what
some men who were in the war had said. They weren't very
eloquent, but it was like that. But I will tell you something which is
not dissimilar. In *Fifth Business* I mentioned that the Bollandists, and
particularly Padre Blazon, wrote in purple ink. Well, I've never seen a
Bollandist, and I think I've only met one Jesuit, and I've never visited
the Bollandist Institute in Brussels, or anything of that sort, but I did
meet a man in New York called Israel Shenker, who knows the
Bollandists very well and is, as far as a layman and a visitor can be, a
familiar there. And he said, How on earth did you know that they
wrote in purple ink? I said, Well, I divined it—and he nearly fell out of
his chair with indignation, because this was a bad answer. But it
seemed to me very probable that they would write in purple ink, and
apparently they do.

Cameron: But you didn't check.

Davies: How would you check? Would you write to them and say,
Please, do you write in purple ink? It isn't a matter of importance,
really. I could have just said that they wrote in ink. But it seemed to
me—wellllll, *purple* ink. And they do.

Cameron: That's quite a chance to take. Certain kinds of reviewers would be very indignant if they were to find out that in fact it was green ink.

Davies: Yes, they would. They'd be very cross.

Cameron: The religious theme that emerged so strongly in *Fifth Business* had been seen primarily in social terms, I would have thought, in the Salterton novels.

Davies: Yes, but not entirely in social terms. In *Leaven of Malice,* the Dean makes it pretty clear what his view is about what has been going on, and puts in his ten cents' worth in a way I hoped was of some significance. Only a very few people have ever commented on the Dean's sermon at the very end of *A Mixture of Frailties,* which is going on contrapuntally to what the girl Monica is thinking when she's trying to make up her mind whether she'll marry Domdaniel or not. The Dean is preaching a sermon on the revelation of God to man in three forms: a revolution of nature for the shepherd, a penetration by wisdom for the wise man, and a sort of natural grace to Simeon. I think most people look at the italics and say, Oh yes, this is the sermon, and hop to where it gets to be roman type next, to see whether the girl's going to marry the old man or not. But it's there, and it's vital to the book.

Cameron: Has religion something to do with your interest in Freud and Jung?

Davies: Yes. One reason I was drawn to the study of Freud and of Jung was my religious interest, because I very quickly found that for my taste, investigation of religion by orthodox theological means was unrewarding. You never got down to brass tacks, or at least nothing that I ever read did so. You started off by assuming that certain things were true, and then you developed all kinds of splendid things on top of that. I wanted to see about the basic things, so I thought that I would have a look at people who had had a wrestle with these very, very basic things, and Freud was one of them. Freud decided that religion is essentially an illusion: well, I read that, I studied it and chewed on it and mulled it over for quite a long time, but it never fully satisfied me, because it seemed to me that brilliant as Sigmund Freud was, there have been men of comparable brilliance or even greater brilliance who had been enormously attached to this concept which seemed to him to be nothing better than an illusion. One of the figures which bulked very large in my ideas was St. Augustine. I was very interested as a very young boy to discover that I was born on the day of St. Augustine, the 28th of August, and also on the birthday of Tolstoy and Goethe; and I thought, Oh, that's great stuff, splendid! This is an omen. But St. Augustine was a man of the most towering intellectual powers, and if he was willing to devote his life to the exposition of this thing which Freud called an illusion, I felt that the betting couldn't all be on Saint Sigmund; some of it conceivably ought to be on St. Augustine. And there were other figures whom I thought intensely significant. I thought a great deal about it, and then I gradually began to look into the works of Jung and found a much more—to me—satisfying attitude towards religion, but it was not an orthodox Christian one. Orthodox Christianity has always had for me the difficulty that it really won't come, in what is for me a satisfactory way, to grips with the problem of evil. It knows an enormous amount about evil, it discusses evil in fascinating terms, but evil is always the other thing: it is something which is apart from perfection, and man's duty is to strive for perfection. I could not reconcile that with such experience of life as I had, and the Jungian feeling that things tend to run into one another, that what looks good can be pushed to the point where it becomes evil, and that evil very frequently bears what can only be regarded as good fruit—this was the first time I'd ever seen that sort of thing given reasonable consideration, and it made enormous sense to me. I feel now that I am a person of strongly religious temperament, but when I say "religious" I mean immensely conscious of powers of which I can have only the dimmest apprehension, which operate by means that I cannot fathom, in directions which I would be a fool to call either good or bad. Now that seems hideously funny, but it isn't really; it is, I think, a recognition of one's position in an inexplicable universe, in which it is not wholly impossible for you to ally yourself with, let us say, positive rather than negative forces, but in which anything that you do in that direction must be done with a strong recognition that you may be very, very gravely mistaken. This is something which would never satisfy the humblest parish priest, but I live in a world in which forces are going on which I am unable to tab and identify so that the tickets will stick. I just have to get on as well as I can. Various kind people in writing about my books have called me an existentialist, and they won't believe me when I tell them I don't know what an existentialist is. I've had it explained to me many times, but the explanation never really makes enough sense to me to cling. But I have tried to state for you what my position is, and I fear that I've done so clumsily and muddily—but if it comes in clumsy and muddy, it's just got to be that way. Better that than slick and crooked.

Cameron: Perhaps people find it difficult to believe that you don't know what an existentialist is because of your public *persona*, your image, to use the ad-man's word, which—

Davies: —my image, if I've got an image—I suppose I have—has been made for me by other people. Nobody wants to listen to what I want to say. They want to tell me what I think.

Cameron: Well, the image presents you as a man of formidable learning, formidable intellect, and fearsome wit, a man who *would* know about things like existentialism.

Davies: I am not of formidable learning; I am a very scrappily educated person, and I am not of formidable intellect; I really am not a very good thinker. In Jungian terms I am a feeling person with strong intuition. I *can* think, I've *had* to think, and I *do* think, but thinking isn't the first way I approach any problem. It's always, What does this say to me? And I get it through my fingertips, not through my brain. *Then* I have to think about it, but the thinking is a kind of consciously undertaken thing rather than a primary means of apprehension. Also intuition is very strong in me; I sort of smell things. As for this wit business, it's primarily defence, you know. Witty people are concealing something.

Cameron: What are you concealing?

Davies: I suppose I'm concealing—hmmm. Well, you see, if it were easy for me to tell you, I wouldn't be concealing. I think I am concealing a painful sensitivity, because I am very easily hurt and very easily rebuffed and very easily set down; and very early in life I found out that to be pretty ready with your tongue was a way of coping with that. You know that is a thing which is attributed to Dunstan Ramsay in *Fifth Business*. He was always "getting off a good one". If you can get off a good one once or twice a day, people don't rasp you as much as they otherwise might. They'll do it enough, however defensive you are.

Cameron: Humour does fend people off.

Davies: It's defensive and it's diverting. You know, you suddenly send the dogs off in that direction, instead of straight ahead.

Cameron: One can't talk about these things as a dispassionate interviewer, you know. I've been known in some circles as a person of fairly savage humour myself, and I've always felt that in my case it had to do with profound feelings of insecurity and inadequacy, the sense that I was surrounded by people who knew their way around the world and were at home in it in a way that I wasn't.

Davies: Yes, there's that, and there's also a thing which I expect you have experienced, and which certainly I've experienced: the narrow outlook, and limited sympathies, and want of charity, and general two-bit character of what is going on under your very eyes, which drives you to the point of great extravagance. It comes out in terms of savage, bitter humour, just because you don't quite want to go to savage denunciation, but you want to blast them like an Old Testament prophet. Instead you just swat them around with the jester's bladder. But the impulse is the same.

Cameron: Isn't the effect actually more powerful through humour, and isn't that something else one easily learns?

Davies: Yes, but you haven't learned enough. If you blasted them like a prophet, they might forgive you; if you mock them like a jester, they'll *never* forgive you.

Cameron: That's true, but it's because making a joke of them is a more powerful thing to do.

Davies: Yes, I guess it is, in a way. Oh, it hurts, it stings, and they never forgive it. Now this is interesting: you have made a confession and I've made one. That's why one makes jokes, very often.

Cameron: To make confessions—?

Davies: No, to keep things at bay. It's a sort of distancing thing very often. Not always: I mean, sometimes you do it out of sheer lark.

Cameron: There's a very interesting interplay in your work between theatre and fiction. I suspect that for you theatre is a metaphor of some dimensions.

Davies: It's the element of illusion in life, the difference between appearance and reality. In the theatre you can be in the know about what makes the difference, and it is fascinating that you can know what creates the illusion, know everything about it, be part of it, and yet not despise the people who want the illusion, who cannot live without it. That's important, you know. So frequently it is assumed that if you know how something's done you despise the people who don't. You don't do that in the theatre. You respect them; you know that they know a good thing when they see it.

Cameron: You were with the Old Vic at one point, weren't you?

Davies: Yes, not for very long. For three years, until the war broke out and there was nothing further to be done there or anywhere else in England, so I came back to Canada.

Cameron: You are very strongly Canadian, aren't you, in that you have a very clear sense of who you are and which national community is yours.

Davies: Yes, indeed, and this became very very clear to me within the last two or three years. I've always felt strongly Canadian, which doesn't mean complacently or gleefully Canadian, but Canadian; and my father, who was a Welshman, had always, during the latter part of his life, spent all his summers in his native country, in Wales. My mother was Canadian and her family had been here for a very long time—since 1785 as a matter of fact—but my father always had this extraordinary pull back to his home country. Living in this college, I live in a house which is attached to the college, which is not mine, and when I retire I will not, of course, continue to live there. So my wife and I thought the time had come when we ought to have some place where we'll be able to go when we retire. Distant though that time may be, now is the time to get on with doing it, because when you're retired you don't want to plunge right into the business of finding a dwelling or building one. So we thought, what'll we do? Will we acquire some place in England and retire there? Now this would have been comprehensible because there was this very strong pull of my father's towards the old land, and my wife's family, who were Australians, were always drawn back to England as the great, good place in which all important things happened. We talked it over and decided that my wife had been a Canadian far longer than she'd been an Australian, and that I was really a Canadian, and that to leave this country would be like cutting off my feet. So we built a house in the country in Canada. That was a decision which went far beyond a matter of bricks and mortar. It would be impossible now to leave with the feeling that you'd left for good. We like to travel, we like to get around to see what's doing, we're both terribly interested in the theatre, which means we like to get over to England where the theatre is most lively, and to the continent. But to live, to have your being, to feel that this is where you're going to get old and die, that's another thing—and that's *here*.

Cameron: That doesn't surprise me now, but it might have before I met you.

Davies: Well, as we've said, the popular notion of what I am and why I do things is very wide of the mark. The mainstream of what I do is this sense which I can only call a religious sense, but which is not religious in a sectarian, or aggressive, or evangelistic sense. And also, you know, I really think I've now got to the age where I have to consider what I am and how I function, and I can only call myself an artist. Now people hesitate very much in Canada to call themselves artists. An extraordinary number of authors shrink from that word, because it suggests to them a kind of fancy attitude, which might bring laughter or might seem overstrained—but if you really put your best energies into acts of creation, I don't know what else you can call yourself. You'd better face it and get used to it, and take on the things that are implied by it.

Cameron: What sorts of things are implied?

Davies: A duty to be true to your abilities in so far as you can and as deeply as you can. I think this is where Leacock didn't trust himself, didn't trust his talent. He never thought of himself as an artist, which he started out, I'm sure, to be; his early work has a lot of that quality about it. He decided he was going to be a moneymaker instead, so he didn't become the writer he might have been, and I think that's what you've got to do if you have a chance. I couldn't have said this until fairly recently—you know, you step out in front of the public and say, I am an artist, and they shout, Yeah? Look who's talking, and throw eggs. If you step out in front of them and say, I am a humorist, they say, All right, make us laugh. You can do that fairly easily, but if you say, I can make you feel; I can maybe even make you cry, that's claiming a lot.

Cameron: And do they want you to do it?

Davies: They really do, but they want to be sure that they're in safe hands before they let you do it, because you might be kidding them: you might make them cry and then say, Yah, yah, look who's crying; I did that as a trick—and that's what would hurt them. They're sensitive too. It's an awareness of approaching and retreating sensibilities that is not very easy to acquire.

Cameron: W. O. Mitchell refers to the reader as a "creative partner".

Davies: *Yes!* Exactly! And you've got to find the way to make it possible for him to create without being ashamed of himself afterwards. Only an artist can do that.

Robertson Davies
Paul Soles/1972

Transcription of "Take Thirty," CBC Television, 3 January 1972.
Copyright 1972 Canadian Broadcasting Corporation. Reprinted
by permission of the CBC, Robertson Davies, and Paul Soles.

PS: Professor Davies, we can look back on the course, the path, our lives have followed up until now, and I think the route is not what most people would have expected at the start. I'm wondering if in your case you are what you thought you wanted to be.

RD: Well, I had only vague general ideas about what I wanted to be. But I certainly had no idea of being the kind of thing that I am now. I never thought, that I would be, for instance, in academic life, and although I thought I would probably write things, I never thought that I would write quite the sort of things that I do write.

PS: You're not a disappointed man that it didn't work out the way you expected?

RD: Oh, no. Not in the least. It's all been better than I'd expected because, you see, my ideas were vague. I just generally wanted to do something interesting, but I hadn't clear or determined orders to give to destiny about the matter.

PS: I think it was Winston Churchill that said your fate is your character. Would you believe that?

RD: Well, if he said it, he was saying something that people have been saying for about three thousand years. And, of course, to some extent, character is destiny; but it's very difficult to determine precisely what character is because you're confronted so often by people who seem to be admirable characters but who never have any luck. You remember that Napoleon used to say when someone was presented to him as a possible candidate for high command, "Yes, but is he lucky?" And that's very important. You can have all kinds of talents sometimes in a man who never gets a break, and it's inexplicable. Now it may be something in his character but it's not something that you can see from outside.

PS: Well there are various things that determine the way our lives go and they're like instruments of fate. I'm thinking, first of all, of world events. Now in your own case, the Second World War had an influence on your career because you were with the Old Vic, and the Old Vic closed shut.

RD: It's true. And, of course, the war had an effect on virtually everybody who was living at that time, and all kinds of people—I was only a trivial instance—but all kinds of people had things pulled out from beneath them which they'd been depending on. Luckily, I was a young man and could sustain that kind of change. But there were many people whose lives were very sharply wrenched out of line by that sort of thing.

PS: And then sometimes a person can see more in you than you can in yourself, and an outside person can be an instrument of fate.

RD: Yes, they can, but it is not always a happy thing when someone sees a possibility in you of which you are unaware because very frequently such people are exploiters, and they find something in you which they then work to death. I've seen this happen very frequently and it happens not infrequently in the theatre where someone finds that someone is good for a particular kind of part or to create a particular sort of situation, and they're worked to death, and pretty soon they're through. This happens very strikingly and rapidly with mannequins, you know, fashion models: they're the girls with rumpled hair, or the girl with the black eye, or the girl whose mouth is dribbling, or something like that. In a year there are fifty pictures of her like that and in eighteen months she's gone. Nobody wants her any more. They've had all that she can do. She'd have been better off if she'd just been somebody who posed like an ordinary girl and not a special sort of girl.

PS: But then the accident of where we're born can have an influence. Now what do you think of Canada as a country in which to realize one's life?

RD: Well, I don't know. It's extremely difficult to say anything that makes sense about a thing like that. Certainly, there are reasons why, for instance, it wouldn't be a good thing to be born at this moment, in say, the city of London. It's hideously crowded, there are a great many people for almost every job that's available. It is a country which is, in some ways, tired, and the outlook for a beginner isn't perhaps as good as it is here, but on the other hand, if you want to practice certain sorts of trades, or professions, or crafts, there's not much use in trying to do them in impossible places. Canada is a bad country if you want to be the world's foremost orange grower. And there are an awful lot of people trying to grow oranges in Canada, and they're not having much success with it.

PS: But, it's a kind country to some occupations, and it's a cruel country for other occupations.

RD: Yes, that's perfectly true. And yet, the situation changes. Now I can remember—and so can almost any other Canadian who isn't really quite a young person—when the theatrical profession in Canada was hardly existing. It was a kind of orange-growing profession. But within the time of my observation, it has become an extremely alive and good profession for a lot of people. Tyrone Guthrie said a few years ago that the prospects for a young actor of talent in Canada were probably better than they were anywhere else in the world. There were more openings and a more understanding world for him to confront.

PS: You've written quite a bit about Canada in the past. And I wonder if I can take a quotation out of context as people in the media often do. You said: "Canada has one of the highest rates of insanity in any civilized country and one reason might be that life in many places is so desperately dull." That was written some time ago. Have things improved?

RD: I'm not sure that they really have. I think I would have to change that statement about the insanity rate in Canada now because it's changed. It's not as high now as it is in some other countries. And our suicide rate, we've lost our lead in that, too, though still we have a high rate. But, as for dullness, I think we are disposed toward dullness, that we're perhaps more nationally conscious of it than some other dull nations.

PS: I think in the past you've felt that it's a country that doesn't favor cheerfulness, too.

RD: That's very true. We don't favor cheerfulness. I think this is a kind of pioneer hangover. The pioneers were not a cheerful, high-hearted lot. They were courageous, and they were enduring, but they were pretty difficult to live with. I can speak with some certainty about that because on my mother's side, all my family were pioneers. And there were a long series of family stories going back several generations about them, and, oh, they were a grim lot. But they were the characteristic of the generality of the time. They suspected joy, they suspected any unforeseen good fortune, and they suspected strangers, and they were suspicious of just about everything. Mind you, if you lived your whole winter eating salt pork and punkin' sass, you'd get suspicious.

PS: When you talk about the role that destiny plays in our lives, it suggests that fate intends changes in one's life, and I think many people fight change, don't they?

RD: Yes. Fear it. Many people are desperately afraid of change, they think that what they want is change. But it isn't genuine change. They just want an improvement in what they already have, they want more of the same: they want the same job, but they perhaps don't want the same boss; they want more pay, but they want the same or perhaps less work. They don't really want change, they're afraid of any true change.

PS: Now in your own case, in 1960, when you described yourself as well into middle age, you changed from being a publisher of a newspaper to the academic world. Is this a disappointing change to go from the exciting environment of the newspaper world into the remote and isolated university life?

RD: No. No. The university is not dull, and newspaper life, as I experienced it, was not exciting. You see, I was an editor and a publisher, and this is not the exciting side of newspaper life. This is the side which is routine. You have to make things happen, and you have to make them happen almost at split-second timing. You know, in a newspaper, unless you start the rotary press within three minutes of the same time every day, you'll be late getting your paper out, you'll be late getting it to the newsboys, you'll be late catching the trains for the people who carry the rural routes. It's just like a theater, the curtain must go up on time, and *your* job is to see that it does that. Now, there's a lot of nonsense, really, about the excitement of the reporter's life, but any honest reporter will tell you that that sort of excitement, like the excitement of war, is something you've exhausted before you're thirty. A newspaper life is an interesting life, and it's a very good life. But it is a routine life, and I had had enough of it.

And so I was glad to go to another kind of life which was the academic life, and although it has its areas of rigidity and its routine, which must be followed, there was for me an expansion in the realm of the kind of people that I met and the circumstances under which I met them. A newspaperman—an editor that is to say—usually meets people professionally when they're angry or when they want something. Now an academic, meets a different sort of person, and although a lot of absurd things are said about the pleasure of teaching and meeting young and inquiring minds, and so on and so forth, there is a lot of pleasure about exploring truly interesting things at considerable length with other interested people, and that is what my work area allows me to do now. And I enjoy it very much indeed.

PS: Do you think that this is the last change you're going to see?

RD: No. No. No, no. I don't imagine so at all. I shall retire from academic work eventually, and then I will be doing something else, and there's so many other things that I can think of that I'll be doing that it's really hard to determine only a single one.

PS: You don't plan to retire permanently at 65?

RD: Well, what does one mean by retirement? There are a lot of things that I want to do that I haven't had a chance to do, so far. When I was a boy, my kind and thoughtful parents had me, quite elaborately and expensively, instructed in playing the piano. I've never played the piano well. Now when I retire, I should get down to work and see if I can really do anything. That'd be interesting, that'd be interesting to do. I've got so much work put aside that I want to do after I cease to do a sort of regular daily job that I don't imagine that I will have very much time to worry about whether I'm retired or not. I remember when my father retired, he never had the slightest doubt about what he was going to do, and he was busily occupied until he was in his eighty-eighth year when he finally died.

PS: When I was told by a man who works for a large company that a survey revealed that people who retired from the company at the age 65 lived an average of one and one-half to two years. They were presumably hale and hearty until they retired, then they didn't last.

RD: Yes. Well, there are a lot of people, I suppose, like that.

PS: Is it a good idea to take up something else?

RD: Ah, well, you know, really, taking up something, saying "Ooh! I'm 55, in ten years I'll have to retire, I'll take up collecting moths." It's ludicrous. It makes you want to do moths, in which case you've probably been doing it all your life. You're just really focusing your fear of retirement on the hobby or whatever it is. The world is full of sad people who are trying to make themselves happy with something they don't really care about or like, but they feel they must have an occupation. I heard about a man whom I knew for many, many years who had had an extremely absorbing job which he was doing very well indeed, and he was indeed, the head of his company, and why he retired, I don't know, but when he got to 65, he retired and he was dead in about fourteen months. But he tried to occupy himself with a miserable little dog. A man who has been running an important and interesting business all his life can't devote his attention to a small dog. There's nothing wrong with the dog, but it's not a life, for anybody.

PS: I've met people, too, who are about thirty-five years old and who felt somehow that they'd reached the top of their careers, they couldn't see any place to go, and they felt life was empty for them. They were discouraged because they couldn't see where to go next.

RD: Yes, and I expect that hell is very heavily populated with just exactly that sort of person because, you know, somebody who fears that he has exhausted what there is for him to do and what he can do at thirty-five, is a fool. What he means is that he's become the sales manager of International Widgets or some wretched thing. That's not a life, that's not a thing that should occupy a man. People drive themselves terribly hard at these jobs, and they develop a sort of mystique about something which does not admit of a mystique. A thing to have a mystique must necessarily be—have many aspects, many corridors, many avenues, many things that open up. Well, this is not to be found in the business world, and I've known a lot of first-class businessmen and they all tell you this. People have told me that in their particular business there's nothing to be learned that an intelligent man can't learn in eighteen months. But if you've learned it in eighteen months and if you're exhausted by the time you're thirty-five, it's nobody's fault but your own if you haven't found something else to do.

PS: That's right, I can see that. If your own career has gone as you said, did you purposely go after jobs with a sense of reaching for them or did they come to you?

RD: No, jobs came to me. But I don't mean by that that I sat grandly and waited until the job approached cap-in-hand. There was a job around and I grabbed it because I wanted the job. I never felt that I was one of those gifted people who could wait and pick and choose. When there was a job that would provide a living nearby that I could do, I wanted the job and tried very hard to get it. But it wasn't always a job which I had foreseen. I mean I became an assistant to B.K. Sandwell on *Saturday Night* and it never crossed my mind to do that. But there was a job and I needed a job, and, well, I just needed money, and I was delighted to be able to and get a job, to get a job that was such a pleasant job.

PS: What about the importance of willpower in life, of knowing what you're trying for and going after it?

RD: Well, I don't know. I've known some people who've had a lot of willpower but it seemed to me very often to betray them. They tried too hard. You know there is a thing that psychologists sometimes talk about, the law of overcompensation. You know, you try too hard, and you inhibit success. It's like when you're playing golf, you're trying too hard to do it right, and you stiffen up, and you foozle the shot. This can happen in a great many other things, too. If you're always telling life what to do, life won't like it, and will revenge itself very sharply upon you. And that's not mystical nonsense. It's a thing that you can observe. The people who are always bullying their careers, are, well, you know, it's like picking at a sore, it will never get well, nothing good will come of that. You've got to be a little bit easy and take what's coming to you and sometimes what's coming to you may not be entirely what you want or very pleasant, but you can't always have it your own way [laughs]. You know people are always saying that, but it's perfectly true and a lot of people never realize it.

PS: Is it important also that we should know what we are, each one of us?

RD: Yes, that is extremely important, but it is uncommonly difficult. And it is virtually impossible, I think, until you get to be quite old because you're perpetually changing, you're perpetually unfolding, you're perpetually becoming a new person. I remember when I was just a little boy, when my seventh birthday was approaching, my brothers told me that you change completely every seven years. When I became seven, there wouldn't be a bit left of the person I'd been when I was a baby. I woke up on my seventh birthday, expecting to be somebody quite different. Well, I wasn't really, but in a way that is true. You're changing all the time, so to know what you are is virtually an impossible thing, but to try to know what you are is a duty of ordinary mental and moral health.

PS: What do you see as what a person is, if you can break it down? The brain, for instance, the intellect?

RD: Oh no, no, no. That's only a part, and often an extremely deceptive part because we all know people who haven't got very much brains but they are very good and useful people because perhaps they're extremely reliable, or perhaps they are, well, they're people who can be trusted, or they're people who are brave, they have some quality which is other than purely intellectual, which is extremely important, or maybe they're just enduring, to be able to hang on when things are really tough. That's important, and an awful lot of very brilliantly intelligent people, can't do that. Very intelligent people are frequently extremely enduring, but people just below that level snap sometimes, very fast. So just intellectuality isn't by any means the whole story. In fact, it's a betrayer.

PS: But then our own constitution in each one of us has something of what we can do in life, doesn't it?

RD: Exactly. Everybody, well, it's very old, everybody knows this. Anybody who's interested in the astrology in the newspaper knows that if you're born under one sign, you have trouble with your chest, and if you're born under another sign, you have trouble with your digestion, and this, that, and the other. Everybody is physically different, and their points of stress and their points of endurance are different.

PS: What about the soul in all of this? Is there a place for religion in your scheme of things?

RD: There is no place—well, life without religion, I think, is out of the question. But, of course, when I talk about religion, I am not referring to a sort of fixed creed, or a sort of churchgoing belief, or the desire to rush out and convert people to some other form of thought or feeling. But to be aware all the time, even if you haven't got your mind directly on it, of the existence of things which are infinitely greater than yourself, and in the face of which you and your desires and your hopes are trivial. I think it's very important, and that is what I mean by religion, a sense of the great things of life.

Death is one, and an awful lot of people, you know, who are extremely unwilling to spare any thought for that circumstance. And when I say death, I don't simply mean that eventually everybody is going to peg out and be put away. I mean that you have to be aware that there is a termination to your life, to your career, to everything about you, and, that therefore, you should try perhaps to give some shape to your life and that not all of your life should be devoted to really self-serving and self-applauding things.

PS: Well, if you think of the things that people so often believe they want from life, you think of things like wealth, fame, and happiness. What have you found those bring?

RD: Well, I haven't got wealth or fame, but I really think I might say, and I know how dangerous it is to say this, particularly on the air, I think I have happiness. And happiness, you know, so many people when they talk about happiness, seem to think that it is a constant state of near lunacy, that you're always hopping about like a fairy in a cartoon strip, and being noisily and obstreperously happy. I don't think that that's it at all. Happiness is a certain degree of calm, a certain degree of having your feet firmly routed in the ground, of being aware that however miserable things are at the moment that they're probably not going to be so bad after awhile, or possibly they may be going very well now, but you must keep your head because they're not going to be so good later. Happiness is a very deep and dispersed state. It's not a kind of excitement.

PS: We're coming into a new year, we're into it already. As you look ahead to the unknown that lies ahead of us, what do you feel, then, is the importance of change in our lives, because change is the one constant that we're all facing.

RD: Oh, I wouldn't really have anything to say about that. It wouldn't make much sense to anyone, except that a year from now we'll all be a year older, and unless we're a lot of fools, we ought to try to be a year wiser. Now a year wiser doesn't mean very much wiser, but it means some wiser, that we might have made some attempt to establish ourselves a little more firmly, and sensitively and intuitively in the world in which we live.

PS: Thanks very much, Professor Davies. It's been pleasant talking with you, and I hope our viewers have found what you said, particularly about happiness, as interesting as I did. We'll look for it.

RD: Thank you.

"This Country in the Morning"
Peter Gzowski and Vivian Rakoff/1972

Transcription from CBC Radio, 23 October 1972. Copyright 1972 Canadian Broadcasting Corporation. Reprinted by permission of the CBC, Robertson Davies, Vivian Rakoff, and Peter Gzowski.

PG: I welcome now, with great pleasure, Robertson Davies, a man whom I've been reading for years and have not had the pleasure of meeting until this morning, and the first question I had to ask him as he arrived in the studio was "How does one address the Master of Massey College?" because my experience with that title is almost totally from the novels of C. P. Snow where people are always calling one another, or calling the master "Master," but you don't say that outside the college?

RD: Well no. It's silly, I mean it implies particularly, I think, to Canadian ears, a type of superiority which I would not dream of [chuckles] assuming and it's just that I don't like Principal or President or Provost or whatever it was, and I was called the Master of Massey College because it was one of the few academic titles left when I got there.

PG: I suppose it was. There are a couple of things I want to ask you about Massey College, which is at the University of Toronto for people who are not aware of it. It is a unique institution I believe. But, Mr. Davies, another thing that I didn't know about you was that before you began your career as a journalist, which is what I knew you as first, you'd been an actor with the Old Vic. What was that like?

RD: Well, it was very interesting and I enjoyed it enormously and there were two things that I think made me relinquish that life. The first, of course, was the war which came along and there were fifteen hundred out-of-work actors in London, and I was one of them. And it seemed very unlikely that, as I was a very humble actor, I would be likely to get a job in a hurry, and I couldn't get into the services anyway, because at that time they didn't want any people; it was the "phony" war. And so it seemed, you know, I just had to have a job and eat and all that so I gave up being an actor and never went back to it. And also the fact is, I don't think I was ever a very good actor. I was all right in some things but not in a very wide range, and it's stupid to persist in something like that. You don't want to be fifty years playing Romeo's father and that kind of thing.

PG: That would be pretty difficult. You came back then and started in the family business.

RD: No. I started on *Saturday Night* where I was the book editor for B. K. Sandwell for a couple of years, and then I went to one of the family newspapers because they needed somebody to be an editor and I was a likely person.

PG: Did you start at the top?

RD: No, no. I didn't start at the top, I started under very considerable tutelage from the managing editor, who is a first-class man and a very good teacher, and I learned the job.

PG: The family newspapers were the *Kingston Whig-Standard* and the *Peterborough Examiner* owned by your father, Senator Davies. Were you resented at all as the son of the Senator who would come in, and . . . ?

RD: Not inside the newspaper. I was somewhat resented in the city of Peterborough I think for a time because I was thought to be very young to be doing what I was doing and I suppose I was, but there it was.

PG: And you wrote a great novel, *Leaven of Malice,* which is not about Peterborough, is it?

RD: No, no.

PG: But everyone in Peterborough says the opposite, do they not?

RD: Well, some people do, but you know it is so obviously about Kingston that it couldn't be about Peterborough.

PG: [Laughs] How did it go over in Kingston?

RD: I never knew. Kingston is a very quiet place about that sort of thing but the university in Kingston, Queens University, figured quite largely in that novel and subsequently Queens University gave me an honorary degree, and I thought that was very decent of them after what I had said [Laughs].

PG: Imagine me doing that, Peterborough—Kingston [Laughs]. What I've always thought of you as—may I risk applying a label to a

man whom I'm sure distrusts and dislikes labels?—as a "man of
letters." If someone were to ask me who is a Canadian man of letters,
the name Robertson Davies would spring instantly to my lips. Do you
accept that label?

RD: Well, I would be delighted to accept it. In fact I think it's an
entirely honorable and desirable title but you know people are
beginning to despise it. There was an extremely interesting book
written two years ago called *The Decline and Fall of the Man of
Letters* rather sneering at the idea of the person whose life is very
much taken up with literature and who writes books and occasionally
reviews books and writes criticism and that sort of thing. The
suggestion was that such people belong to a period before the First
World War, but 'there have always been such people and I just do
what I do and I don't care what anybody thinks about it.

PG: What do you think the Canadian attitude is right now toward
a man of letters?

RD: I don't know. It's very difficult to tell. Some people I think are
not very pleased with that idea because it seems to them perhaps to
be remote and unsympathetic and un-Canadian. There is a curious
notion that a lot of people have in Canada that the literary world is
somehow or other a remote and cold world and, therefore, they're
suspicious of it. Of course the opposite is true. This idea that the
literary world is cold and remote drives some authors to act in ways
which are obviously not cold and remote in order to kill that
suspicion, but . . .

PG: You have a twinkle in your eyes as if you're thinking
specifically of one or two authors.

RD: Oh, I was thinking perhaps of one or two, yes.

PG: We have a man coming on later whose initials are F.M. and
who occasionally wears a kilt.

RD: Oh, yes, yes!

PG: He wouldn't be one of them, would he?

RD: Yes, yes. Well, he might be, but I think he is authentically
colorful; he doesn't invent his color. Farley Mowat is a wonderful
fellow and writes admirable books and what he does is really and
truly of himself. I'm thinking of people, whom I will not specify, who
rather invent a personality of great sincerity and they're not as sincere
as they would like you to imagine.

PG: What's the "literary world" mean? I don't know who the literary world is.

RD: Well, I don't know who the literary world is, either, but there are apparently some people that do and who, I gather, have strong associations with one another and decide who is a new writer of talent and who isn't, and who is old-fashioned and who is not old-fashioned, and who is an old-timer and who isn't an old-timer. I'm an old-timer now.

PG: Are you old-fashioned?

RD: Well, they said so. As a matter of fact, William French said about my novel, *Fifth Business,* that it was a very old-fashioned novel. I was interested in that and so in the last one that I wrote, which was *The Manticore,* I did something which I hoped that Mr. French would notice. And I did something which I thought was rather tricky. The first part of it is written in American style with American punctuation and American vocabulary; the second part in British style with British punctuation and vocabulary; the third part is Continental. Well, he didn't mention it at all.

PG: Oh, good heavens. You don't suppose he didn't notice?

RD: Well, I think he must have noticed because the punctuation is so very, very different, you know.

PG: Are you conscious of the critics then when you're writing a novel?

RD: You have to be conscious of the critics, yes. You mustn't let them worry you too much but, of course, you think about them, and they do influence you to a considerable extent, particularly the ones who take the trouble to give you detailed and careful criticism.

PG: Do you think your attitude toward the world as it's shown by your writing is changing or has been changing over the past decade or so? In many ways you are—well, I was going to say a humorous writer which would certainly not be accurate or fair—but so much of your Marchbanks books and *Leaven of Malice* itself, I always thought of being very witty and your early works as full of wit and humor, and now with *Fifth Business* and with *The Manticore* growing more and more toward—I can't say more serious, can I?

RD: Yes, I think you can, and that's probably true, but you see wit and that sort of thing is likely to be a disguise, and it is a disguise because you dare not say what you really think. I now can say what I really think, I'm old enough. Both my parents are dead, I can say what I truly think about things which was not the case before. You know, although I was not—it would be absurd to say I was afraid to say what my parents might say if I wrote what I honestly thought about the world and about life; nevertheless, one is influenced by their attitudes.

PG: Isn't that interesting? Is there then any sense of roman à clef in either *Fifth Business* or *The Manticore*—

RD: No, no.

PG: —because people do seek out through your work "keys" as they did in—I keep mentioning *Leaven of Malice* as though that's all you've written; in fact, you've written twenty-four books.

RD: Yes, well, no there isn't really because although all that I write is somewhere or other rooted to personal experience, it's not direct reporting of personal experience and there are no direct portraits of people that I have known in the books but of course they reflect an attitude toward life, and that's it. As you grow older, you change and it's interesting what you were saying about writing sort of funny books when I was younger. That is true but when you get past a certain age, if you are going to be a humorist, you're a humorist in a different way, perhaps not quite such an obvious way as when you're young, and you notice that humorists who don't do that explode. Now there have been some very famous ones who didn't make any change in middle-age. One of them was Robert Benchley, and Benchley ceased to be an interesting writer in middle-age and then not very long afterwards, he died. I don't know whether the two things are related or not.

PG: What about from the same period in the same country? What about Thurber who never really changed but I always thought was a very serious writer.

RD: Oh, Thurber's a very serious writer. Thurber wrote hilariously and marvelously and beautifully but Thurber's attitude toward life was always extremely serious. The attitude of many humorists is, of course.

PG: I'm seeking one exception that might prove the rule. S. J. Perelman is a man whose humor it seems to me has never faded or never failed. Perhaps it does to you.

RD: Well, it's exactly what it used to be, and I will tell you this: I admire Perelman enormously and I've always read his stuff with keen enjoyment, but whenever one of his stories turns up in the *New Yorker* now, I say, "Oh yes, I must read that," and I go on and read the other things and then perhaps I get back to it. It used to be that I read it first. Because I know what it's going to be; it's going to be the same kind of word play, the same attitude toward life, and yet, I don't agree with you that it is as identical as it was. It's getting quite sour, he's always griping about something, he went to live in England. Well, now he writes things which are sour about England; he wrote formerly about what was sour in the States. I think he's becoming discontented and disillusioned with life—if a man who had worked for the Marx Brothers retained any illusions about life—and I rather sense this disappointment, this disillusion in this work.

PG: I wonder, would there be parallel things to be said about your own work—disappointment, disillusion—when you talked about, when you said your attitude had changed a little bit. Are you more cynical now?

RD: No, no, I'm much less cynical than I used to be. I think cynicism is a thing you can really only afford when you're young, if you're not going to pay the price of a life for it. I'm much more accepting and easygoing than I used to be.

PG: We've talked about so many books and scarcely touched on *The Manticore,* your book which has just been published, but because of the particular form it takes, we thought it would be interesting to bring in another guest and hear the two of you talk about the form and the novel itself, and I'll eavesdrop and perhaps join in. I'll be back very shortly with Robertson Davies.

*   *   *

PG: When I said that Robertson Davies' new novel, *The Manticore,* takes, I can't say unique form, but an unusual form and that form is the psychoanalysis of its protagonist who is David Staunton, a man who appears in younger form in *Fifth Business,* and David Staunton is forty years old as a lawyer in Switzerland in *The Manticore* going through a psychoanalysis which is the form the novel takes. And to talk about that, we thought it would be interesting to bring in Dr. Vivian Rakoff, psychiatrist from the Clark Institute here in Toronto, who has, I hope now, who has become a fairly familiar personage on this program. And Mr. Davies may I ask Dr. Rakoff in your presence if he believes that the description, the form of the psychoanalysis is a valid one in this particular book?

VK: Sure, the description is valid. This is what happens between people in terms of physical aspects of sitting and even the framework of the theory underlying it. Whether or not this is valid to a particular life, that is, the content rather than the form, that is after all the problem of talking about this particular novel. The shape of it is certainly, I mean, you know, in terms of realistic reporting of what goes on, this may well have gone on. I think the explicit unfolding of the man's life in this particular form is after all very skillful but it is a novelist's device and as a novelist's device, it requires, perhaps, a different kind of comment from a case history. You see, case histories are generally confused, always, no, almost invariably dreadfully written. The subsidiary characters get dismissed in one or two words, they lack symmetry. Whereas the essential thing about a work of art is that it's got symmetry. It imposes its unfolding on a life and makes sense of it. It's much better written, the dialogue is sharper, the rejoinders are better, the figure of the therapist is much more fully realized, is a much more interesting person. I noticed that Robertson Davies couldn't resist the patient's tremendous curiosity about the therapist, he couldn't resist leaving this lady anonymous, he had to have someone come in from the side and tell him, "Oh yes, I know Johanna very well. I know her husband, etc., etc., etc." This is what the patient always wants to know.

PG: The patient always wants to know what the psychiatrist is like outside the . . .?

VR: Oh yes, it's an essential part of the game, and *The Manticore*, in particular, explores the psychoanalytic problem of transference very carefully, the way in which the patient, because of personal needs and personal history, transforms the therapist into a kind of joker in the pack, a polymorphous person who will fit the needs of any particular moment so that he can be a nice person, a bastard, someone you fall in love with, someone whom you hate, and someone whom, if the therapy is successful, you'll finally cool off to and leave sitting in that anonymous chair.

PG: Mr. Davies, why the particular form? What turned you toward . . . ?

RD: Well, because I wanted to tell the story of the life of David Staunton, and it seemed to me that this was a possible, economical way of doing it. You know, so many stories which are life stories, are rather self-indulgent and rather, they're told rather in length. And it seemed to me that this would give an opportunity to describe Staunton's life in sharp and in vivid detail but without all that connective tissue which can be an awful bore in a novel. Also I was very much interested in writing one in terms of an analysis according to the theories of C. G. Jung because so far as I know that has not been done before.

PG: Because Staunton deliberately picks out Jung, he deliberately goes to Zurich where Jung's whole school is flourishing and he dismisses Freud. Was there some particular reason behind that? Is it of interest to you?

RD: Well, yes, Jung is of tremendous interest to me, and I used to be enormously interested in the work of Sigmund Freud, and, of course, still am, but I think that what happened to me was what Jung says does happen to people. When you get to be middle-aged or close to middle-age or over forty, his way of looking at things is a great deal more appealing and a great deal more explanatory than Freud's because Freud's method of analysis tends to be a reductive. It reduces what happens in somebody's life to things which are caused by small incidents frequently occurring in childhood. And the Jungian attitude allows for a wider exploration. Now I am not so bold as to assert that Jung's ideas are superior to those of Freud but from a point of a novelist, they are very, very, much more interesting than tracking down the mainstream of somebody's life to some incident in childhood.

VR: Of course that very sense of a continuing life is one which is not necessarily heretical within the psychoanalytic world, in which, if you like, Jung and Adler constitute the heretical churches against the orthodoxy of Freudian psychoanalysis. Other people have also been concerned about the psychoanalytic theoretical refusal or incapacity or lack of interest in pursuing life beyond forty. But the existentialists, in particular, have added this as a separate dimension and in very much the same kind of terms, it lacks the mythological resonance which is so attractive in a novel. But the sense of a life that has to constantly be made even after forty is something that the existentialists certainly had and in fact oddly enough Freud often accepted this; the thing is he never quarreled with Jaspers as he did with almost everybody else because that was on one side. And then, of course, the very influential theorist at the moment, Erik Erikson, has written about the way in which lives continue after forty and curiously enough, Erikson is usually seen as the man connected with adolescence and the time of having to make oneself. And yet, the most interesting things that Erikson has written, have been about men who reach round about forty and then suddenly decide to remake themselves in this usual way which you describe in *The Manticore,* that between thirty-five and forty-five men come to a turning point in their lives and they either take or bash in to a brick wall, I think is your phrase.

PG: Has anyone put a name on that phenomenon yet? It seems to me something that more and more writers are being concerned about.

VR: They talk about middle essence, and they talk about the crisis of the middle-aged man—but just to complete that thing Erikson writes about Shaw who I think writes his first play at forty or forty-one, he writes about Martin Luther who doesn't really come to himself until he is 30, and Gandhi, in probably his most elaborated work, who doesn't, in fact, find his great political technique of passive resistance or civil disobedience until his forties. So, in that extent, certainly Jung has kind of staked out the territory.

PG: May I just insert one comment of something we have learned from this program? We had an essay by Harry Bruce, which I read, a very casual essay and very brief, four or five minutes. (I'm talking about this phenomenon in much different terms and not examining it very deeply.) Very seldom have we had such a response from people who wanted copies of it for their husbands, or for themselves, who wanted to know—It's obviously striking a very strong chord in numbers of people. I haven't heard this phrase, "middle essence" before.

VR: Just one second to take a moment on that. I did a radio talk on middle-age that I don't think I ever got as much response to, for anything else.

PG: Well, we will not leave *that* subject alone. Back to *The Manticore,* if I may. Or perhaps, Mr. Davies, you have a comment on that whole . . . .

RD: No, except that I agree with what Dr. Rakoff said. Middle-age, I think, is enormously interesting. As a novelist, I get very tired of the insistence on young characters in novels. They are interesting and they have interesting things to do, but one gets sick of the repetition of the clichés of youth, including their experiences with sex and love. It all has a strongly similar ring. I think life gets to be much more interesting when you get a little older. Stranger things happen to you, don't you think?

VR: Well, the point about youth is that it's all promise and, therefore, character hasn't yet had a chance to resolve itself into action. You make a . . . I think it's in *Fifth Business:* there's a very interesting phrase which really jolted me, and you throw it in so casually, as one sentence hanging loose, a paragraph by itself at the end of a chapter, that "before people die, all they are left with is their characters." And the point about being very young is that the way in which character and personality works itself out in the world isn't yet established and by the time you're middle-aged, you've suffered both the disasters and the rewards of your particular character in the world, and, I think, it makes it much more interesting, it's much more elaborately different.

PG: One specific point raised in *The Manticore* about the difference between Jung and Freud—and I think applicable to what each of you is talking about here, and is it valid psychoanalytically, Dr. Rakoff? because I'm sure it is—that Jung sort of de-emphasizes the sex drive as being behind everything and that David Staunton points out there are more interesting and more important things to him in life than sex? Does that all hold true?

VR: This is a bit like the medieval argument about whether or not the wafer—not medieval—the wine wafer and the wine actually became the body and the blood, or whether it didn't, because when one listens to these arguments in detail, the essential thing, is this, that libido, the life imagery, that force that keeps you going, that gives you the capacity to latch on and do and energize is seen almost substantially in sexual terms by Freud whereas Jung defines it nonsexually as a more generalized, almost Bergsonian *élan vitale* at which you share in, an energy for your life but which is not specifically sexual.

PG: We have to pause for a couple of minutes, and I'll be back again with Dr. Robertson Davies and Dr. Vivian Rakoff.

* * *

PG: We're back now with Dr. Robertson Davies and Dr. Vivian Rakoff discussing—occasionally—Dr. Davies' new novel *The Manticore* and from time to time other things as well. "The man freed to be human" is a phrase that just came out. Mr. Davies, could that possibly be inferred as the theme of *The Manticore?*

RD: Yes, certainly. You see, David Staunton finds himself in a dreadful situation, he thinks that he is losing his mind, he knows that he has become a serious alcoholic . . .

PG: He denies that in a curious way.

RD: Well, he does, because all alcoholics do—

PG: I drink a bottle a day, he says.

RD: —because all alcoholics do, as Dr. Rakoff says. But he is in bad trouble and he needs help and he goes to get it in a place where he thinks he can find it, and he does find it toward the end of the book; he has been released, partly by his work with his analyst and partly by another and very dramatic experience.

PG: Which we will not give away.

RD: Yes, to be his best self more of the time than before.

PG: Can I ask you a very personal question?

RD: Yes.

PG: Relating to our earlier conversation, you talked about freedom in a personal context and freedom to say the things that you wanted, and it involved, you said, the death of your parents in a way—

RD: Yes.

PG: The event which starts the novel, *The Manticore*, is in fact the death of David Staunton's father, Boy Staunton. Is there a relationship?

RD: There is a relationship, but not a direct one. I think that this is a thing, perhaps Dr. Rakoff could throw some light on it for us. But I think that in everybody's life there are certain reticences which are observed while one's parents are living, out of respect for them, and for a variety of reasons for which virtually everyone recognizes as quite good and sufficient reasons. But that is not to say that anything that happens in that book is drawn from my own life because it isn't. But it is true that David Staunton is able to say things after his father's dead that he couldn't say while his father was living, and it would be a funny world if this were not so.

VR: You know, all fiction is ultimately rearranged autobiography.

That doesn't mean to say that it is direct reporting, but you can only write out of what you know, and what you know is everything that has happened to you. You know, Freud himself, after all, reports the crucial event of his life as the death of his father, the point which he suddenly had to come to himself, and this wish, or this need, or this terror that sons have about surpassing their fathers is one that he wrote a great deal about in a most remarkable essay of his called, I think, "A Disorder of Memory on The Steps of the Acropolis" in which he suddenly realizes how far he has come because he gets to Greece and his father always wanted to and never did. And this is very important. The problem that I have with a novel "as analysis" as opposed to "as a novel," is its neatness.

PG: But isn't that the novelist's license?

VR: That may be, but that is precisely the problem of reality and fiction, that the most excitingly union symbolic—I won't say what specifically, you've given me that hint—the mystical thing that happens to this man is not in his interior journey which is full of exciting things anyway, but something so spatially real, something in geography, something in the very crust of the earth, something in real time, not personal time. I'm certain that Mr. Davies will take this in good part, but it's almost to me like those traffic smashes that kill off a lot of novels. When the characters cannot be resolved internally, an external force is brought out. Now you may say this is, after all, the novel is a fantasy and, therefore, even this which occurs is a fantasy.

RD: Well, you know, I wouldn't agree with that, and for a lot of reasons, but one which came into my life very early when I was a young man. I remember exactly when it was, it was when I was twenty-three. And I had at that time the opportunity of doing some study and some work under very agreeable terms with the late Dr. Robert Gillespie—you remember him—the psychiatrist, and Gillespie kept saying, we attract what we are, we attract what we are, and he thought that external happenings like the happening that occurs in this book to David when he is venturing in the Swiss mountains, or all kinds of things—even like motor accidents—happen to people because they needed them. Now this is something that you probably wouldn't or mightn't like, but because I have always remembered what Gillespie said—I was immensely impressed by him—it seems to me that I have in various times of my life, without being impertinently

know-it-all about other people's lives, seen that they terminated or
suffered some sort of grave change when it was inevitable and they
needed it. Now this may be a novelist's way of looking at life, but that
was what Gillespie put in my mind.

VR: You know, I would be very stupid to reject what you say out of
hand because I think that much of what you say is true, and one has
after all, only got to see in one's own life the kind of novelist's devices
at play, the coming together by accident of things that you just
wouldn't have dreamt of, and I often find myself saying to someone
that coincidences are so colossal that they would be rotten in a novel.

RD: Yes, yes. Exactly.

VR: Or you know, when one is in a personal situation, and one
says gawd, this is badly written because it's so trite, because literature
reflects back, and yet, I must persist with as much politeness as I can,
that one of the devices after all in the novel is to prevent this
coincidence, coming together too neatly, appearing to resolve too
quickly. Oddly enough, the novelist, and particularly a fictive account
of a life, has to be much more—here I am teaching my—to put it
mildly—my grandfather in all sorts of ways to suck eggs—but it
would seem to me that one of the technical problems in reporting a
life is in fact not to make it come out too neatly.

RD: Yes.

PG: So you can't have reality.

VR: That's precisely it. That in fact you know Francis Bacon, the
painter, for example, when he's finished something that looks too
real, goes across and quite arbitrarily just scratches up the surface
because the paradox is that reality is the enemy of that necessary
enclosed world which is a work of art.

RD: Yes. I think you're entirely right. Shakespeare says something
about that in one of his plays. Someone says if this were presented
upon the stage now, I would condemn it as an improbable fiction,
and it is true that if you want to present life as an effective sort of
realistic representation of life, you must not be so daring about
coincidence as fate is. But Jung wrote so interestingly about this in his
theories about synchronicity, and so forth, that I have been greatly
tempted to have a bash at it [Laughs].

PG: Gentlemen, if we have done nothing else, I'm sure we have
interested a number of people in having a look at *The Manticore*, and

we won't even tell you what "the manticore" means for people who don't know. It's interesting to get through this discussion and not define that word, but Robertson Davies' new novel is called *The Manticore*. It's published by Macmillan, it has a price on it somewhere, and I don't care what it is.

RD: Awful! Frightening!

PG: [Laughs] Awful in price and—

RD: [Laughs]

PG: I thank Mr. Davies and Dr. Vivian Rakoff, very much indeed. Thank you.

Acta Interviews Robertson Davies

Renée Heatherington and Gabriel Kampf/1973

From *Acta Victoriana*, April 1973, pp. 69-87. © 1973, reprinted by permission. All rights reserved.

February 28, 1973. Furnished with a tape recorder, we arrived at Massey College. The Master's secretary greeted us and led us up a few steps to another door which curiously swung open. Robertson Davies motioned us into his study, a rectangular room lighted by large windows at one end. We sat near these windows beside a glass-fronted cabinet. Davies sat several feet away in front of a large French provincial desk. On its face were papers beneath a rounded dark glass paperweight, ash trays and an ivory-handled letter opener. At the back of the desk were several small wooden boxes, beautifully carved. Parkinson's painting of a scene from the original production of *She Stoops to Conquer* hung above the desk. The Stratford Festival based their costumes on this painting when they produced the play last season. There were busts of Shakespeare and the actor Henry Irving in the room. The wooden floor was covered by several small but exquisite Oriental carpets.

Robertson Davies is a handsome and gracious man. The atmosphere was relaxed and cordial. He met us wearing a green velvet jacket and smoking a long thin cigar. He spoke slowly in a clear and resonant voice. After several questions about *Acta* and student writing the interview began and lasted an hour.

Acta: Through *Fifth Business* you have achieved great international recognition. Why do you think this novel has gained such widespread renown?

RD: I really haven't any idea. All my previous novels have done quite well in the States, not so much in England. I suppose that it touched some particular chord that was popular at the time. From

111

the letters that I get I think that the interest in saints and in magic was
what attracted a large group of readers.

Acta: How did you become interested in magic?

RD: Well, I've always been interested in magic.

Acta: Are you familiar with Aleister Crowley?

RD: Yes, oh yes indeed. I'm interested in that kind of magic but
I'm also interested in just ordinary magic, illusions, tricks.

Acta: Can you do tricks?

RD: No, I'm very wanting in skill. I'm clumsy, and though I'm
interested and know how it's done, it's rather like playing the piano.
I'm intensely interested in that. I play the piano a little but I'm a very
poor player. But I know how good players play.

Acta: What first led you to becoming a writer? When did you first
think of it as a profession?

RD: Nothing led me to becoming a writer. I was born a writer the
way the son of a chimney sweeper is born to be a chimney sweeper. My
father was a writer. Both my brothers wrote things. I had a great uncle
who was quite a remarkable writer. I had another great uncle who was a
quite eminent medical writer, and writing just ran in the family.

Acta: Was it more the result of inherited talent or because of the
environment in which you were brought up?

RD: I suppose it was environment. There might have been some
degree of inheritance in it. But my parents laid great stress on it, and
they were very keenly interested in language, and in the use of
language, and in grammar and in techniques of language.

Acta: I remember that in *Fifth Business* Mr. Ramsay says that you
can't adequately write English without a background in Latin. Do you
believe that to be true?

RD: No, but that's a thing many people say, and it's the thing that
an awful lot of Scottish people say. You remember that Mr. Ramsay
was a Scot, and he went when he was a boy to quite a celebrated
Scottish grammar school, Dumfries Academy, where a lot of my
forbears went, and they all thought you couldn't write English if you
didn't know Latin, but I'm not sure that this is true. I know too many
people who write English as if it were Latin. They actually use Latin
structures, like the ablative absolute, and think that they're being very
elegant. You know, "The river having been forded, Caesar advanced

upon the camp." They think that sort of thing is great, but it's not, it wasn't English. It's cart before the horse writing.

You learn to write English by writing English. Nobody says you cannot write a fine French style unless you know Latin. It would make even more sense than in writing English, because French and Spanish and those languages are much more allied to Latin. But nobody says that you must learn to write French.

A classical education is good because it teaches you other languages, and other modes of thought. Really, just learning another language is not enormously enlarging except that you can associate yourself with the culture and literature of that language, but it is learning to think like another race that is important.

If you learn languages very unlike our own, such as an oriental language, you have to learn to think that way. Their ideas about time are all revealed in the way in which they use verbs. And this is true, for instance, of Hebrew. If you are going to know any Hebrew, you must learn the Hebrew time sense which is rooted in the present.

An enormous amount of the Bible is written in the present tense as though it were happening right now, which is a different way of thinking about the past. And this is like Welsh, which is a language of which I know a little because my forbears were Welsh people. In Welsh, if you talk about something that has happened, you indicate that it has happened in the past and then you tend to describe it in the present tense, which gives it great vividness.

Acta: That influence has shown in Dylan Thomas.

RD: Yes, and it influences the way people think. A friend of mine was telling me a story recently. She was a Welsh woman and she was immensely amused by this because some American friends of hers had told it to her. They were travelling in North Wales, and they had hired a car to drive them through the mountains. They were saying to the driver, "What a good road this is. Has it been here a long time?" And he said, "Yes. We built it for them. But you know, they never paid us for it." They said, "Who?" He said, "The Romans." Well, you know, this is the way they think. The past is much more present than in English, for instance.

Acta: It could be the length of the tradition.

RD: Yes, and length of resentment.

Acta: I see. What sort of environment do you like to work in? Does it matter?

RD: No, it doesn't matter tremendously. I can work almost anywhere, because of newspaper training, where you must work in hotel rooms, in corners of village grocery stores, wherever you happen to be when you're reporting what you're reporting. What I do like if I can have a luxurious surrounding in which to work is lots of quiet. But that is almost the ultimate luxury in the modern world. So I like to work in the country if I can, where it is, on the whole, more quiet than in the city, but it's not perfectly quiet.

Acta: Could you describe a usual working day?

RD: A working day for me when I'm writing begins when I get up at about eight o'clock. By nine-thirty I'm writing and I go over what I wrote the day before. Usually that takes until about ten o'clock and then I write fresh material until half-past twelve, on a typewriter, without break. Then I have a break for lunch and in the afternoon I do the things that you do in the country, trim trees, etc. At five o'clock, I go back and very carefully revise what I wrote in the morning. Then during the evening I pretend to be doing other things but I am really thinking about what I'm going to write the next day.

Acta: Do you keep a notebook?

RD: Oh yes. I keep notebooks all the time. I've got a desk full of notebooks. I carry a notebook all the time and make notes all the time. [We were shown a red-covered, palm sized book containing pages filled with tiny, neat handwriting.] Books like that. They're little books with thin leaves.

Acta: What role do your hands play in your writing? Do you think of the act of writing as something physical?

RD: Oh yes. But I don't write by hand, because for one thing it has a bad influence on my writing. I'm a very persnickety writer. I write italic hand and if you did that for two and a half hours you'd have a very tired hand. That gives you tired writing and you begin to write in a very compressed way because you don't want to write any more words than you can help. That's no good. I write on an electric typewriter and it's just the same when you begin as when you stop. And then you can revise very carefully. Also, you are not interested in your own handwriting. If you look at a badly written page, you think, "that's terrible" and you think that what you've said must be bad. On a typewriter, good or bad, it all looks the same so you can revise without having to worry about the appearance of the thing. I'm very much influenced by appearances, and so a dirty, messy scribbled page would bother me.

Acta: The names of your characters are fascinating. How do you devise names for them?

RD: That's a subject on which I have rather unusual views. People do have very, very strange names. And so I try to give the characters in my books names that people will remember, and yet they're not extraordinary, queer names. Now for instance, the chief character in *Fifth Business* is called Dunstan Ramsay, which is not an odd name at all. And yet it is not a name which is hard to remember. It identifies him as what he is. He's a Scot. And his mother's name, Dunstable, which he was christened, is a Cumberland name and so it identifies him as a man of northern British background. And that's what he was; he was one of those rather cold, considering, strong-minded people.

Acta: According to Elspeth Buitenhuis' book, you chose the name Dempster because of the faculty of judging. Is that true?

RD: No. There are a lot of things in that book that I never said and don't agree with but she must say what she thinks. There's a lady at McGill who teaches *Fifth Business* in a course on Canadian literature and she says that the stone which Ramsay carried all his life and which Boy Staunton had in his mouth when he died is the stone of judgment out of the *Talmud.* I have never read the *Talmud.* I don't know anything about the stone of judgment, but when you fall into the hands of academics you're a gone goose. They will interpret and say what they think and there's nothing you can do about it. It doesn't really very much matter unless we take it too seriously.

Acta: How much do you admit modelling your characters on real people?

RD: Not very much, really. But I'll tell you something that happened to me last week which really made me jump. Perhaps you remember that in *Fifth Business* there is an old Jesuit named Ignacio Blazon. He was a Bollandist, but I don't know any Bollandists. However a friend of mine who is a Jesuit sent a copy of that book to the Bollandists in Brussels, and he got a letter in reply which he has sent to me. It amused me but it also startled me because it was a

most excited, sad, bothered letter. I had made ridiculous dear old
Père Grosjean whom they all loved so much. They admitted he was
an eccentric and he certainly was rather curious in his personal habits
but he was a fine man, a great Christian, and I had made him look
foolish. I don't know anything about Père Grosjean, but there it is.

The next day I got a telephone call from a man who identified
himself and said, "I'm going to Zurich and I want to have a Jungian
analysis. Will you introduce me to your analyst?" I said that I had not
been analysed and didn't know any analysts. He said, "But when I
was in London they told me you'd been analysed by Marie-Louise
von Franz and that she is the model for Dr. von Haller in *The
Manticore*. She must be, she's just like her." The same day I got a
letter from a Jungian analyst in Chicago who had reviewed the book
for a psychological magazine and she said that this woman was Dr.
von Franz. I don't know Dr. von Franz; I've heard of her, but I know
nothing whatever about her. People tend to assume that you must
model characters in books on living people. But you don't, certainly
not like that. It is in the mind of the reader rather than in the mind of
the writer.

Acta: How do you go about developing a character?

RD: You don't. The character arises in your imagination and then
you go ahead. I know this sounds terribly pompous and grandiose,
but you don't really do it; it's something that happens and you write it
down. You can't sit down and say, "Now, I think I'll think up a funny
Jesuit," and do it because you'll get a mass of eccentricities; you
won't get a live person. But if one arises in your mind, and he's got
all his oddities and you see him hopping around and doing things,
then you just write down about it. This is what imagination is. It's not
invention, you're more passive than that. You listen to your ideas;
you don't tell them what to do.

Acta: We were thinking along the lines of what Kipling said, "Drift,
wait, and obey." Do you also have this inner voice?

RD: But this is absolutely the way it is. You "Drift, wait, and obey."
And if you're lucky, you don't have to drift very far or wait very long.
But you jolly well have to obey. Because if you start pushing your
characters around they'll go dead. And if you just keep quiet and let
ideas come to you, you may get some good ones.

I met a man in New York who knows a lot of Bollandists. He said,

"How did you know that they wrote in purple ink?" I said, "I don't know that they write in purple ink." And he said, "You said so in your book that Ramsay received a letter from Père Delehaye that was written in purple ink." I said, "Well, yes, I did do that." But I didn't tell him that about nine people out of every ten in France and Belgium write in purple ink. I let him think it was magic.

Acta: Who would you consider to be your literary antecedents?

RD: I don't know. You see, I admire many writers, but I'm very careful not to imitate them because imitation is another thing which is exceedingly dangerous. And if you imitate, you're going to end up, if you're lucky, with an imitation. And if you're not lucky you're just going to end up with a mess. So I don't really imitate anybody. But I am very interested in certain writers whose work I admire enormously. I think that perhaps at the top of the list I would put Thomas Mann. But I am not in the least like Thomas Mann, though I was very much complimented when a New York *Times* reviewer said that *Fifth Business* reminded him of Thomas Mann. But it can't remind him very closely because it's not a bit like him.

Another writer who is an enormous enthusiasm of mine and a very unfashionable one is Dickens. I think he is the greatest master in English literature after Shakespeare. People say that Dickens' characters are so wonderful and so various, but that they are not like people. That is not true. They are like people, but they're like people seen by a great artist. And the thing about Dickens which really is fascinating is not so much his power of creating, or bringing about fascinating characters, as the enormous creative energy which comes through the books. It's like the kick of a mule, really. Last summer, I had not for a long time read any novels by Thackeray, and so I read some Thackeray, and then immediately afterwards I reread Dickens' *Our Mutual Friend,* and it was astonishing because Thackeray was supposed to be Dickens' great rival when they were living. Yet Thackeray was a man who was working only on about four cylinders compared to Dickens' twelve. And great writer though Thackeray was, he just hadn't got that extraordinary creative energy that Dickens had.

Acta: How do you think that transforms a character? Why are Dickens' characters as they are and Thackeray's as they are?

RD: I think it is because Dickens was not so afraid as Thackeray.

Thackeray was brought up a gentleman, had many things in his life which made him a very sad man and a sad man is likely to be a very compassionate man. You know Thackeray's wife went mad, and he had a very unhappy love affair with a lady who was the wife of his best friend, but because he was a very honourable man he didn't carry it very far. And he had to bring up his two daughters and look after them without any wife to assist him. This all made him a very compassionate, but a rather too compassionate man.

Dickens hadn't any more compassion than a tiger. He was a brute and a monster! And in his private life you know he was a ferocious person. What he did to his wife was just murderous. And he was a sort of moral crook as well. Because you see when he sent his wife away, he took as his mistress a girl called Ellen Ternan. He set her up in a house that he acquired for her and then he made his daughters and his sister-in-law invite her to tea and treat her as an intimate friend. He said they must be kind to her because she was such a sweet girl and needed help. Now this seems to me to be a very queer man indeed. He was trying to kid himself that he wasn't a middle-aged man, desperately unhappy, who'd taken up with a young actress. He was trying to turn the world upside down. This is moral crookedness. But he did it because he had the drive and the compelling energy to dominate his world in that way, and it made for a very unhappy life. But it certainly made for some great books.

Acta: You said that you didn't have any specific literary antecedents. How would you describe your own style?

RD: I don't honestly know. I just try to write as clearly as I can. And this is not a thing which I absolutely approve of, it's just all I can do. Now a modern writer whom I admire very much and who writes fascinatingly, I think, is Lawrence Durrell. He is a poet and he writes like a poet and it is a joy to read his novels, but I could no more write like that than I could fly to the moon. So I don't attempt it. All I can do is try to get it all clear and put it down.

Acta: How do you see the function of drama?

RD: If I told you what I thought was the function of drama, you would probably leave this room in indignation. It's to entertain and amuse people, like novels. You know, this awful business that the drama has got to illustrate social problems, rub people's noses in troubles they hadn't thought about, is all very fine except that you can only do that if first of all you get people into the theatre and charge them a dollar or whatever it may be and give them a full dollar's worth of entertainment. You get a dollar's worth when you go to *King Lear*, but you don't get a dollar's worth when you go to something which shows you how tough it is to be a blind paraplegic with syphilis, or something of that sort.

Acta: To what extent does drama influence your fiction?

RD: I don't know. To some extent it must, because I am intensely interested in the theatre; it is my great pleasure. I am a student of drama. I teach drama and I am enormously interested in it. But I also get great pleasure out of music and I'm very enthusiastic about that. But nobody ever asks me how music influences how I write but it does, you know.

Acta: How does it?

RD: The way that it influenced the writing of James Joyce. I'm always thinking in musical terms and there are various devices which are common in symphonic music that are transferable to the novel. One of them is the disappointed climax. If either of you study music you know that symphonies are full of disappointed climaxes; so are novels. You lead people right up to some extraordinary expectation, then cut it off. And they're much better pleased than if you went on and boomed and crashed and groaned your way all through it. You leave it to them to complete what has to be said, or heard. I think one of the problems about writing is that a lot of writers think their readers are stupid. Well this is a very bad frame of mind to be in. You must assume that they're at least as intelligent as you are and probably more so. And then you won't insult them. A lot of novels insult their readers. They go on and on after the point has been made.

Acta: One of the major themes that everyone is talking about in connection with your novels right now is the Jungian influence. In a comparison between Jung and Freud you said that Jung is the more truly revealing explorer of the mind. Could you describe for us your interest in Jung, and how it came about?

RD: Yes, I can. When I was about fifteen, I became aware of Sigmund Freud because a friend of mine was reading him. He said to me, "I'm reading some stuff by this fellow Freud. He's a madman. Everything he says is crazy. Look at his picture. His eyes are the eyes of a madman." And it was one of the usual pictures of Freud that you see reproduced often. I looked at it and I thought, "He doesn't look like a madman to me. He looks pretty sharp as a matter of fact." But this fellow didn't like what Freud said because of its strong sexual emphasis. And so he assumed that Freud was mad. I became interested from that time in Freud. In fact I would say that I had read just about all of Freud. When I was at the university, I invested what was for me at that time an awful lot of money in the collected papers of Sigmund Freud and I read them all through. Five long volumes. And I read the main books on dreams and the pleasure principle and wit and its relation to the unconscious. And for a time I was a very keen Freudian, and tried to see life through Freudian eyes. But there was a thing which struck me then and which continued to impress me. Because not so much Freud but his followers were always knocking somebody called Jung. So I began to read some of the works of Jung, and it interested me and satisfied me as Freud had not.

I have enormous admiration for Sigmund Freud. I think he's one of the very great figures in the cultural history of mankind. He set mankind free from a lot of crippling ideas. But, one of the things about Freud which bothered me right from the beginning, though for a long time I didn't quite understand what it was, is that he is a reducer. Everything that comes into the Freudian method is reduced to something less than it was. Why is somebody a writer? A Freudian will say, "It is because he had never lost his dread of the pre-oedipal mother." Well baloney! That's not why he's a writer. He must be a writer for some better reason than because he was scared of his mother before he developed his oedipus complex. Anyway, I don't think this is a thing which is very easily provable.

So I began to read Jung, and one of the things that fascinated me about Jung was that his method was not reductive as the Freudian method was; it was constructive. And if somebody went to Jung and said, "I have mental troubles which are worrying me"; instead of pursuing the Freudian method, which would be to say, "Let us go back to your infancy and find out the root of this trouble," Jung was quite likely to say, "What's chewing you now?"

Some of his most famous analyses are sort of jokes, the old man himself thought so. There is one quite famous one. A man came to him and said, "I have acute anxiety and it is related to the fact that I am engaged to a girl that I am very much in love with but I think that she is having an affair with another man." And Jung said, "What you need is not an analyst but a detective. You see if you can find out about this and tell me what you discover." And in a month the man came back and said, "It's true. She is carrying on with another chap and I've called off the engagement." And Jung said, "And your anxiety?" And he said, "It's gone!" This makes far more sense to me.

Some of Jung's analyses were prolonged and fascinating. They investigated all kinds of obscure, strange things. But always they attempted to relate the patient to the whole world, not only the world in which he lived but the world of the imagination, the world of myths, legend, humanity, mankind. I thought, "Now, this is really marvellous. This is something I can wholeheartedly associate myself with."

But you must not imagine that because I am very interested in Jungian psychology that I live my whole life in terms of it. I just find that it is a fascinating way of looking at the world and at certain problems which occur in the world. It is an interesting way of looking at literature because Jung was marvellously rich in his knowledge of literature, particularly in the literature of the middle ages.

He keeps recurring to an idea that I find immensely attractive and helpful to me, which is that the intellectual growth of mankind is exceedingly slow and that the difference between us sitting here and a man living six hundred years ago or more is really only a matter of externals. Psychologically he was just like ourselves and therefore we can associate ourselves with the history of mankind in a very special and sympathetic way. And this is immensely interesting to me.

Now one of the things in *Fifth Business* which interested a lot of readers was my concern about saints. You see, they think of saints as people who lived an awfully long time ago and whose validity has disappeared. I think of them as people who didn't live such a long time ago, only a few hundred years or so, and this is possibly the Welsh way of thinking about time that we were talking about earlier. There must have been something about them that impressed people who were very much like me. What was it? And they must have been much more like somebody living today than we commonly think. What was behind it? What made these people special and what made a lot of other people regard them as special, either hating them or loving them?

This is fascinating. It enlarges the whole world, and because it does so, it gives you great hope and sympathy with the future. You find yourself not an isolated miserable little wretch who has got seventy or eighty years to struggle along and then perish like nothing. You are the continuer of a very great tradition which you are going to pass on to the next lot. And you're right in the middle of the great stream of life. You see? Wonderful thing.

Acta: What kinds of research and special preparation preceded *Fifth Business* and *The Manticore?*

RD: Nothing very particular. I had been working for about twenty years on my study of Jung so I didn't have to do much about that, but I was rather worried because I had never had a Jungian analysis myself and I never had been on very close terms with anybody who had done so, so I had to invent that. I was worried that it might be all wrong and that the Jungians would jump on me, despise me, but they didn't; they thought it was all right.

Acta: Anne Montagnes has asked why you still locate the big spiritual adventures outside of Canada.

RD: And she also asked why all the pretty girls in my books were not Canadian. Well, I met Anne and told her directly that this was not true. The wife of Boy Staunton was a pretty Canadian village girl. And that the big spiritual adventures happen outside Canada is just not true. The whole of Ramsay's life happened in Canada. He was a Canadian soldier in the Canadian army when he saw the vision on the battlefield. He returned to Canada as soon as he could get here and lived his life in Canadian terms.

Acta: Do you consider Canadian literature to be regionally separated? segregated?

RD: To some extent. I think that is becoming less true than it was. Canadian literature is developing very rapidly and in an extremely optimistic and promising way, I feel. Now at last we're getting some real dispute and interest about Canadian literature. I think that there will always be a considerable measure of regionalism about it. All literatures of gigantic countries are regional. People talk about Russian literature. They should talk about Moscow literature. The great Russian novels were and very much still are related to three or four big cities. Those are the places upon which they converge. When Dostoyevsky or Tolstoy wrote a Russian novel, he wasn't thinking of some fellow living in a goatskin tent, three thousand miles away, eating dog cheese; he wasn't writing for him. You can't write for all your fellow citizens; there are too many of them.

I don't think any Eskimos read books of mine. Although I had a postcard the other day from a student of mine. It says, "I am five miles from the Arctic Circle and I found a paperback copy of *Fifth Business* sitting beside Simenon, Balzac and Hesse." I was delighted by that so I can't throw that away. I must keep it. It reassures me.

Acta: How did you develop the symbol of *The Manticore?*

RD: Shall I tell you or shall I try to evade the question? (Pause) I dreamed it. It was a mural on the wall of a building. A sibyl was leading the beast by a gold chain. The sibyl was a very beautiful, naked young woman, much more beautiful than the one they put on the cover.

Acta: You write in your most recent essay on Leacock that, "A woman's intellect at its best, is not the same as man's, and that its differences make it fascinating but not inferior." What are the differences?

RD: I can't tell you because this would take us into the middle of next week. But this is a decidedly Jungian attitude. A woman looks at life from another angle and it is one which lays emphasis on feminine values: the continuance of the race, the continuance of culture as it relates to the continuance of the race. And the application of the principle of Eros to everything that is important in life as opposed to the male principle of Logos. Men are great ones for law and rules. Women are great ones for feeling and understanding. I think that to educate women on a Logos principle which our university is soaked in the way a railway tie is soaked in creosote, is to wrong her, is to try to change her into something which she is not and to belittle and betray what she is. A lot of people think that I am hostile to women. I am not hostile to women. I am fascinated by women and enormously appreciative of them, but I don't think that they are men and I don't think that the finest thing you can say about a woman is that she is just exactly like a man.

The most fascinating thing about a woman is that she's not a man, and to try to educate her along masculine lines and to treat her as though she were a man is to ignore what she is. It is to treat a flower as though it were an onion. It's an absurdity. You can eat the flower and you can smell the onion, but you are not going to get the best out of either of them that way. I think that eventually when women's lib has achieved its immediate ends, the next move will be towards education of women which takes account of what women are and of the Eros principle of life, which doesn't get anything like the amount of emphasis in our western world which it ought to have. Consequently, we have endless Logos-created problems: wars, constant wrangles, disagreements, economic misery, because people try to do everything according to a system of rigid rules.

Acta: Your writing is always so poised, controlled, and self-assured. The Survival theory doesn't seem to apply to you. Do you agree with it?

RD: The Survival theory is a very fascinating one which works admirably for some people. I don't personally find that it works for me because I've never felt that way. I think I belong to a Western world rather than specifically to a threatened culture in Canada. And our Canadian culture is part of that Western culture, I think. It's not something you can identify specifically as our own. This nationalism's a lot of nonsense. Let's think of ourselves as sharers in the great wealth of western culture. Let's get the best out of it that we can wring from it and let's give it the best that we have in us, but let's not pretend that somehow we're fantastically special. We're just one part of the Western world which includes the United States, Great Britain, Australia, New Zealand, South Africa, all the English-speaking countries.

Robertson Davies
Ramsay Cook/1973

Transcription of "Impressions," CBC Television, 8 July 1973.
Copyright 1973 Canadian Broadcasting Corporation. Reprinted
by permission of the CBC, Robertson Davies, and Ramsay Cook.

RD: [Photograph] Well, now that is me in the part of Dogberry in
Much Ado About Nothing, and I played that part when I was at
Oxford with the Oxford University Dramatic Society, and you can see
I'm done up with a bald wig and a false nose, and stuff in my cheeks,
and everything possible to make me look different. But the problem
was I didn't look really very different because once the lights had
come on, I looked exactly like myself, everybody told me.

RC: Mr. Davies, you were born in Ontario, were you?

RD: Yes.

RC: As you were growing up, did you have the sense of being a
Canadian or an Englishman?

RD: Like a great many boys at that time, I was very much troubled
as to what I was because if you read anything, you were always
conscious of the fact that you were reading about someplace other
than the place where you were. When I was a boy, I read a very great
deal and I read both American books and English books about boys
and what boys did, and also I read magazines. I remember I used to
read a magazine which my parents bought for me which came from
Boston, it was called the *Youth's Companion*. It was always about
American boys and they were always looking up to Abraham Lincoln
and celebrating Washington's birthday, and doing this, that, and the
other, and I was sufficiently a Canadian boy to know that Washington
was a scoundrel, and I wanted nothing to do with him, and I couldn't
understand why these boys whom I admired were taken with him.
And, you know, always you were reading about someplace else and
another way of life. You were reading about English schoolboys who
went to boarding schools and who were taught solely by men
whereas I went to schools where we were taught almost exclusively

by women, and it was all very puzzling, you didn't seem to be like anybody that you ever read about.

RC: Mr. Davies, among other things, you've been a college master and a newspaper publisher, an editor, a dramatist, and perhaps these days above all, we think of you as a novelist. Was there any special time in your career when you decided you wanted to be a writer?

RD: No, no, there wasn't really. I've always been a writer in one way or another.

RC: When you were a newspaper writer, how did you find time to write your novels, for example?

RD: At night. I worked during the daytime and really had quite a lot to get done, but at night I used to work for a couple of hours, or two and one-half hours, many nights, and did them then.

RC: When you sit down to write a novel like *Fifth Business*, does that all come out of your memory, or do you do what I would call "research" to write it?

RD: I tried to remember what I had heard when I was a boy and I tried to make it as general as possible. What interests me is that many people who fought in that war have written to me, and they have seen things in the book which are not in the writing but it was open enough for them to read into it their own experience. And certainly, I know, I was told by people—some of them masters in Upper Canada who are men of great considerable intelligence that the great misery of the war was the almost unrelieved terror of being in the trenches— that unless you were extremely insensitive, trench life was very, very exhausting.

RC: Well, in that novel and, of course, in *The Manticore,* what becomes another impressive feature of your writing is your evidently extensive knowledge of Jungian psychology.

RD: I first began by reading Freud, and I read a great deal of Freud, and then began to read Jung in consequence because I found Freud grated on me. There was a constant reductive tendency about his thought which, although I admired it enormously, I found very, very, wearing and somehow, for me (and I only say for me), false. I found that the Jungian attitude was a much more humane one and much more suitable to my personal temperament. Though I think it would be a mistake to use anything like Jung's thought or Freud's thought as a sort of mechanism for a novel because, brilliant though the insights of both men are, they never provide a really full or satisfactory explanation for what you encounter and what you see in life. You see, I spent 20 years as a newspaperman, and when you do that, you hear about three times as much as you can possibly publish. And you know motives that lie behind actions which appear very, very differently in print.

RC: In your recent novels, you are very interested, it seems to me, in formative influences in the younger lives of your characters that . . . Have you any sense of those formative of influences in your own life at this early stage?

RD: Oh yes. There were many of them. One of them was the fact that my family was one that moved a great deal. You know, in those days people in Ontario didn't move from one place to another nearly as readily as they do now, and it seemed to me that we were always on the move. Before I was born, my parents had lived in several places before they were in Thamesville where they were for a few years, but not for a long time. And this perpetual gypsying around almost, as it seemed, gave me a sort of rootlessness and also a somewhat watchful quality because I didn't belong especially anywhere. When we lived at Renfrew, one of the things which I was very acutely aware of was that almost every child that I knew seemed to be a cousin of half the town. I hadn't any cousins there at all. Well, that was the sort of extraordinary Scottish clannishness of the place. But when we moved to Kingston, everybody knew who everybody's grandfather was and who his Aunt Minnie had married and this, that, and the other. I didn't know any of that.

RC: And your father by this time was publisher—

RD: Of the Kingston paper.

RC: —of the *Kingston Standard?*

RD: Yes.

RC: And was he active in politics?

RD: Oh yes, he was very active in politics. As a newspaperman, he was a liberal and he ran liberal newspapers and he was intensely interested in the local organization of politics, and eventually he became a senator.

RC: That was in the 1920s, was it?

RD: No, he became a senator just about 1943, I think it was, because you see at that time he was president of the Canadian Press, and when the war broke out, it was rather a special job to be done in making arrangements about the coverage of war news, and so on and so forth, by the Canadian newspapers and their news association. And he did it and it was for that reason that he was offered the Senatorship. [Photograph of Senator Davies] That's my father. He liked that picture, that was his favorite picture of himself. Other people said it made him look very disagreeable, but he said it made him look the way he really was. I don't think he looks disagreeable but that's the way he wanted to be thought of. [Photograph.] And there he is much later and that's a sort of official war portrait, and I think he was probably about 80 when that was taken.

RC: That's a Senatorial picture, isn't it?

RD: That's a Senatorial picture by Karsh. Senators had to look like that.

RC: [Laughs] Your father was a successful businessman and he was involved in politics, and you were later a political editor, or editor, and obviously you had to comment on politics, and so I'm somewhat surprised at perhaps how little politics plays in your writing. Have you lost interest in politics or is that another side of your writing?

RD: No. I'm keenly interested in them and I'm interested in successful people, and so on and so forth. But my father was a very strong influence in my life and, you know, he was the only man I ever knew who had quite a bit of money, who said he had enough.

RC: Boy Staunton seems to have pretty successfully frustrated his son. Apparently that wasn't the case in your relationship with your father.

RD: Well, you see my father and I had certain things in common and shared certain interests which made that kind of effect very unlikely. Now he was a man of extremely dominant personality and if I had challenged him in the realm in which he was successful, we would have locked horns and I think very possibly he would have won. But I never did that. I didn't want to do the things he'd done, I wanted to do other things, I wanted to do things in which he was interested and he—and I must say also my mother—were always very encouraging and friendly towards my ambitions.

RC: You started out with some ambition to be an actor I take it?

RD: Yes.

RC: And that was encouraged by your parents?

RD: Yes, because they were both intensely interested in the stage. [Photograph] Oh, now, that is a very dear place indeed because it was the first theater I'd ever attended and the first theater in which I ever appeared, and it was the Ferguson Opera House in Thamesville, Ontario. That picture is from a book called *A Stage In Our Past* which the University of Toronto Press brought out a while ago about the origins of the Canadian theater. And that little opera house has been pulled down now so it's lucky that we have a picture of what it looked like.

RC: What did you play in?

RD: Well, I played in an operetta called *Queen Esther* which was a Bible piece, and I was an Israelite child.

RC: You go back over the kinds of writing you've done, have you any special preference for the novel form over drama, or is it just something . . .

RD: Well, I wrote plays for quite a long time and liked writing plays, and would like writing plays still but it is a cruelly difficult thing to get productions for plays because—. I'm sometimes amused when I hear complaints as I do from time to time or read them in papers from people who produce plays in Canada and about how hard it is to get new scripts. It's not my experience alone, but that of a number of playwrights I know that once a producer has got hold of your script, you almost have to sue him to get it back again. He gets it, he decides he doesn't want it, and then you can try to get it back. This is very, very wearying and somewhat discouraging because getting those things printed and reproduced is costly. And it's a very long, miserable business, and the rewards for having a play produced in Canada are pretty small compared with the rewards for publishing a successful novel, for instance.

RC: Why did you choose to go on to Oxford?

RD: Well, I tell you, that was a grievous story; it was because I couldn't take a university degree in Canada. You see, I never was able to pass my matriculation in mathematics, and in my day, you had to pass your senior matriculation in twelve subjects, two of which were mathematical. I could never do it. It was very, very depressing. I never made more than a zero on a mathematical examination. It was very, very disagreeable. You know, I tried hard enough but if I were to get a degree at all I had to go someplace where they didn't care so much about mathematics.

RC: So your years spent at Queen's, you were not really a properly registered student?

RD: I was always called a special student because they were very kind to me: they let me be a special student. They let me study just as though I was a real person and not a sort of non-mathematical ghost, and I did rather well at Queen's. I am very grateful at Queen's, but I never did get a degree from there. Consequently, I was enormously pleased when years later Queen's gave me an honorary degree because I felt for the first time that I had really finished the business there.

RC: Did you have the intention when you went to Oxford of coming back—was it always your intention to come back to Canada?

RD: I don't think I thought very much about it. I expected, I rather expected, I think, to work in England for a while but I don't think I ever intended to stay there. But the coming of the war smashed up everybody's plans.

RC: Back to the question of politics, you said earlier that you're convinced that the Canadian people, or Canadians at least, are much more complex than people usually believe. Does that in any way reflect your knowledge of a man like Mackenzie King whom your father must have known?

RD: Yes, he knew him, and I do think that Mackenzie King (whom it is now rather fashionable to deride) was very much more representative of Canadian opinion and Canadian character than a great many people are prepared to admit today. But I can remember a time when he was regarded with great respect by all political parties because he was such an adroit political tactician. Now, of course, that he need no longer be feared, it's much easier to see what was wrong with him.

RC: If I may go back and ask you something about the way in which you work. In one of your essays you quote, I think, Georges Simenon saying that "the writer is a man with a vocation of unhappiness," if I have that quotation right. Is that your own view or is it just one of a number that you were citing?

RD: I think that it is a partial truth. Writers are curious people in that they tend to be withdrawn, they tend to be rather grumpy and unhappy, they tend to take offense very readily, they tend to harbor grievances, perhaps more than a great many people do, and they tend to be hypochondriacs. Now that all sounds terribly negative and bad, but it doesn't necessarily add up to a disagreeable personality.

RC: With the kind of busy life that you lead as the Master of Massey College and as a teacher at the University, when do you write?

RD: Well now, you see, I can't do what I did when I was a news-paperman and that is to write at night, because at nights I'm very frequently busy. And you yourself know how unremitting university work is. There's always some stuff that has to be read or marked or something, when you had hoped to get some time off. Consequently I have to try to clear several weeks in the summer and work then.

RC: So in the course of winter, you do very little of your . . .

RD: I do a great deal of note making, and there's always time to reflect about what you're going to write when you're riding on the underground or walking about or listening to a lecture by one of your colleagues [Laughs] or something of that sort, but you can't get much writing done, you just make notes.

RC: Do you write a novel from beginning to end and then do a great deal of revision, or is it a finished product when you're done?

RD: Oh no. I make a great many notes. I carry a notebook all the time, a book like this, and fill several of them with notes and then I transfer the notes into another book in the form of a plan, and I make all kinds of extra notes as the plan develops and then from the plan, I write the first draft. And then the first draft requires very, very ex-tensive revision and after a great deal of revision, that's pretty much the book.

RC: Do you see your novels, and for that matter your plays as well, as part of a Canadian tradition or do you think about that kind of thing?

RD: Yes, I do, I think about it quite a lot. But it seems to me, you see, that what is Canadian about them is the source from which they spring, which is the life that I know, which is Canadian life. But I see it rather differently from some Canadian authors. I see Canadians as often very much more complex, and many-colored psychologically in a way that some people, in a way that people used to think was not Canadian. There used to be an idea that Canadians were a very one-

colored, rather straight-ahead, a simple lot. They are nothing of the
sort, but I've always tried to convey as well as I could some
impression of the complexity of Canadian life.

RC: Are you psychoanalyzing the Canadian character?

RD: No, no. I don't think that that is a possibility. You know that is
something that critics have sometimes said about certain writers. I
mean they say, for instance, that Dostoyevsky has analyzed the
Russian character. I'm sure Dostoyevsky would be horrified by any
such suggestion. Because inevitably what he sees in the Russian
character is reflected through his own personality, and this is one of
the things that makes writing extremely various and, I think, intensely
interesting. Inevitably the evidence that comes to a writer is
interpreted through his own personality.

RC: Do you find that the interest in your novels is primarily in your
recent ones or has this been your experience since the beginning?

RD: The recent ones, but you see the recent ones take the other
ones along with them. And one of the things that amuses me in a
somewhat wry way is that people who think that my recent novels are
good are beginning to discover to their astonishment that there was
more in the earlier novels than they'd supposed.

RC: You read other Canadian writers, do you read Canadian critics?

RD: Well now, do you mean the academic critics or the newspaper
critics?

RC: Well, both perhaps.

RD: Oh yes.

RC: And do they help you? Why do you read them?

RD: Well, I read them because I want to find out what they are
saying, but I wouldn't say that they help me particularly because I
don't think that critics generally do help writers. It's as Thornton
Wilder has said, you must be very, very careful with the critics who
praise you and with the critics who blame you because you begin to
think about them too much and pretty soon you'll find that, in a way,
that critic is looking over your shoulder when you're writing and in a
certain way, he's writing your book. That's the end.

RC: In *A Voice From The Attic* you're pretty harsh with critics it
seems to me.

RD: Yes.

RC: And in that book you talk about your hope for the

development of a clerisy, of an intelligent reading public in Canada. I'd like to ask you two questions about that. Do you still feel that harshly about the critics, that they don't really—. I've forgotten the phrase you use now, but it's a very strong one, almost to suggest that you think that the general newspaper critics are pretty useless and the academic critics—the very best ones—are interesting because they themselves have imaginations and the rest are just people who write rather bad books.

RD: Yes. Well, I do think that. And I wrote that with a great deal of strength because nobody criticizes critics, and it's bad for anyone to be free of criticism. Now critics, I've known a lot of them personally, and they're extraordinarily touchy fellows. And one of the things that really hurts a critic dreadfully is if you suggest to him that he doesn't write very well and yet, you know, it's very often true.

RC: Have you seen a development of a more intelligent reading public in Canada over the course of your years as a writer?

RD: Yes, unquestionably.

RC: Is that because there are more people going to the university or do you have any explanation?

RD: More people going to university and growth of population— growth of population in the middle range, I think. You see we now have so many people who come to Canada who don't come as laborers and do very humble work so that it's really their children or their children's children who are going to be the comparatively educated children. So you get people who come here to do skilled, professional work, or work on a well-paid and intelligent, intellec- tually demanding level.

RC: It seems to me that you've perhaps, in most of your life, you've never done just one thing. I mean you moved on from being a newspaper editor, already a successful novelist and writer. Instead of becoming just a writer, you then took on this job at Massey Col- lege. Does that give you some special kind of stimulation?

RD: Well, the part of that that I like very much indeed is teaching. I find teaching extremely interesting.

RC: It's now been in existence, I think, for ten years.

RD: Ten years.

RC: Has it found a special role for itself at the University of Toronto?

RD: Yes, it has, though I don't think that it has found the role that it will eventually fill. It is not only a place where a certain number of graduate students live, but it's a place where a lot of graduate teaching goes on and where a lot of senior academics write and do the kind of research that you do if you don't have to do it with a laboratory.

RC: When the College first began, one of the criticisms of it, I suppose, was that it was an attempt to impose an Oxford college or an English college on a North American university. How do you feel about that now?

RC: Well, it never was that; though it has some of the appurtenances of an English college, but the model that was actually in the minds of the Massey family (and particularly of Vincent Massey), was not an English institution at all but the Princeton Institute of Advanced Studies. And it was toward that that they wanted to work. But you know you can't create one of those things just by snapping your fingers. It had to grow and it is growing, and we're not there yet by any means and when we get farther on, we won't be a place like the Princeton Institute because there's only one, but we'll be something else and I think we'll be very useful.

RC: I suppose that implicit in that criticism was the idea that this was a very elitist place?

RD: Yes. And it is very elitist, but it's elitist in a way that I don't think anybody can truly complain about because the one standard for admission is high academic achievement. And that's not a thing which depends on money or knowing the right people, or any of those things. It's just something that exists and the people who have it deserve a break.

RC: Do you feel that once your career at Massey College is over that you'd want to retire in Canada or elsewhere?

RD: Oh yes, yes. That is a decision that my wife and I arrived at. Some time ago, because you know, if you ever think about retirement in Canada, you have to make up your mind whether you're going to do it here or whether you're going to do it elsewhere. The only place that we would be likely to retire other than in Canada would be in Great Britain, and we don't think that Great Britain would be a very satisfactory place to retire to now, and Canada has many, many satisfactions for retired people, not that we have any intention of retiring in the sense of just lying down among the daisies.

RC: But I suppose a writer can really never retire, never has to retire; you're always self-employed.

RD: You carry yourself in your head and unless you lose your wits, you ought to go on writing as long as you live.

RC: Are you planning a new novel now?

RD: Yes.

RC: Is it related to the previous two?

RD: Yes.

RC: Are you superstitious about talking about the work that's to come?

RD: Well, I wouldn't dream of telling you what it's going to be about because it almost certainly would prove to be quite different. But it is another aspect of the story that has been told in *Fifth Business* and *The Manticore*.

RC: Well, I'm certainly going to wait for it with great interest.

RD: Thank you.

Author Says Messiah Could Be a Woman
Tom Harpur/1974

From *Toronto Daily Star,* 16 February 1974, p. F5. Reprinted by permission of the Toronto Star Syndicate.

Davies: To give you my religious background, I'm an Anglican by what I suppose you would call persuasion. I was brought up in a Presbyterian family and I found Presbyterianism, even as a child, a strikingly cold and unsympathetic faith. I couldn't say that I was very conscious of what it was, but, at an early age, church chilled me; it seemed to be a combination of concert and lecture.

As I grew older I became much more interested in the sacramental approach of the Catholic Church and the Anglican. As I was very ill-suited by temperament to be a Roman Catholic, it was pretty obvious that I would be better off in the Church of England.

I was confirmed in Christ Church Cathedral, Oxford, while there as a student and away from home, so it avoided disturbing my parents.

Harpur: Are you still a practising Anglican?

Davies: I would hesitate to say that, though I attend church fairly often. You see, here at Massey College we have a chapel and it's ecumenical. We've had many different chaplains; the present one is Anglican, but his predecessor was a Presbyterian. We use our own form of service and it stays the same throughout.

Harpur: You consider yourself a believer then?

Davies: Yes, indeed. But, you know, if I were asked to nail down and defend what it was I believed and why, I would be in a pickle like a lot of people. I think this is the thing which is not perhaps very widely or sympathetically understood.

Religious belief is not susceptible to the kind of discussion and proof which appeals to sceptical minds that generally want to work on scientific principles. They're so imbued with the scientific method that intuition and a sort of native awareness don't count for anything.

Harpur: I wonder if you could enlarge on that a little.

Davies: Well, I mean, you're not asked if you say you've fallen in

love, to give an absolutely water-tight and world-convincing explanation of what you're doing. In a very different way, it's the same with
religion. I don't see why it should be demanded that you justify,
explain and excuse it to people of another opinion.

Harpur: Do you think there has been too much emphasis on
theology, then, in the churches?

Davies: I don't think I'd want to say that. In too many modern
churches there is no emphasis on theology at all. There is a kind of
justification by works or by keeping up with modern trends—anything that will drag in a few more people. I think that if the church
were more, not uncompromisingly but firmly, theological, it might
attract a lot more intellectuals.

Harpur: In your novels, especially the two most recent, *Fifth
Business* and *The Manticore*, you write in some depth about evil.
What is the human problem here as you see it?

Davies: This is something with which I am very much concerned
and think a very great deal about. You see, I cannot consider myself a
totally orthodox Christian because I can't accept the Christian urging
toward perfection. I don't think that perfection is possible or even, in
psychological terms, desirable for human beings.

I think it is absolutely necessary for a man to recognize and accept
the evil in himself. If he does that he is in a position to make the evil
work in a different way; the charges of psychological energy involved
can be re-directed in not necessarily good paths, but at least in understood paths.

When you behave badly, at least then you're sufficiently far ahead
to know what you're doing and to count the cost. It is Dr. Carl Jung
who is always quoting a saying of Jesus from the Gospel of Thomas
to the effect that if you know fully what you're doing, you are
blessed; if you don't know, you are damned. This is a very great
saying and I wish we had it in the orthodox Gospels.

You've got to know yourself and take personal responsibility. Just
to go ahead living blindly, assured you're on the right path, is almost
certain damnation. I don't mean the theatrical damnation of red
flames and torture, but just to be an ineffective nuisance.

Harpur: What of the devil; is he just a mythical symbol?

Davies: The devil seems to me to be not the commonplace
symbol of evil but the symbol of unconsciousness, of unknowing, of

acting without knowledge of what you're intending to do. It's from
that that I think the great evils spring. The devil is the unexamined
side of life; it's unexamined but it's certainly not powerless.

Harpur: What about the rightness or wrongness of any particular
action. Are there, for example, standards for human sexuality?

Davies: I think every act must be weighed individually; there can
be only general principles. Sexual contacts which are primarily just
for their own sake, for thrills, can be very deceptive and, ultimately,
disappointing.

I'm very depressed by a lot of stuff you read nowadays—articles
about sex as though it were a kind of open gate to happiness and
fulfillment. This is not a matter of being puritanical. Sex that is not an
evidence of a strong human tie is just like blowing your nose; it's not
a celebration of a splendid relationship.

Harpur: How do you yourself arrive at the general principles you
use in deciding what is right and wrong?

Davies: It's an endless process and you just have to do the best
you can. It's almost like belonging to Alcoholics Anonymous—you
just live one day at a time and hope you won't make too much of a
mess. Attempting to set up gorgeous principles and then stick to them
is an awful way of disappointing yourself. It's like the way we used to
make New Year's resolutions when I was young. If they lasted a week
you were practically a hero.

Harpur: There are risks then in setting a code for yourself?

Davies: You have to have one which works without too much
pressing. If you're perpetually nagging yourself, there's something
wrong. It's time for some serious self-examination. You have to be on
reasonable terms with yourself; you've got to forgive yourself for
being an awful lot of things which you just are.

Harpur: You spoke earlier of the churches' attempting to keep up
with modern trends. Is this what you feel is happening in the push to
ordain women as priests?

Davies: No, I don't. I think that the bringing of the feminine
principle, feminine values and insights into greater prominence in
Christianity will be the greatest revolution in the faith in the last 1,000
years. But, it's got to be the real thing and not just women's lib.

The trouble with Christianity is that it's too Hebraically based with
its single Father God and its masculine Saviour. We've got to get rid

of that fearful masculine insistence if we're going to have a religion which is a workable, comforting and dear one to humanity at large.

We've got to stop pounding away at the Logos idea (word, reason) and do some serious thinking about the Eros principle; i.e. the principle of love and relationship as women know it, instead of a frosty, disembodied love of God which seems so often to exercise itself in such horrifying ways.

Harpur: Do you believe that religion has fostered discrimination against women?

Davies: The Jewish and Christian religions have been hard on women. When you read how Orthodox Judaism looked at women you realize what a gigantic revolution was ushered in by Jesus. Now the church needs another one. People talk about the coming of Messiah; how do they know Messiah isn't going to be a woman? It's a fair deal!

Harpur: I take it you don't accept the Christian claim that Jesus is the unique Messiah for mankind?

Davies: No, and I don't think He would have either. It seems to me that Jesus as an ethical teacher and Jesus as the symbol of the best in man are different creatures. When they're mixed up together you get some bad results.

Harpur: You think there was a myth that grew up around Jesus after His lifetime?

Davies: Yes, and I think that the myth is of infinite value, but the teaching also must be realized as that of a man of an astonishing degree of insight. In my view, the symbolic Jesus and the historical Jesus are just not the same creature. This, of course, would get me into the most awful wrangles with theologians, but that can't be helped.

Harpur: You don't like the ideal of struggling for perfection. What would your definition of a truly good life be?

Davies: I think—and here I run counter to virtually all theologians and a lot of others, too—it's the fully realized human life, the fulfilling of one's potential. The person who lives that way can't help but be enormously valuable to an awful lot of people. And he's not going to do harm, because he knows himself.

But, when I talk about goodness it's with inverted commas. What goodness so frequently means is giving to community chest or cam-

paigning against cancer, etc. while at the same time leading an utterly
unexamined life which may be a source of despair or less effective life
for others. The place to start living a better life is at home instead of
using it as a launching pad from which to sally forth to impose virtue
on other people.

Harpur: What do you think of the current widespread interest in
meditation, mysticism and other religious experiences? What is this
trend saying?

Davies: Well, it depends so much on the individual involved. I
think that the attempt to incorporate Eastern religious practices into
the Western world is enormously suspect, because I don't think we're
temperamentally and psychologically well-suited for it.

Meditation is a good Hebrew and Christian practice, so why do
you have to sit around with your legs tied up in knots saying: "O
mani padme hum," which nobody understands, in order to promote
spirituality? If you want to meditate no one's stopping you, but do it
in a manner which is historically yours instead of kidding yourself
you're an Indian.

I think the romance of it, eating sesame seeds and funny foods,
appeals to some; but, it's a mechanical way to perfection. You know,
the idea that if I stop eating meat I'll be more spiritual. Baloney!
Some of the greatest saints ate meat every time they got their hands
on it.

Harpur: What do you think of the role of the clergy today and of
trends toward priests who earn their living in a secular job?

Davies: A committed person who works at something else while
authorized to lead worship, etc., seems to me to be in the truest
Christian tradition.

There's great value in having men who are committed to carrying
their beliefs into some kind of daily work and who don't walk around
as professional victims for every beggar and hustler or for every
neurotic woman or whining man.

Often a minister is just a kind of poorly paid, ill-equipped psychiatrist. I don't mean this cruelly. You can't expect these fellows to
be Jesus Christ, Sigmund Freud and John Paul Getty all rolled into
one! A minister is expected to be able to scale the pinnacles of
finance while he's usually getting a rotten stipend himself.

Is the Day of Davies the Dramatist Finally at Hand with *Question Time?*
Herbert Whittaker/1975

From The Globe and Mail, Toronto, 15 February 1975, p. 14.
Reprinted by permission.

"The right honorable gentleman has repeatedly called attention to his candor; he protests he has nothing to hide. No indeed, Mr. Speaker; he offers us the first example in the political history of this House of full frontal nudity, for he stands before this House shamelessly displaying his engorged ego and his shrivelled principles."

It was this Parliamentary reference to the Leader of the Opposition from Robertson Davies' new political fantasy, *Question Time,* which caused Prime Minister Pierre Trudeau to break into laughter, appropriately enough during the House of Commons' question period. Trudeau had just received a script sent by St. Lawrence Centre's nimble press agent, Fiona McCall.

Question Time, which is to have its premiere at the Centre Feb. 25, with Kenneth Pogue as the prime minister, examines the intellectual, spiritual and personal responsibility of this country's chief representative against a setting of Les Montagnes de Glace, where the dramatist has isolated the PM after a plane crash.

"Nobody could be foolish enough to mistake my characters for the present Prime Minister and his wife," announced the author over a chicken crepe. "Or should that read 'his lovely lady.' "

Davies regards *Question Time* as an extension of his earlier *Jig for the Gypsy,* revived by the Lennoxville Festival last summer. Like that Welsh comedy of argument and magic, the new work is a frankly political play.

"I've always been interested in politics. My family was always interested in politics. My father (the late Senator Rupert Davies) was interested in politics. I've been especially interested in the costs of politics and that's what *Question Time* is about, incidentally.

"A prime minister who devotes himself to power and the good of his people can be drained of all energy in his private life. And the public life is a reflection of the private life." Davies warmed up to his proposition. "Those schlemiels in Ottawa haven't a vestige of private life left to them." (Names deleted at the request of the interviewed party.)

Dr. Davies, does not your Prime Minister's wife also lash out at the media which help deprive public servants of private life? "That is the essence of your squalid art," is what she says to an interviewer while awaiting word of her husband's survival. "Getting across what you mean without saying it; making somebody else say more than they had any intention of saying," is what she says.

Davies assures me that "the media" always refers to television interviewers. If he has objections to newspaper interviewers, he is tactful enough not to mention them at this point. His scorn for the printed press he confines to antiquated front pages and the content of editorials.

But he is delighted that Lloyd Robertson's handsome face will be seen, via film in the St. Lawrence Centre production. The chief announcer for the Canadian Broadcasting Corp.'s National News was happy to oblige, so it will be his face and voice which break the news in Davies' play: "Ottawa announces that the plane bringing the Prime Minister, Peter McAdam . . . back from Moscow is missing . . . "

During the play PM's delirium on Les Montagnes de Glace, he is attended by a shaman and a highly symbolical nurse. They act as sounding boards for the questions Davies posits in his play.

"In Question Time, my Prime Minister learns about himself. He also learns about Canada. He learns that the Queen of Canada is not Elizabeth the Second; it is the country itself.

"We live on the oldest land mass in the world and we live on it as if it were created when we got off the boat!" Davies can look quite formidable on occasion, a prophet no longer minor.

"Question Time is about the same thing that all the plays I've written are about. The Casanova play, King Cole (his name for King Phoenix), Fortune My Foe, Hunting Stuart."

And what is that? "Self-exploration!"

Question Time is Davies' first new play since 1967, since The Centennial Spectacle, which was planned to be acted in front of the Parliament buildings, with Tyrone Guthrie directing, Louis

Applebaum composing the music and Gratien Gélinas as its leading player.

"At one point in it, a man was to leap from the Peace Tower, but instead of plunging to his death, he was to fly heaven-wards." Davies plainly regrets that this never took place. What happened?

"Tony Guthrie got high-handed with the Ministry of Works (responsible for the stage and the seating) which then announced that nothing could be built on Parliament Hill, because the Queen was expected.

"I also contributed to The Centennial Play that year, a five-writer project conceived by Nicholas Goldschmidt for groups to stage all across the country." And whatever happened to that?

"It had its tryout in Lindsay, then its premiere in Ottawa, where the director took it on himself to alter it so as to be more favorable to the Province of Quebec. It wasn't done again, as far as I know."

That did it. Davies, who would rather have been a successful dramatist than anything in the world, had been finally discouraged. Previously, he had been roughed up as a dramatist by British adjudicators, Canadian critics, Broadway producers and the great Guthrie himself. We had spoken of this struggle a year ago, when he accepted Leon Major's pressing invitation to write a play for the St. Lawrence.

You have had some rough experiences in the theatre, Mr. Davies?

"Yes." His answer was firm, but he did not whine. He has high hopes for this one. He is impressed with Major's energy and excitement about what he does.

"It is a spectacle. I had long admired Leon's work as a director of opera and spectacular plays and I didn't want to miss the chance of working with a master of this sort of theatrical art," he has written for the St. Lawrence Centre program.

When discouraged by those Centennial experiences, Davies settled down to a major trilogy of novels. Fifth Business and The Manticore have already won him outstanding response here and abroad. Before he could respond to Major's invitation, he had to finish the third book, and it is now completed.

"It is called World of Wonders and carries on the story of Eisengrim. Part of it is a description of a tour from Montreal to Vancouver by an actor-knight playing melodrama."

The actor is plainly Sir John Martin-Harvey, whom Davies had seen in his early youth and who represented the great tradition of Victorian theatre. Davis was tickled when his editor checked dates to see if he had been old enough to have been on one of Martin-Harvey's Canadian tours.

We talk of Martin-Harvey and Davies recalls the great stage trick which allowed the actor to play the twins' role in *The Corsican Brothers*. Does Davies have such tricks in his new spectacle?

"Better," he says, fully confident of the St. Lawrence's Murray Laufer as a stage designer. *Question Time* calls for a great phantom bear, for the melding of its two very different locales, Les Montagnes de Glace and the House of Commons, in a sequence in which Ken Pogue seemingly plays both the Prime Minister and the Leader of the Opposition.

But *Question Time* is not to be seen as an exhibition of stage techniques, an extravaganza on the level of an ice follies. It follows through that early line of theatrical self-exploration with the confidence of his more mature work as a leading novelist. Davies has been exploring himself more frankly, more rewardingly.

"I seem to be able to write more frankly about what I feel," he agrees. "Part of this is because of the change in the environment. I've changed, but I think Canada has changed.

"The writer today can say things in public—I don't mean shocking things—and expect to be understood. Canada's growth in this direction has been phenomenal in the last 20 years.

"This sets the writer free to say things that he couldn't say before. And it is splendid that we have a theatre to match that new freedom. The writer can now work in Canadian theatre. Look at the relationship between James Reaney and the Tarragon. Canada's supported theatre can now afford to be civil to writers."

The Davies philosophy is Jungian rather than Freudian, as readers of *The Manticore* realized. In fact, he rejects with scorn such Freudian dramas as O'Neill's *Long Day's Journey into Night*.

"I submit the question for examination papers: Is Sean O'Casey right when he calls *Long Day's Journey* a long sodden whine?" but the examiners never let it pass.

"I have a sense of humor," he announces. "Can you name a major humorist who has become a national hero?" I venture Mark Twain, and he accepts Twain. "Any others?" Charles Dickens could be pretty amusing, I say, although he was perhaps accepted basically as a social reformer.

"Charles Dickens attacked social evils after they had been recognized and corrected," he scoffed.

With that comment, it was plain that the dramatist Davies was turning back into his other identity, the Master of Massey College, the terror of the conventional, unthinking undergraduate. Our interview about *Question Time* was plainly over.

But while Davies set out resolutely marching over the white snow in the direction of Massey College, to correct examination papers, I knew that he was keenly anticipating with pleasure his attendance at St. Lawrence Centre of dress rehearsals for his new play.

The day of Davies the dramatist seemed to be at hand at last. Toronto's municipal theatre is giving *Question Time* its world premiere. The Shaw Festival has announced his *Leaven of Malice* will be in its new season at Niagara-on-the-Lake and the Lennoxville Festival has plans to follow up *A Jig for the Gypsy* with another early Davies work, *Hunting Stuart.*

With the publication of *World of Wonders,* 1975 may well be viewed as the Year of Robertson Davies, one in which magic and satire become meaningful once again to the Canadian public.

"Sunday Supplement"
Margaret Penman/1975

Transcription from CBC Radio, 19 October 1975. Copyright 1975 Canadian Broadcasting Corporation. Reprinted by permission of the CBC, Robertson Davies, and Margaret Penman, M.A., Ph.D.

MP: In your trilogy—it's been called the Deptford Trilogy by at least one critic—you fold three main characters—Dunstan, David, Magnus—as they've gone through a kind of confessional and come to some sort of self-revelation. I'm wondering how much of their confessional revelation you see as being part of the Canadian psyche.

RD: Well, I don't know. I wouldn't have thought of it in quite that large-scale way, but it seems to me that they demonstrate three aspects of Canadians as they appear to me. Dunstan certainly is very much a Canadian, and Staunton is very much I think another recognizable Canadian indeed. A lot of people have rather bothered me to give him a name and they put forward all sorts of candidates among eminent Canadian businessmen and so on and so forth and I won't have anything to do with that, but I think that Magnus demonstrates the possibility, the potentiality. This is what a Canadian very well might be and sometimes I think is.

MP: If you took the chance?

RD: If you took the chance, yes.

MP: Well, I'm interested in Magnus in another way and the connection between magic and religion. When as Paul, still a very young boy, he first goes to the fair and he meets Willard, he's been primed with psalms, with difficult teachings, he sees and he is absolutely overwhelmed like the evangelist and his heart pounds for him like the hart for running waters. Is this connection between magic and religion something you see as . . . ?

RD: Oh, very decidedly, and it used to strike me very, very strongly when I was a small boy that the Bible stories with which I was diverted and instructed, as children were in those days, seemed to me to be just side by side with the stories from *Arabian Nights* and

146

Grimm and Andersen and so forth. They were equally marvelous.
They were full of extraordinary characters whom you certainly
wouldn't encounter every day but who were very real in another way.
I think that for a child, certainly, a person who appeared in the
gorgeous aspect of a sideshow magician might very well seem to be
almost like an angel, more interesting than what we hear about most
angels.

MP: Well, I'd like to pick up on the angel and the devil out of this.
The film-makers and the BBC producer who are listening to Magnus,
his subtext, as you call it, his life, say that they don't think Canada is
perhaps a very good place to go to hell from. Is it a good place to go
to hell from or to heaven from?

RD: As good as any. But you see this is the image of Canada that I
protest against and it is one which is certainly very prominent in the
minds of a lot of people in other parts of the world and far too many
people in Canada, that it is an inferior: spiritually inferior, intellec-
tually inferior, inferior in all the really important subliminal ways to,
oh, you know, the rest of the world and parts of Europe and so forth.
But I've travelled fairly extensively; I've been in some terribly dull
parts of Europe and met some uncommonly, dull-minded people
there. And I don't believe this nonsense. I think that Canada is just as
full of extraordinary potentiality in this area as anywhere else in the
world and perhaps greater than most because it's a fascinating, very
old, extraordinary country. But as long as we insist on concentrating a
sort of peanut 19th century association with it, well, of course, it looks
dull.

MP: Well, what associations would you take out of this old
country?

RD: Well, its enormous age for one thing and the fact that it's been
inhabited for an extraordinarily long time, it seems to me that almost
every few months you read in the paper that they've pushed back the
time area in which North America has been inhabited by a few more
million years. There have been people here since there were people
anywhere, doing *what*, and doing it *how*, and the remains of it are
being discovered or rather we're beginning to recognize them. And
we must associate ourselves not with a European past of a few hundred years or a few thousand years but with the past of our own
country which is reckoned in millions of years.

MP: Well, I've got to pick up on that again. Two points here really. Magnus has had an extraordinary past and an extraordinary life. At least one critic has said that in *World of Wonders,* he turns out to be really rather a nice, decent, middle-class Canadian. Now further from that in *The Manticore,* you have David Staunton going into the caves in Switzerland finding the bear that used to be worshipped by the peoples in the past and that Liesl still worships. If Magnus or a Canadian were to go back into the cave of the unconscious, what would they find? And would they turn out like Magnus at the end, tucked up in bed and—?

RD: Ah, yes, but you see I didn't see the critic who said that Magnus had turned out to be a nice symbol, a middle-class, Canadian chap, and I don't believe it for one instant. In fact . . .

MP: He's not nice.

RD: Oh, he is not nice. Look what he did to Willard the Wizard. He killed him in a most appalling fashion. What did he do to Boy Staunton? Did he withhold death from him? Did he put out a hand toward him? Did he show any kind of Christian charity toward him? None. If this is a typical Canadian and, of course, it may be, I don't think he's a nice guy. I think that critic ought to take another look or stop measuring Magnus Eisengrim by himself. Criticisms generally say quite as much about the critic as they say about anything else.

MP: Well, Dunny was trying to get away from dull and gray Canadian respectability which you said many people see Canada as. This is a personal question really: were you trying to get away from it when you went to Oxford and then in your years at the Old Vic?

RD: I never really believed in it, but I found that so many people did believe in it. I felt alienated from my own country and my own people. I didn't think it was dull, I didn't see why it was at a disadvantage in connection with other countries. But so many of my contemporaries and elders did, and it was only when I got away from Canada that I was able to look at it from elsewhere that I saw that certainly, for my money, I was right and they were wrong. It was just as extraordinary as I'd always thought it was.

MP: Is this why you came back?

RD: Oh, yes. Oh I never really thought of going away for good.

MP: I know that you've worked in the theatre: you did work at the Old Vic. Have you ever worked in a circus?

RD: No, no, never worked in a circus. I don't think I'd be much good in a circus. You've got to be a special kind of person to be effective in a circus. You've got to be terribly good at, you know, the sensation side of life. I mean judging distances, doing things actually bang on time: marvelous eyesight, wonderful coordination, all the things I haven't got. I think I'd be a dead loss in the circus.

MP: Well, how do you explore? How do you find out, let's say, about the circus? How do you find out about people like that?

RD: Well, you see, that is the thing I can do that they generally cannot. I've known some circus people and they're not very curious about one another. They're remarkably easygoing and charitable toward one another but not very searching, not very penetrating in their investigation of one another. This is where I can do something they can't do. I can see things that they don't see about themselves.

MP: Will they talk to you?

RD: Oh yes, yes. Yes. And people generally will talk to me. I'm not stalking them as a man stalks an animal. I want to know about them, and I want to know about them not for some horrible reason but I do want to know. I want to know the real thing, I don't want just to pretend.

MP: Well, I was wondering how Robertson Davies, the Master of Massey College, can get to know the people at the subway stall. I think of Virginia Woolf here who had really just one side to her life, didn't she?

RD: Yes.

MP: She couldn't know the fishmonger's wife really or know what it felt like.

RD: Ah, but you see Virginia Woolf was a lady of upper-class birth and education and she had no touch with ordinary people at all; she hadn't very much touch even with people of her own class and this just happened to be something about her. I on the whole can get on with most people, and I don't have to pretend or do awful patronizing things about it. People don't respond to patronage but they do respond to genuine interest, and they will talk.

MP: Leon Major tells me—this was when you were working on *Question Time* with him—that you complained that people sometimes called you the Canadian George Bernard Shaw.

RD: Yes.

MP: And you said, "No, I'm too emotional."

RD: Well then, of course, it's absurd. Nobody is the anything George Bernard Shaw and also from childhood I protested against the fact that if a singer is any good, she's the Canadian Melba or if a Canadian writer is any use, he's the Canadian somebody else. Why aren't they just themselves? As for Bernard Shaw, you know, he was a immensely cerebral man (though he had his very emotional points) but I am not. I disagree with Shaw on just about every vital aspect of everything, and I'm different (and I'm quite prepared to admit a vastly inferior creature). But I'm not him. I'm me.

MP: It's the emotional that I'm interested in.

RD: Yes.

MP: I think in this trilogy there is a new departure, there are many more emotional feelings, too. You know, real emotion comes through, they're not so detached as novels, not so cerebral. Would you agree?

RD: Ah yes, I would, because you see these novels are all written in the first person, somebody's talking all the time. The other novels were written in the third person. They were written by an author and that was the only way I could write at that time but you see I try to get so that I can do things that I couldn't do before. And I do not believe in the popular nonsense that as you get older you can't learn anything, so I try to learn things. I try to learn to do what I've been doing better than I did it before, and I hope I'm getting on with that, and I think that being able to communicate more directly with readers is one of them.

MP: Do you find it difficult to reveal yourself?

RD: Oh terribly, terribly. It's very, very difficult, but it is possible if you will take the pains and go through the difficulties of doing it. You see, I think that where a great many people suffer and are terribly unhappy is that they cannot reveal themselves, and they can't reveal themselves even to themselves. Self-revelation is not pleasant but it's better than staying all tangled up.

MP: Ah now, you did write—this is through the analyst in *The Manticore*—that to live is to battle with trolls. That is Ibsen's poem.

RD: Yes.

MP: To write, that is to sit in judgment over oneself.

RD: Yes.

MP: Are you sitting in judgment over yourself as you write?

RD: Well, I suppose I am because I have the greatest admiration for Henrik Ibsen and when he said that, he was talking very intimately to a personal friend and I'm sure that he was talking truthfully and I think that that is true. You see a lot of people ask me if I have ever undergone a Jungian analysis because there's one in *The Manticore*. No, but, believe me, writing books is another kind of self-analysis, and you don't blat out everything that you discover in what you write but you have to do a lot of self-investigation before you can write anything at all.

MP: What are the main things that you reveal about yourself in this trilogy?

RD: You reveal the quality of your perception and your really important attitudes toward very big things: mankind, mankind's relationship to whatever else it is that is a part of our universe—if you want to call it God or whatever you may want to call it, it is that. It is your relationship to time and to the circumstances of age and where you stand in life, whether your life is at the point where it's shorter to the end than it is to the beginning. All that kind of thing. These things inevitably color your writing. You don't put them down in so many words but they color every line you write.

MP: Now you mentioned the Jungian analysis here and you haven't undertaken one; I've wondered if the three—Liesl, Dunny and Magnus—can be construed as components of the Jungian self with Liesl the Anima linking the Conscious, Dunny, and the Unconscious, Magnus.

RD: Ah, now I think that's a very, very shrewd analysis indeed, and I didn't do that, you know, on a scheme but it's the way it came out. This is something that I'm sure you understand but a great many people don't. You don't make a kind of intellectual plan and then hang a novel on it like hanging clothes on a scarecrow. If you've got something that is like a novel to write, you write it and then either you see the plan when it's done or other people see it, but you don't do it to demonstrate anything. But I think that you are probably right and that occurred to me when the books were all done and I was rather surprised, particularly as Liesl is not everybody's idea of an anima figure, which is, you know, a woman of great beauty and rather a mute type who is talked at rather than talked to. Liesl is a tireless talker but I think she's fascinating, and I think that it is interesting and probably a Jungian would have something interesting to say if one wanted to talk about it, as to why I made her so hideously ugly.

MP: But she's sometimes beautiful as the men see her.

RD: Of course.

MP: In their view of her.

RD: Of course, and she is delightful and she is embracing. She is stimulating. She is magnificent. She's more fun than a dumb boob like poor old Leola Cruikshank in *The Manticore* who was just a sad, pretty girl and that is unfortunately what an anima figure is in the lives of many people.

MP: Except that these people do project onto the anima figure, don't they?

RD: Oh yes, yes, indeed they do.

MP: Good or bad witches, the good or bad breasts in Freudian terms?

RD: Yes. But you know Liesl is all kinds of fascinating things. She's a delightful, young woman; she's an extraordinarily perceptive, intelligent, middle-aged woman; and she is a terrifying brute when she's aroused. Well that's great. [RD laughs]

MP: She changes a lot.

RD: Yes.

MP: And she does have something of the fierce witch in the earlier novel and then in *World of Wonders* she becomes more the good witch or almost the therapist; she is the link between them. Did you intend this or did this just spring from your— ?

RD: No, it was not intentional. But, you see in *World of Wonders,* we find out how Liesl became the way she was and, of course, when she smashed up her grandfather's collection of beautiful, little toys, she wasn't a very nice girl.

MP: Did the trilogy change, did it end differently from what you had originally planned when you wrote the first volume, *Fifth Business?*

RD: Well, you see I never planned it as a trilogy. It just came out that way, there was more story after *Fifth Business* was done than I had told and *The Manticore* continued it, and then it was obvious that something had to be said about Magnus and so I had a book about him. But I never really, truly planned it to be three volumes, you know, starting at the beginning and piecing out what was to go in each one. It was pretty obvious what was to go in each one but it was not a planned scheme.

MP: Now what about David in *The Manticore?* In some ways it seems that perhaps that will go off at a tangent, in that he is not taken up again in *World of Wonders.* The impact of his meeting with Liesl and Magnus and Dunny in Switzerland, it's quite something, and one might expect perhaps in volume three [chuckles] that there would be a confrontation, that there would be a tremendous impact on all four of their lives as the story unravels itself.

RD: Yes. But you see, at the end of *The Manticore,* the question is open what's going to happen to David, and the reader may think for himself what he chooses about that. But, you know *The Manticore* was written as it was for a reason, which is not perhaps the very best reason, but critics are always having a good deal to say about the way people write books and one particular critic said of *Fifth Business* that it was very conventional, that I never attempted to experiment or anything of that sort. So I thought, all right, my fine friend, field this one! So I wrote *The Manticore* which is all about Boy Staunton but he isn't the principal character: it's the way he's reflected from his son. And did that fathead see it? No, he did not, predictably. But there it is and really the second volume is about Staunton.

MP: Boy Staunton?

RD: Yes. And what he did to people and how he influenced people and what a miserable father he was.

MP: Had you decided his death right at the beginning and then, of course, you reveal it, how he did die, really in *World of Wonders?* Or was that the form of his death? Was that something that came to you as you were completing *World of Wonders?*

RD: Well, no. It was inherent in the thing from the beginning because you see I have ideas about death which I very roughly summed up in saying that most people die of being themselves, and this means that their death arrives from a variety of different causes. Why do they get particular diseases? Why does it come at a particular time? When does it seem that the end. damn the end, has arrived? Or why with some of them is death deferred so long after the end has obviously arrived? Well, the reason that a man dies—I think in one of the books, I forget which one, I say something about this—is an immense complexity of reasons, and it was so with Staunton. But the vengeance of Magnus Eisengrim, or rather his rather subtle vengeance in refusing to do anything about it, is part of it, and we don't know in how many deaths somebody's refusal to do something is not a factor.

MP: Well, he's repeating himself, isn't he, Magnus and Willard, he's true to character?

RD: Vengeance is a strong element in all three of these books.

MP: Dunny worries a lot about God and the Devil, the intervention of God and the Devil who's been dreamed at least once in Magnus' life or perhaps an Angel Mary in his own life. Have you any conclusions about God and the Devil?

RD: The kind of conclusions as you'd expect from someone who is enormously influenced by Jungian thought and almost anything I say in this area is going to get me in trouble with somebody. But it seems to me that if you're going to have a really satisfactory notion of God, you must include evil in it because evil is a part of the universe as we know it, or what we think is evil is part of the universe as we know it. We think that cancer is a dreadful thing; we think that the plague is a dreadful thing, and so on and so forth. But if we were keeping the heavenly book of statistics, we might think quite otherwise and I don't think we're in any position to sit in judgment on God and say that he's either all good or partly bad or that there's a separate entity which we for shorthand call the Devil, who is the father of evil, this, that, and the other. We must have some more comprehensive idea of the universe and its mainspring than that.

MP: Is the Devil God's sense of humor? One character at least speculates on that.

RD: Yes, though you don't think the Devil's very funny when you look at some of the things with which you'd associate him, like the wards full of dreadfully malformed children and so on and so forth. You'd have to have a very refined sense of humor to consider that funny. But then, you see, we're looking at it from a very special point of view. We're not God, and we don't know what he needs or how he's running things or anything, but we do know that we somehow or other got from a protoplasmic atomic globule to you and me sitting in this studio with a fascinating amount of wire devices around us which make it possible for a lot of people to listen to us, and that's not just a tiny step and so we must assume that there is some kind of purpose somewhere however strangely it manifests itself.

MP: Which character are you closest to? People generally assume that it's Dunstan.

RD: Yes, but then, you know, it's like dreams. When you have dreams, you're all characters in a dream, however strange they may be. All snakes and monsters and beautiful girls and so on and so forth that appear in the dream are some aspect of yourself, and I leave it to you to conclude what relationship I have to these characters in the book.

MP: Well, I would assume that part of you is in all those men, or that they are all in you in some way or other drawing on your vast unconscious, drawing on archetypes and so on. These are all part of you in one way or another.

RD: It must be so.

You Should Face Up to Your Death, Says Author

Tom Harpur/1975

From the *Toronto Star,* 15 November 1975, p. B8. Reprinted by permission of the Toronto Star Syndicate.

Robertson Davies, Master of Massey College, well-known playwright and novelist, has recently written *World of Wonders,* the third in a trilogy of novels which brim with religious themes. Davies, an Anglican, talks with *Star* religion editor Tom Harpur about the basic religious question—death.

Harpur: As a novelist and playwright you have a unique insight into the human condition. How do you think people in our society look at death?

Davies: When people talk about it, they are, I think, inclined to joke about it or to regard it as a kind of inevitable evil that brings oblivion. Generally they pass it off without giving it the kind of thought and serious investigation they apply to other things.

They don't want to talk about it for long; you can't work up much of a prolonged conversation about death! For example, you don't hear many sermons about it, or how to approach it, or what it might be.

Harpur: There seems, then, to be what some have called a conspiracy of silence. This has not been, and is not still, the case with many other cultures, for example, the Canadian Indian. Why do you think it is true of ours?

Davies: Many of these other people have lived closer to death. Our civilization has removed death from the observation of most people. Today a person dies in the hospital whereas they used to die at home—just as they were born at home.

You don't usually see someone die and in many hospitals even the

156

relatives are asked to leave the room when the moment of expiry comes.

Doctors, in my experience anyway, are very resentful of any discussion of the way in which they allow death to come about. There was a book written recently about the way in which death is handled in hospitals and it's a very sore touch with many doctors.

Harpur: Do you think that this reflects the doctors' own unwillingness to come to grips with death or is it because it represents for them a failure of their healing art?

Davies: I think that in part it's because it's a failure of their practice; they tend to regard it as simply a medical and physical happening just as they sometimes seem to regard birth as a purely medical business. They don't seem to want to investigate beyond what they can know.

Something has always interested me in my study of literature, that is that doctors so frequently appear in books and plays as atheists or free-thinkers or advanced thinkers of some kind. It's supposed to be because they are men of science. Now, very few of them are men of science in any very serious sense; they're men of technique.

Thus, while they're frequently brought face to face with death they're not at all ready to consider it as a psychological or spiritual happening.

Harpur: Do you think that coming to terms with death, not morbidly, but trying to think it through, investigate its meaning for yourself, is important for one's own quality of living?

Davies: I do, indeed. I would go even further and say that if you think about death seriously for any length of time some of your thinking is going to be morbid because death means the cessation of the ego, the cessation of the person that you recognize as you, the disappearance of your face from the mirror, and the end—or the fear of the end—of contact with a world that perhaps has grown very dear to you.

But, there are other kinds of reflection about death which are by no means morbid. One of the things that puzzles me is that so few people want to look at life as a totality and to recognize that death is no more extraordinary than birth.

When they say it's the end of everything they don't seem to

recognize that we came from somewhere and it would be very, very strange indeed to suppose that we're not going somewhere.

We have always been present in the world as a possibility and when we die it is, I think, reasonable to assume that we're still going to be in the world as a fact.

Harpur: Could we explore that a little further? Do you think that there is life after death?

Davies: That is extremely difficult to answer because when people talk about life after death they insist on thinking about life in some form which is recognizable to them.

People in the past have had ecstatic notions of some kind of eternal bliss or horrifying notions of a life of eternal damnation; but it has always involved a life which is to some extent in the flesh. They say it's in the spirit, but they never conceive of it in the spirit.

We cannot escape from the bondage of our own humanity, but surely we have reached a point in thinking where we can consider the possibility of something which is other and beyond this present existence.

Harpur: You don't look forward, then, to working on some "master novel" in another dimension after death?

Davies: Oh heavens, in the life to come, novels will be utterly irrelevant. I haven't any notion of what I might be or whether I'll be capable of recognizing what I've been, or perhaps even what I am, but I expect that I shall be something.

Harpur: Do you believe that in this kind of spiritual survival of which you speak something of our individual consciousness will remain?

Davies: There have been numerous cases of people who have been considered dead or who were close to death. Their experiences, while perhaps not firm evidence, have nevertheless been very striking.

I have a document in my possession given to me by a Toronto doctor, based on an incident at the Toronto General Hospital, where a man died from a medical point of view and then came round again. The description he gave of what happened to him is fascinating.

He was at a distance from the room, but he saw himself in bed; he saw the doctors working around him; and he was concerned about it, but not to the extent that he was struggling to return.

Of course, we also have a very remarkable account by Dr. C. G. Jung of an occasion when he was quite an old man. He seemed to die and be absent from his body for quite some time and then came round again.

However, when this sort of thing happens, the medical answer is, "well, he was never really dead." But, if to all appearances they are dead, you wonder who is in the right.

Harpur: Could you describe briefly what Jung said of the period between his "death" and his reawakening?

Davies: He said that he saw an extraordinary vision of a very large land area which he recognized from certain features as the land around the city of Zurich. He then was able to focus in on the room where his body was lying surrounded by relatives and medical staff.

He later described the experience to a friend who was a geographer and expert in mathematics. He was told that to see Zurich and its surroundings the way he did he would have to be about five miles directly above the city!

Harpur: What do you make, then, as a Christian, of the statement in the Creed which affirms belief in the "resurrection of the body?"

Davies: I don't know, and I'm prepared not to know. It's there and I say it because I am not in the business of inventing new creeds and I don't think it's very wise to pick at old creeds which contain so much that is good. When we say body we mean the carcass. That may not be what the creed is saying at all.

Harpur: Do you foresee a time when science, through conquest of diseases, transplants, cloning, or whatever, might be able to give people "immortality" and so render obsolete the belief in life after death?

Davies: I don't know—I suppose all things are possible, in theory at any rate. But, I don't know that the master plan of the universe is going to be greatly changed by what people do on one small planet.

Harpur: In your trilogy, *Fifth Business, Manticore,* and *World of Wonders,* and recently again on radio, you have put forward the idea that a person dies of "being himself." Could you enlarge on that?

Davies: Well, in the simplest terms, if you eat like a wolf and drink like a fish, you will die the death of one who has obviously overdone things. But, this is just on the physical side.

Similarly, if you've been intensely anxious all the time about your health, you're more likely to end up sick than if you seldom think about it. But I think this holds very much so in the spiritual and intellectual realm as well.

If you haven't taken on any cargo earlier in these areas, inevitably you're going to wear out the equipment you have—if it hasn't been renewed, restored, or refreshed—and you get pessimistic.

I think that pessimism, depression, and mournfulness and a sense of despair are great killers.

In my book, *World of Wonders,* there is a fortune teller who comments to a little boy that all the people who come to her, young and old, say to her so often: "Is this all that life has for me?"

I think a lot of people feel that. They have unreasonable expectations because they never stop to consider what life actually has to offer them. They're always looking for some great epiphany from the skies. They never stop to consider that fact which human beings find hardest to recognize: "Maybe I'm not worthy of an epiphany."

Harpur: You have an interest, I know, in an idea which is prevalent in the East and has at times been a feature of Western civilization as well; i.e. the preparation for death. What does this mean for you?

Davies: I mean by it: Preparing yourself to die well. That is, to die like a creature who has been worthy of life rather than just sinking into senility and oblivion and feebleness.

The more we know of children today the less likely we are to accept the silly limitations we used to put on their consciousness and understanding. If it's that way at that end of life, I think that at the other end of life there is a change and an unfolding and a new kind of splendor to life which should be seized and enjoyed.

By preparation for death I don't mean folding your hands or going around forgiving a lot of people you don't want to forgive: it's preparing for a richness, a good and glorious end.

Harpur: But how does one prepare?

Davies: You have to come to terms with yourself and your place in the scheme of life—something a good many people don't want to do. In the last century we have extended the normal life-span. Many seem to believe that this means we have extended the period when they should enjoy the things they enjoyed in youth. But, I don't think they realize that we've also expanded the period of life when we can learn to think, feel, and experience the largeness and the splendor of life.

Making Most of Myth, Mysticism

Louise Lague/1976

From *The Province* (Vancouver), 29 June 1976, p. 11. Copyright 1976 *The Washington Star;* all rights reserved.

Question: Myths and reason have coexisted since the beginning of time, of course, but they seem to have risen to the surface in popular literature or the mass awareness with special intensity at this moment. Which do you see the age favoring, myth or reason?

Davies: We are at an age of superstition. Of course, people very rarely recognize that they live in an age of superstition, but we do. Look how many newspapers and publications carry astrology columns. And some of them are obviously ridiculous, contrary to the whole theory of astrology. It's interesting that in a magazine for people who are by definition sophisticated—*Vogue*, they carry a big astrology section. Take unidentified flying objects. Well, that's one of the great things of our time. Whether this is superstition or what it is I'm not prepared to say, but there are apparently very, very large numbers of people who believe in that. And other kinds of super- stition which disguise themselves as science.

Q: In what way?

A: You read every day of some new threat, something which is going to kill you. It sometimes takes the form of some new thing that is going to cause cancer. Bacon is dyed red, it gives you cancer. This funny stuff in the milk. It gives you cancer. Cancer is the big sort of bug-a-boo and curse of the day. Not all these things can give you cancer because people have been eating these things for a long, long time and they haven't all had cancer, but it seems as though we were perpetually looking for new threats to our peace of mind and that is in a measure superstitious. We're inventing problems.

Q: Is this a reaction against the 19th-century Western belief that life could be scientifically controlled?

A: Yes, that we had the world by the tail. We've realized we haven't and we're very superstitious. What interests me very strongly

162

is that we're very much in the position that the Roman Empire was in before it began to go downhill. It took the Roman Empire 500 or 600 years to finally play out. But at about the time that's in agreement to where we are now, they were immensely superstitious. They were full of new religions and they had swamis and maharishis and all kinds of Eastern teachers who invaded the capital. They taught meditation, and they taught this, that and the other thing. The Roman ladies of the privileged class were great on this sort of thing. At that time, Christianity was only another of the sorts of voodoos from the East that invaded Rome. And I think that we're probably going to see the rise from the midst of all this queer, superstitious searching for something, a new religion. Perhaps not an entirely new religion, but at least a new form of religion.

Q: Does the goodness give rise to myth? Why do we have such dramatic tales of saints?

A: I think that is because mankind has a built-in yearning for marvels. I think that we will see them where they do not exist. They want extraordinary people and they invent extraordinary people and are very, very angry if you question a miracle, for instance. They want a savior who was a miracle worker and are happier to believe in miracles than not. I certainly have no intention of saying that miracles are out of the question. All sorts of extraordinary things happen that certainly look like miracles. The fascination of a saint is the fascination of the extraordinary person, the remarkable person, the outstanding person.

Q: In general, there is a kind of an upheaval going on in all the orthodox religions. Is this actually going anywhere, though?

A: Yes. I think it is going somewhere and I think it's going somewhere quite specific. I thoroughly agree with C. G. Jung that the most significant religious statement that's been made in recent times was the Pope's declaration that the orderly Assumption of the Blessed Virgin was a matter of doctrine and faith. What this really means, when you boil it down, is that finally they've got a woman into heaven. And with the Trinity, the Trinity is now a foursome and one of the foursome is a woman. Now this is something which the women's lib women never mention because that's not their line of country, but I think it is of enormous and psychological importance.

Not because a tremendous number of people are thinking about it and believing it, but because it could happen.

Q: We don't seem to talk about heroes anymore. Do we have one? Do we need one?

A: Well, you know this is a thing you regain as you get older. It's often disappointing when you're a kid, you love to meet heroes. Then when you get older, you're disappointed because they're not as wonderful as you thought they were. And then when you get older still, you think: "They really are wonderful, they did do the thing which made me admire them. They can't be wonderful right from top to bottom, but they're more wonderful than I am, so that's good enough." We live in what is called as the age of the antihero. But again the antihero is an extraordinary man. He's more miserable and damned and unlucky and rotten and generally unsatisfactory than anybody ever could be if he tried. You see a lot of romantic young men who obviously think of themselves as antiheroes and they go around being miserable and dirty and this, that and the other. And then something happens to them, they get over it and they clean up and realize that that is only fun for a limited time.

Q: Are there any new myths or are we still running on the old classics?

A: They are constantly renewed. One of the things that has puzzled me in the last few years is that the men going to the moon didn't create any new myths. They went out there and they left a lot of junk behind them. It sometimes depresses me when I think there's a lot of trash up there. The worst thing those fellows did was to go and litter it up, and you know they didn't really achieve anything marvelous. I think it was quite a blow to the romantics the way they went to the moon, floating around in that big machine and drinking their own urine. Horrible.

"Gzowski on FM"

Peter Gzowski/1977

Transcription from CBC Radio, 5 February 1977. Copyright 1977 Canadian Broadcasting Corporation. Reprinted by permission of the CBC, Robertson Davies, and Peter Gzowski.

PG: What is your fascination with Richard Strauss in particular and opera and *Ariadne Auf Naxos?*

RD: Well, I like Strauss because I think he's a very great composer and he is a composer who is (although at times without being really very) modern. I like modern music and I follow it and I try to understand it. But the very latest and the most extreme modern music is not very congenial to me and Strauss is, because it has, or it seems to me to have, a tremendous psychological quality in it. Of course there's a psychological quality in all music but I found the Strauss quality particularly sympathetic and I think a lot of that has to do with the superb libretti by Hofmannsthal from which he works. And of course *Adriadne Auf Naxos* I'm particularly devoted to because it embodies, in a magnificent operatic form, an idea which is very dear to me and that is that life is composed of comedy and tragedy intermingled and that there's nobody who's watching the shows completely sure which is which and that's the way things seem to be to me and it's wonderfully set forth in that opera.

PG: That life is comedy and tragedy intermixed is one of my difficulties. I did not have many in reading *World of Wonders* and in listening to you read was—. Partly in reading it I think I was taking things more seriously than you were because as I heard you read I heard a kind of pleasure and joy and sense of comedy that in fact I laughed when I heard you read in places where I did not laugh as I read quietly to myself. Perhaps I approach your work with too much reverence.

RD: No, no, several people have said that to me and I have been rather puzzled by it because they've said to me that (in the first part of the book) where the little boy is traveling with the show is so dreadful, his fate is so terrible that it pains him to think of it and that the squalor

165

and the misery of his life is to them very hard to bear. I didn't feel that when I wrote it because it seemed to me that although the boy certainly had a hard time he also had excitement and a kind of lively approach to the world that an enormous number of children do not get. One of the things in the book which I was quite serious about was that our modern education tends to breed the sense of wonder out of us but that the boy had no education and whatever approached him that was wonderful or extraordinary, he was able to sense and appreciate to the full. So I find it essentially cheerful, but I can understand that it may not seem that way.

PG: It's very hard to get cheerful about a boy who spends 10 to 12 hours a day locked up inside an automaton and hidden from the public view operating the mechanics of a "magical" in quotation marks—not in quotation marks—of a magical device and talking about the smell of the dwarf who was in there before him and becoming conscious of his own bodily smells. Except that at one point he does say that he was strangely happy at that time, doesn't he?

RD: Yes, yes. Well, children are happy if they're left to live a kind of natural and developing way. And of course being in a prison as that boy was, imprisoned inside that automaton, was not very natural but he did develop along the lines that were congenial to him. He became a conjurer, he practiced for hours on end inside the automaton, and he was brought face to face with the realities of life. He had to please his master and he had to keep going just in order to exist and I think that in some ways the really extraordinarily easy life that children have nowadays inhibits their development They haven't much to protest against and so many of their protests, therefore, are manufactured.

PG: It's hard to put that abstract idea into the concrete realization of Magnus' boyhood locked inside that. Are you making out—is that idea behind this scenario?

RD: Yes, I think that it is. He had a terrible boyhood, but he survived it and I think that that is one of the cruel but inevitable things about life. Extraordinary people survive under the most terrible circumstances and they become more extraordinary because of it. The ones who can't stand it go under, perhaps they die, and this again is a very cruel thing about life. But it's something that we're trying to hide from ourselves nowadays, but which is inevitable. I was just reading in this latest life of Bertrand Russell that he said something which I think many people find chilling. He said: "I never help weak people." Life doesn't help weak people either. It disposes of them.

PG: That is such a cruel idea.

RD: Well, I think I know what Russell meant. You help weak people and you've got them and they're on top of you and you're carrying them. And it's very, very hard to shake them. You don't help them once. You never help a weak person once. They're always back for more and pretty soon you find that you're sort of a psychological and financial and spiritual and energy-producing milch cow.

PG: Isn't that strange? I remember my grandfather telling me that he had run a gravel pit on Vancouver Island during the early part of this century. Of course most of the labor was Chinese and they were working out into the sea. If any of the Chinese coolies fell off the boat or the barge, or whatever, the others would not go in and save them. My grandfather at one point was going to dive in and save one of these poor nonswimmers lying invisibly under the ocean, and the Chinese said that, no, no, you don't do that because once you've saved that man he owes his life to you and the whole relationship becomes impossible. So in the culture of those people that was explicitly—what you're saying was explicitly put forward.

RD: Yes, yes. Well, it is painfully true. It is against a great deal of our modern culture and particularly against the Christian ethic, which is to help everybody. But you know if you look at what happens in individual cases and in large cases of government action of that kind: you start helping everybody and pretty soon you're sitting on top of everybody. We've now in this part of the world got a government which is devoted to rescuing the perishing and succoring the dying and doing everything for everybody and now they're going to stop us smoking, and we're all going to sit in seat belts and the police are going to be able to take our cars away from us and every mortal thing that can be done to us is going to be done to us for our own good. I think that compassion has become almost a disease in our society.

PG: Compassion, a disease?

RD: Yes. Let people alone. Let them find their way. Let them find their level and you may sometimes be delighted and astonished at the extraordinary high level to which they'll rise if they're let alone.

PG: If you bring that down to personal terms, it means turning your back on the dying Chinese coolie, personally making that decision, saying I will not help my weak brother.

RD: Yes. I have never been faced with that situation and would find it extraordinarily difficult to bear because among other things I'm a non-swimmer. If I dived in, I'd be gone, too. But I would not like to think that if I fell off the dock, nobody would give me a hand. Still, that could happen if I were among people who thought that way.

PG But you couldn't live up to it yourself? Let's take the metaphor aside. If someone came to you, I bet you're a softy.

RD: Well, unhappily I get myself into messes trying to help people, but it is true as Russell suggests. If you help somebody, they never can get enough. Sometimes you're almost driven mad with their demands.

PG: Well, I'll never help anybody again!

RD: Oh, don't do that. Don't say that. There must be some middle way.

PG: We'll come back to the interplay between comedy and tragedy in some of the places. In the fourth piece you read for us from *World of Wonders*, that's Liesl the psychiatrist speaking, Ramsay's "sort of" mistress; it's hard to establish that.

RD: When people are as old as that, that sort of thing becomes difficult.

PG: Well, they're only 72 and 62 or something like that.

RD: I know, but [chuckles] they've gone beyond the mere pleasure of the bed by that age.

PG: Well, I don't know why.

RD: Well, I do and I think I'll tell you why. I think it is because people do not physically become incapable of sex but they have more interesting things on their minds. Sex is for the first part of life, and then in the second part of life it is sort of affirmation of humanity, of tenderness, of love, of all those things, but it isn't the sort of driving, snorting, me-first passion that it is with the young. Sex with the young is sort of bull fighting and domination. With the old if it isn't real love and if it isn't something that can be expressed in other ways, it's a pretty bad show.

PG: Robertson Davies just winked. She talks, Liesl, Dr. Liesl talks of, she's quoting Spengler?

RD: Um-um.

PG: And she talks of digging into the dunghill?

RD: Yes.

PG: Why did that image catch your ear, and Liesl's, and why is it in the book? Because some people would say, particularly the first portions of the book are digging into a very dunghill part of life.

RD: And what grows out of it? Flowers. And what do you put on your flower bed if you want it to flourish? Dung. This is the thing which we have to keep our eye on very carefully and which modern civilization is perpetually tring to distract us from. It is from this combination of the gross and earthy and creatural in life that the magnificent and splendid things grow. The minute we begin to become what we might call "refined" we're sunk, and this is not just some wild point of view of my own. You'll find it running through the poems, for instace, of W. B. Yeats, that love has pitched his tent— ah—love has built his mansion in the place of excrement. And that's one view of sex.

PG: That's curious because the word refined which you've just used in a perjorative sense, is the one that so many people would apply to you perhaps before any other Canadian.

RD: But they don't know me. A foolish image has grown up of me as a cheese taster and a wine sipper, and a snuff taker, and this, that, and the other. It's all a lot of rubbish and it is because people have a mythmaking instinct in them and when they think that somebody knows something they don't know, they attribute to him all kinds of absurd things that they think belong to that kind of person. They don't. I think that I try to be simple. Being simple is very, very hard. It's, I think, the last thing that you can perhaps achieve. I haven't achieved it, but I seek simplicity. Ah, whereas, as a great many people seem to think that any kind of, whatever you want to call it, "wisdom," is an infinite complexity. Nothing of the sort.

PG: Simplicity?

RD: Simplicity. Yes.

PG: You mean in the end if you reach the ultimate guru or the ultimate moment, all life can be compressed into one sentence, or one thought?

RD: Things become very simple. Yes.

PG: Talk to me about chivalry which is what you read about last and it's obviously a very important statement to you and again it's about the relationship between men and women and I guess its kind of a simple idea.

RD: Yes. Well, you know, when people talk about chivalry, so often they think it's a one-way street. They think it's a thing men do to women. You always get up when they come into the room. You always open the door for them. You always give them a chair. You do this, that, and the other. It's also a thing that women do to men. It is an agreement to exist together on a high plane of affection and courtesy, and I think that it works. There's a wonderful scene in that one wonderful play, *The Way of the World,* in which Mirabell and Millamant are agreeing that they will marry and they say to one another, "We shall be very strange, we shall be as strange as if we were not married at all, and as polite as if we were not married at all." And I think that a great many marriages would be saved if people would behave toward one another with the same courtesy that they would extend to someone whom they really didn't know as well as a marriage necessarily implies. Chivalry is, to some extent, treating the people who are nearest to you and whom you love most with the same consideration as you would give to a distinguished stranger. How do you like that?

PG: I like it a lot as a thought. I'm wondering how much easier it is to say than to do.

RD: Well, it's not very easy to do, but it is surely easier to do than to haggle and nag and fight and bitch and yelp at one another as you hear a lot of married people doing and there's a lot of people who think that they're in love do. They seem to feel that the familiarity of affection permits anything, including insult. And you know with love it has two sides. There's the good side and then there's the shadow side and if the shadow side is allowed too much run, some very ugly things arise. There's too much familiarity, too much knowing everything about somebody. I am always chilled when I hear, and I do hear it about once every six months, some woman or some man say to her husband or wife or a lover, I can read you like a book. That's the beginning of the end. I they can read them like a book, bring down the curtain.

PG: A little mystery?

RD: There should always be surprises.

PG: Mystery is another thing that patently fascinates you through the whole trilogy and specifically in *World of Wonders*. Have you ever been an amateur magician? I mean you've done everything.

RD: I was never good enough even to be an amateur magician. I was interested in it, but I couldn't do it, I could only learn about it.

PG: Where did you learn about the world of the carnival about which you wrote and read?

RD: By going to carnivals and watching them. If you watch a carnival, you see an awful lot of things that they don't intend you to see. You go into a carnival and somebody's always telling you what to look at. Don't look at that, look at the whole thing. Look all around you. Particularly look at the people who paid their money to go into the carnival. They're daring the carnival people to excite and enchant them and generally they're getting what they went for, one way or another.

PG: But you know, I mean, how did you know that they drugged the snakes and that you can kiss a snake from the top and that's a safe act to do? I'm not going to do it, in spite of what you said.

RD: Well, I mean I know some scientists who will tell you this, that there are other things you can do to snakes. If you want to deal with a venomous snake as a snake charmer, you'll find that in India they sometimes have their mouth sewn shut. They don't live very long because all they can do is suck in a little milk through a tiny hole. They don't last long but you can do all kinds of extraordinary things with them. The kind of people who go in for that sort of business don't belong to the Humane Society.

PG: No.

RD: And when I went, I used to go to the carnivals when I was a small boy at the CNE, one of the things that astonished me was the racing monkeys. They were terrified little creatures. They were strapped into little cars which ran round and round the track and the monkeys were supposed to be racing when the electricity was turned on. They were scared to death and they were all drugged and you could see that they were.

PG: So the knowledge that you show of the carnival is all perceived knowledge, nothing is firsthand?

RD: Yes. No, I never traveled with one or had anything directly to do with one. But, they're very, very, very, very peculiar. I remember also a thing that I observed when I was very, very young and that was when people went into the show. If there was a congress of little people or midgets or something of that kind, they were always getting the knife in first. They looked for the shortest man in the crowd and said, "Hello, Shorty." And they'd got him first you see, and everybody laughed at him before they laughed at them but there was a terrible defensiveness about it. I don't wish to set up shop as an extremely sensitive or unusually aware person but I have got my eyes open and I used to see these things and they fascinate me.

PG: To take you about back to something you said just a few minutes ago and it's still ringing in my head and I would imagine in the heads of many persons. I should have said at one point—were I presumptive enough, but I'm not—I think I should have said "Rubbish!"

RD: Well, say it now.

PG: Well, when you said that you were not a refined man and that you've been created by the media and, imagine, making the cover of *Time* magazine, are you ashamed of that?

RD: No, no, I was very pleased.

PG: The character, the Robertson Davies who is seen by the public by those of us who do not know you is the man not only of the sherry parties at Massey Hall and going back to the Oxonian rituals and the unlost accent from your days at Oxford and with the Old Vic and the editor of *Saturday Night,* the man of an incredible variety of knowledge going through everything from the drugging of snakes into the examples from *The Way of the World* and Richard Strauss. You're a very, very cultured man and that's at the point when you said that you're not. I think I should have dared to say rubbish.

RD: Well, I don't think so. I don't think—. I am an exceedingly curious man, I am interested in everything and that's rather a different thing. You know I just can't find out enough about anything.

PG: How about sports? You're not interested in sports?

RD: Yes, I'm very interested.

PG: Are you?

RD: I don't go to them because I'm not much interested in the games. I'm interested in the players, and the players are fascinating. I don't know many players, though I've met some interesting ones, but I know a lot of sports writers, and they'll tell you an enormous amount about the real inside of sports.

PG: How about the world of finance? Are you interested in that?

RD: Yes, immensely interested in it, immensely interested in it: interested in the world of money and interested in what people eventually want to do with their money. I'm interested in benevolence and benefactions and foundations and these giveaway projects where people are trying, sometimes—they'll never admit it, but they're trying to buy an immortality. In the old days they used to found a chapel and put down some money for a priest to pray for them for the rest of time. But now what do they do? They'll found a chair in a university and set up a professor to keep their memory green for the rest of time. It's the same old business. It's an attempt to beat death.

PG: That's a very, very dangerous thing for the Master of Massey College to say.

RD: Well, I know it is but I'm fonder of truth than I am fonder of money [laughs] which is a terrible thing to say but I think that this is true. And I don't see anything wrong with it, I don't see anything reprehensible about trying to keep your memory green by laying down some good hard cash for something which is going to be serviceable to other people.

PG: In writing, is there any attempt on your own part to become a piece of immortality or is it, am I—?

RD: I would like to think that my writing would last but I can't guarantee or undertake to say that it would do so because, you see, I am a teacher of literature by profession and I know how many people have done very, very good work who are as dead as a doornail and others, for reasons which you really cannot understand, still seem to be read and attract attention. It's very difficult to tell which way the cat's going to jump.

PG: Are there writers that instantly spring to mind that you have enjoyed and feel should have enjoyed more kinds of immortality, we should be paying more attention to that we are not?

RD: Well, one of the funniest writers that I know is a writer called Thomas Love Peacock who lived in the early part of the 19th century and his books are extraordinary and delightful and amusing and beautifully written, but you know, he doesn't seem to get studied in the universities and you read comparatively few people who read him. Not long ago a publisher that I knew set to work to bring out Peacock's novels again in a new edition. It gave up after two, and I said, why did you do that? He said, well, there was no demand for them, nobody wanted them. That's an example.

PG: What about the other extreme, someone who through luck or some kind of circumstance has become a part of Literature 3-B and doesn't deserve it in your estimation.

RD: Well, I don't think I could mention any who possibly didn't deserve it but you sometimes wonder why, for instance, a writer like Henry James who was undoubtedly a very great novelist, nevertheless bulks a kind of colossus in the world of the novel when a writer like Joseph Conrad seems not to do so, though I think Conrad was a finer novelist than Henry James, and you wonder why a poor chap like Herman Melville (who could hardly get accepted as anything but a foolish hobbyist, almost, in his lifetime) is now regarded as one of the giants of the American novel. There is no justice in this. It is part of the mingling of comedy and tragedy we were talking about.

PG: Testing your own lifetime, a great deal of which is left, there was a paragraph in one of my favorite columnists in all of Canada the other day. His name is Dennis Braithwaite. He writes for the *Toronto Star.* I often think he writes with his tongue in his cheek just to see how many people he can make angry from time to time. But he had a little paragraph saying, "Will the media please leave Robertson Davies alone?" And within the past just, *Fifth Business* was 1970; *The Manticore,* 1972; and *World of Wonders,* 1975; and now with this trilogy which now puts your output at 26 books, I think?

RD: Yes.

PG: Suddenly you are being celebrated and toasted and things are being named after you and *Time* is publishing covers about you, and things. Do you see any irony or comedy or tragedy in that at all?

RD: Yes, of course, but it is cliché to say so. When I was—30 years ago, it would have given me so much pleasure. Now it rather makes me feel bashful and I know that that sounds a very improbable thing to say to you but it is true. I, well, I won't say that I wish it were otherwise because, of course, I like being recognized and I like people reading my books but I wish it didn't involve me being represented as a kind of ultra-refined fellow who, you know, lives always with his little finger crooked. I wish I could somehow or other be disassociated from the thing but that cannot be. Everybody wants to know about you and what they want to know about you is what they've already made up their minds is true. The real truth doesn't interest them very much.

PG: We have instituted a bit of a game on this program but we find that it sometimes is more than a game, and I don't know if your Jungian leanings and passion and anything whether you would be, would try at performing: but what it is is we have asked people from time to time to tell their whole life story in one minute. And we have given them no more notice than I have given you now. And if I were to say in seven seconds, could you condense your entire life story into one minute, Robertson Davies, beginning right now?

RD: Well, I was born of poor-but-honest parents and my parents remained honest but they ceased to be poor. This influenced my life extraordinarily and I now seem to be regarded as a person who has always lived a wealthy and privileged life and that has influenced me profoundly.

PG: You have thirty seconds left.

RD: Well, I don't know that there's a great deal more to be said but I know life from poverty to well above the poverty line and it looks awfully interesting along the way.

PG: Less than one minute. Was it Scott Fitzgerald that said "I've been poor and I've been rich and rich is better."?

RD: I didn't know he said that. It's true.

PG: I thank you very much for talking with us and I thank you even more for reading from *World of Wonders.*

RD: Well, thank you. It was a delight to do it.

PG: Write another book and come back and—. You don't have to write another book to come back but if you do, perhaps you would read for us again.

RD: Thank you.

PG: Robertson Davies.

"Sunday Morning"
Bronwyn Drainie/1979

Transcription from CBC Radio, 18 March 1979. Copyright 1979
Canadian Broadcasting Corporation. Reprinted by permission of
the CBC and Robertson Davies.

BD: Twelve-thirty by the clock in the Massey bell tower on an early
spring day: just outside these gates the bustle of an enormous
university in the middle of Toronto. In here fountains splash, bells
ring, and scholars glide quietly from study to high table in an almost
perfect imitation of a medieval Oxford college. Massey is a stately
anachronism and the same could be said with some qualifications for
the Master of Massey, Robertson Davies, former actor, former
publisher of the *Peterborough Examiner,* essayist, playwright, professor of English, and a highly successful novelist. Professor Davies is
a man who seemed old even when he was young, an imposing figure
with a long, reddish gray beard, a man much taken with the surface
amenities of the privileged academic life—grace in Latin at the dinner
table, frequent sherry parties, and sparkling witty conversation in the
English collegial style—a man whose early novels smacked too much
of our quasi-British colonial stature to be taken very seriously by
Canadian critics. But all that changed in 1970 when a novel called
Fifth Business appeared. Here was a Robertson Davies no one had
known before, a man steeped in magic, mysticism, history, religion
and the highly symbolic psychology of Carl Jung. In *Fifth Business*
and in the two novels that followed, *The Manticore* and *World of
Wonders,* Davies applied his highly sophisticated perceptions to the
drab world of WASP small-town Ontario, adding extaordinary
dimensions to our notion of ourselves as Canadians. Today,
Robertson Davies continues to be both men, the rather pompous,
formal academic and the mature, passionate artist. He is a man very
much alone and apart from his fellow Canadian novelists.

    RD: I really don't know very many of them personally though I
know a great many of them in a casual way and I don't feel that it is
my job or any writer's job to fit in with any particular group. I am

176

older than they are, my attitude towards a great many things is not theirs for, among other excellent reasons, the fact that I am older than they are and that my notions about Canada were . . . they're not set in cement, but they have a longer time of existence and they have a different origin.

BD: If there is any kind of hallmark to these young writers, any kind of common feeling among their books, it's a kind of dry, tight feeling of repressed passion somehow. Your work seems so very different and so very un-Canadian in many ways. Did you set out in some way to really change our image of ourselves with the Deptford Trilogy particularly?

RD: No, no, by no means self-consciously. But what you have said is what I do think about Canadians. They are a Northern people and I think that if there is a national comparison to be made, it ought to be made with the Scandinavians, or even with the Russians, and you know what the Scandinavians are. You've seen what Ibsen, to begin with, wrote about them, people who were living furiously passionate lives and always worrying about their overshoes and whether their collar button showed, and that's Canadian all over. I think one of the most Canadian figures was Mackenzie King and everybody makes fun of him now, but Mackenzie King was two men, he was an extraordinarily adroit and successful manager of people and affairs, and he was also a man with a mass of unresolved passion inside him which found its outlet in all sorts of extraordinary ways. But you can duplicate that in Canadian life and we're all a lot of Mackenzie Kings. We're a rather plain-headed race on the whole as compared, for instance, with, probably, the Americans, but inwardly we're all colored bright red with big dobs of purple.

BD: Anyone who has read the Deptford Trilogy will know that you're a student and an admirer of Jung. One of Jung's ideas, it seems to me, is that people can undergo an enormous change of character, an enormous change of ideas in the middle of their lives. Is that something that happened to you?

RD: Well, you see, it is the sort of change which happens to virtually everybody one way or another. In the first thirty-five or forty years of your life you've got your work cut out for you, you've got to first of all drop out of childhood, acquire all the things that an adult needs, including an education. You have to find what your sexual

orientation is and what you're going to do about that. You've got to
find how you're going to greet the world in terms of expecting the
world to reward you, what job you're going to do, and you've got to
do that. You've got to get a place to live. You've got to buy some
furniture. You have to pay your debts. You've got a really busy time.
But then, quite suddenly, that's all been done and what are you
going to do then? Are you going to buy more furniture and are you
going to try to continue your sexual involvements by that thing which
so many people do, of chasing around rather pathetically trying to be
young when quite clearly they are no longer young, or are you going
to try to settle down to find out what's inside yourself and what it's all
been about? So you must enlarge your way of looking at things and
that is what I did. But the first three novels that I wrote were about a
particular kind of Canadian society, WASP society. They treated it
somewhat satirically but then, you see, when I came to write, there
was quite a gap between those novels and the Deptford books, and
when I came to write those, I was writing, as it were, from a different
place. You see there were a variety of things which conditioned my
life which people don't seem to be aware of. There seems to be an
image of me—I discover this because students speak of it—that I live
very grandly, that I drink an awful lot of sherry, and that I'm very
"refined" and live a sort of curious, privileged, unreal kind of life.
Well, that's not the way that I've seen it. The thing that people don't
generally know is that when I was born, my parents were very poor.
We were like the Ramsays in *Fifth Business*. We didn't think we were
poor, but in the eyes of the world, I suppose we were poor. I've been
an outsider all my life and I can put on an insider disguise, but I never
really think that I'm an insider. Writers aren't insiders. They're
watchers, and perhaps I'd be cold fish in a way and so that made a
very considerable difference to my writing and my attitude toward the
work that I'm doing now. I don't sit in this college thinking of myself
as a kind of crusted old academic making jokes in Latin. I think I am
a man who is doing a particular kind of job but whose real center is
somewhere else and the place where the center is is the place where I
write.

   BD: It seems a very great distance from the formal psychological
systems that Jung, particularly, and Freud developed around the
beginning of this century, a very great distance from that to the truly

incredible proliferation of pop psychology, self-help books that clog the bookstores now. What do you think all of this new move is trying to accomplish?

RD: I know what they are. They are for people who want to have their circumstances changed without changing themselves. They want to be happy without doing any of the things which might possibly create happiness in their terms. Happiness I've said is a by-product. It is not a primary product of life. It is a thing which you suddenly realize you have because you're so delighted to be doing something which perhaps has nothing whatever to do with happiness. But you see, so many people when they talk about happiness are really talking about clinging to youth. So many things that write about happiness talk about rich and fulfilling sexual lives. The plain fact, it seems to me, is that sex changes its character very decidedly in your life as you grow older. If you're lucky, you have formed a happy association or perhaps more than one happy association which provide you with a kind of companionship which has its roots in sexual difference but is not rooted in hopping into the sack every eight hours because that is something which the very nature of the human body [Laughs] makes impossible. If not impossible, less fascinating than it used to be because it is no longer the primary symbol of affection. Now at the time of life which I have reached, which is 65 (I always talk as if I were Methuselah but I'm not actually), you do get a chance to see some things that you weren't able to see earlier because you were either too much in the thick of affairs or you hadn't quite seen the end of enough third acts to know how the drama of life works. And that's a great happiness, to have lost some of the scales over your eyes.

BD: I have a notion that you might subscribe to the rather controversial theory that came out just recently about the difference between the male and female brain and the possibility that perhaps we should be educating men and women in different ways because of the differences in their brain. Did you read and follow that research?

RD: Yes, I read it and I couldn't make much out of it because I don't know anything about the scientific background of it and so I didn't pay a great deal of heed to it, but it seems to me that it would be a loss to the world if we did find that men and women were sort of interchangeable units because there are so many things that women have brought into the world which I don't think it would have occurred to men to emphasize in quite that way and, of course, what I'm talking about is this sort of Jungian idea that a man's brain works on a kind of logos line, that law and order and rule and logic and precedent are enormously important to him, and the women are more inclined to function on the eros principle which means that they would consider every case as a particular case and that, on the whole, they are less rigid and conformist in their attitude toward the important things of life. Now I think that it's possible to talk endless rubbish about the differences between men and women. They have been grossly exaggerated, but I do feel that we must get the best out of both sexes rather than trying to have a kind of unisex attitude which makes a woman who is not really functioning with femininity going full out and a man who is not giving the kind of firm direction that perhaps belongs to his role. I don't know, but I don't want to be dogmatic about this. I always get into awful trouble about it and I have been attacked by some women writers on the grounds that I'm an intolerable sexual tyrant and so forth, but you can't help that. Any man with a beard is bound to look like a tyrant to somebody, you know. [Chuckles]

BD: You've drawn a parallel between the American Civil War and what we are going through right now, the confederation crisis we're going through with Quebec right now. Are the situations really parallel do you think?

RD: The situations are psychologically parallel. They're not at all parallel in concrete terms. I don't think that we're going to come to a shooting war. I can't conceive that we would ever do anything so dreadful, but the tensions and bitternesses of a psychological war are very, very great. I personally tend to be, in the long term, optimistic. I think that we will come to a better understanding with Quebec and that we will come to a better understanding of the kind of Que- becquer that we in the rest of Canada have always known and among whom we have found our Quebec friends, and that is the much more solid kind of Quebec citizen than the university and artistic group who are really the strength of the Separatist movement. Now that is where you would expect to find revolutionary feeling. You always find it in the universities—particularly in Latin societies—

and some portion of what they say is so obviously right that it cannot be denied. Some of it is just raising hell for hell's sake. I think that actually what will hold Quebec to the rest of Canada is first of all the very deep loyalty to the notion of Canada which has evinced itself on two or three occasions in our history. I think the first occasion was when the American Revolution was imminent and Benjamin Franklin visited Quebec to try to buy the French to revolt against the English, and they wouldn't, and they didn't do it because they loved England but because they loved where they were and what they were. And on more than one occasion, they have shown themselves to be our friends and much more like us than they're unlike us, and I think that those are the people who are going to really have the say in Quebec eventually and that the unity of Canada will persist but it won't persist in exactly its present form.

BD: Will you be sorry to see the old Canada pass away?

RD: No, I won't. I knew the old Canada pretty well, and I've written about it, and I saw lots of things that were wrong with it. It had its virtues. It served its purpose. It served its time. But I think the time has come for something new and it's going to mean changes which will be painful for all kinds of people and some of them I suspect that I will not like, but that doesn't say that they are necessarily wrong. They're part of something which is very much more important than individual loyalties and likes and dislikes.

BD: Robertson Davies' outer life as Master of Massey continues in its formal, stylized way from year to year. His inner life teams with energy and change. He has just begun the actual writing of a new novel which he won't discuss. It should be out, he estimates, in two or three years. This is Bronwyn Drainie in the quadrangle of Massey College at the University of Toronto.

"This Country in the Morning"

Peter Gzowski/1979

Transcription from CBC Radio, 17 August 1979. Copyright 1979 Canadian Broadcasting Corporation. Reprinted by permission of the CBC, Robertson Davies, and Peter Gzowski.

PG: Robertson Davies joins me now. Mr. Davies, *Leaven of Malice* won the Leacock Award? Did it?

RD: No, no.

PG: But you won it?

RD: I did one year, yes.

PG: But not for *Leaven of Malice*?

RD: I don't think so. I don't remember exactly.

PG: Does it matter very much?

RD: Not greatly, no.

PG: It was written, first published, in 1954?

RD: In '54.

PG: May I tell you an embarrassing thing, embarrassing for me? As I began, I don't remember when I first read it. All I can remember is my pleasure in reading it and I thought last night since you were going to drop by this morning and talk a bit about the play that is taken from it, that I'd read it again and I took it up to bed and I thought I'll just skim through and refresh myself. It was a total new experience for me, rereading it, and I may be a decade late, but I didn't finish it because I was cherishing it as I went. It was just a lot of fun; it hasn't lost anything in the years.

RD: Well, that's very complimentary. It's been in print since '54 and I find that a lot of people seem to read it in college and sometimes in the upper grades of high school.

PG: Maybe that's where I should be.

RD: This is rather alarming.

PG: It's Salterton, Ontario, where it's at. Let's not care whether it's a real city or not. It's a university town, and how much do you feel that kind of town has changed since you first recreated it?

RD: Oh, very substantially. In those days, you know, before the 1939/1945 war, those towns were very much more isolated than they are now. And I remember, of course, people identified Salterton with Kingston, which is where I grew up. But I can remember it as being a city which, without being in any objectionable way isolated, was nevertheless a long way from both Toronto and Montreal. It was a five-hour motor journey to Toronto and farther to Montreal, and the isolation was by no means a bad thing. It meant that it had a rather more intense community life and a more intense concern with immediate things under your nose than there probably would be in such a place now, and also it was necessary to make your own things. We had to have our own music club if we were going to hear any serious music and that sort of thing.

PG: The University plays a small part in the novel . . .

RD: Yes.

PG: And a large part in the life of Kingston, I'm sure.

RD: A considerable part in the life of Kingston, though it is not as dominant as many people believe. You see Kingston has not only the University but it also has a very large military establishment, very large medical establishment. It has a very large what used to be called a hospital for the insane. Now I think they don't call it that any more. It had two penitentiaries, one for men and one for women— oh, and a third, very near by, sort of for high grade prisoners, and this civil service and legal and military group of people played a very large part in the city's life.

PG: Were you editor of the *Peterborough Examiner* at the time you wrote the novel?

RD: Yes.

PG: Because there's some delightful passages with the editor of the Salterton *Bellman*. I won't give away too much of the plot for people who have not yet had the pleasure, but where he's fooling around with letters to the editor among other things. Did you used—tell me about what you used to do to letters to the editor.

RD: Well, I used to have a regular routine; of course everybody on the newspaper has to have a routine in order to get through the things they need to do, and my routine first thing in the morning was to go through the editorial pages of about forty other newspapers, most of them from within Ontario but some of them from other parts of Canada to find out if there was anything we ought to comment on or reprint.

PG: Steal?

RD: Well, no. It was always attributed to the other paper, and we published it under a heading which said "Comments From The Press," and then I had to read the letters (and there would sometimes be twenty or twenty-five of them) and decide about publishing them and edit them and prepare them for publication. One of the most irritating jobs was correcting the grammar and making sense out of a letter which was knocking the newspaper. But this is something that we felt obliged to do. It would have been cruel and vindictive to print some of those letters in the form in which they arrived.

PG: You said that was an irritating job but the editor of the fictional *Bellman* takes pleasure in doing that. So a little bit of hypocrisy sneaks in . . .

RD: Well, he likes to do that because it makes him feel a sort of Christian brother to the person who is getting after him.

PG: Is it perhaps he's a nicer man than you are?

RD: No, I don't think so.

PG: Your background which has led you to become Master of Massey College includes a great deal of experience within the theatre as actor and playwright and critic. Why would you express *Leaven of Malice* both as a novel and as a play? Surely there are different forms for different expressions.

RD: There are different forms, and it is not, I think, completely satisfactory from an artistic point of view to make a play out of a novel like that. But I was asked to do so over ten years ago by the Theatre Guild. They thought that a play could be made from it and so I was not going to kick the good luck in the face and set to work to do so. And it was extremely educative but painful experience because I found that one of the very first things that the Theatre Guild wanted was the removal from the play of any suggestion whatever that it was laid in Canada. And I could not explain to them—

PG: Is that true?

RD: Yes, that a story of that kind would be most unlikely to happen in the United States, that the attitudes that lay behind the people, and particularly the young people, were not those of the U.S.A. and that it couldn't be done. So I lost, of course, as I lost on so many other things. Then the director, who was the late Tyrone Guthrie, said that he thought the newspaper stuff was extremely dull and that nobody liked editors anyway and, therefore, we must cut out virtually everything about the editors. So that had to go. And then the people who played the lovers felt that there ought to be more about the lovers who were not primary characters in the novel, and then the funny man, the "star" funny man who was hired to play the part of Humphrey Cobbler, kept insisting that he must have more and more material. So eventually, what emerged on the stage of New York was, what I felt, was a travesty of the novel and certainly a travesty of the play as I'd envisioned it. Now the play that we're going to do . . .

PG: Can I, that was *Love and Libel*?

RD: *Love and Libel*, yes. The play that we're going to do at Hart House is the play as I originally wrote it, and I don't pretend that it's a wonderfully good play but I think it's a very amusing play. And I see rehearsals, and I see that they're having a very jolly time with it and that's what its meant to be; it's meant to be sort of a fantasia, not a grubby little situation comedy about a comic star and a couple of loving kids.

PG: Well, I think I really—I like that. Here's a novel which reeks of Canadian Ontario and small town life, centers around an episode in the newspaper. I will give away the fact that the ad is, of course, the key that triggers the whole, all the events that take place. It was planted by someone and causes incredible furor. It is not a true engagement but it hinges around attitudes that are all Canadian and all about the newspaper business. So what they say is you can't have the newspaper business, you can't have those attitudes, and you can't have it Canadian. They might as well have asked someone from Miami to write a new play altogether.

RD: Much better, much better. It was a very painful experience dealing with that situation but there it was, and I learned a good deal from it.

PG: What gave you the idea of someone coming along and announcing the engagement of Romeo and Juliet of small town Ontario?

RD: Because it happened on my own newspaper in Peterborough. Someone brought in an engagement notice and a clever girl at the desk spotted it immediately as a fake and checked on it. It was a fake and so we were very rough with the man who tried to put it in. But I began to think, "What would happen if that had appeared?" And so, away we went.

PG: And you spent your time in the evenings writing while you

were editing the paper and doing seventy-five other things? Do you
go to the theatre much these days?

RD: Yes, I do. I go a great deal.

PG: What kinds of theatre do you enjoy a lot?

RD: Every kind. I go to see a lot of the new plays, and I go to see
anything in the more traditional vein that comes along and my wife
and I generally get away about once a year, and we do a lot of
theatre-going when we're traveling, particularly in England and in
Austria and in Germany.

PG: Are there any new or younger Canadian playwrights who
have caught your attention?

RD: Oh yes. There are several of them, too many actually to
mention but I don't suppose a year goes by that I don't see a very
interesting play by at least one new good playwright. And not all of
them last, of course, because a lot of people are one-play men. It's
astonishing, you know, when you study the history of the theatre how
few playwrights there are whose careers have lasted more than ten
years. The Noel Cowards and the Somerset Maughams are very
uncommon.

PG: [Pause]. And that's the reason for the silence. I'm thinking
and, of course, you're right. Are you a comic author?

RD: Ah, well, I don't think of myself as a comic author but a lot of
other people consider that I am, but I think, you know, that people
tend to have a sort of dominating attitude of mind. And certainly
mine is comic rather than tragic. There are people who think and,
indeed, act and conduct their own lives farcically, and there are an
incredible number of people who live in terms of melodrama.
Everything with them is a great crisis. Everything with them is the
biggest thing that has ever happened and has never happened to
anybody before. But my attitude toward life tends to be, in a general
way, comic (which does not exclude pathetic and unhappy and very
serious things but I try to see them rather coolly, and I suppose that's
part of what comedy is).

PG: You said a very moving thing when you were here on an
earlier program talking about *The Manticore*, which is your latest
novel. You said that you were able since the death of your father to
write more freely about truths within yourself and your relationships
with him. Looking back at *Leaven of Malice* now, the work of almost

twenty years ago, a comic novel, and really in a different genre than *Fifth Business* and *The Manticore* (the ones that have been talked about so much on this program), have you changed in a way, would you approach *Leaven of Malice* differently now?

RD: I don't think so, and I must say that my father liked *Leaven of Malice* enormously and he read it several times. He enjoyed it enormously because you know newspaper novels are not very common, and he recognized what he felt to be truth in that. I would not write it differently now but I would not probably write that novel now. I am interested in different things. That is a novel of immense complication among a very large number of people and now I'm interested in inner complication in a single, one character.

PG: You're more interested in all the diverse things that go on in one person's mind rather than putting a group of interesting people together?

RD: Yes. I can tell you something about that. At the moment I'm getting ready to write another play which I've been asked to write and I'm very interested in writing and, I am working on the theme and, you know, all I can find is one character. And I don't think that'll make much of a play. I'll have to find some other people, but I'm so interested in one person that I don't want to spread the action out over a large group.

PG: Who is that person?

RD: Ah, the Prime Minister of Canada at the moment. Not the present Prime Minister or any Prime Minister, but a man in that position.

PG: Can you tell me a bit about what sort of man he is?

RD: Couldn't really, no. It would be not merely unwise, it would be unlucky to say anything about it now.

PG: Do your characters change as you get to know them?

RD: Oh, very much so.

PG: Did Boy Staunton, for instance, change as you got to know him?

RD: Very much so, yes.

PG: They exist in your mind all the time?

RD: Yes.

PG: Do they talk?

RD: Oh yes.

PG: They write their own dialogue for you?

RD: Yes indeed. Ah, this is, I hear, one of the things that one must try to do when writing a novel and yet if you have to try too hard, it's a sign that you're failing. Every character ought to talk in his own voice, and with his own vocabulary. It's always very dull in a novel when everybody talks one way. You know the novels of Ivy Compton-Burnett are enormously admired, and I think rightly so, but when you read them, you have an awful job knowing who's saying anything because she never says "said John" or "said Annie," she just puts down what is said and then you have to figure out who said it and they all talk in exactly the same way.

PG: I thought they were always the same person. I never finished one of those.

RD: I think they are.

PG: A little malice there from Robertson Davies. The play will open with your wife in it?

RD: No, she can't be in it unfortunately. She had to go away and was unable to take part in it.

PG: But you'll be there on opening night with a critical eye?

RD: Well, with a friendly eye.

PG: What will you do if no one laughs?

RD: I'll laugh. [Gzowski laughs.] I go to the rehearsals and I laugh at those. I don't know why I shouldn't laugh at the performance.

PG: Even though you know all the jokes?

RD: Sure!

World of Wonders
Alan Twigg/1981

From *For Openers: Conversations With 24 Canadian Writers.*
Madeira Park, B.C.: Harbour Publishing, 1981. Reprinted by
permission.

T: Why have humourists fallen from fashion in Canada?

Davies: Oh, I think it's because of the extremely sore skin of our
times. Humour very often consists of shrewd perceptions about
people. It's usually funny at someone's expense. Nowadays if you're
funny at anybody's expense they run to the U.N. and say, "I must
have an ombudsman to protect me." You hardly dare have a shrewd
perception about anybody. The only people you can abuse are
WASPs. They're fair game. But most of the people who want to
mock them aren't very good mockers because they don't understand
what a WASP is.

T: But humour always makes a comeback.

Davies: Of course. It has to find an outlet because it's a basic
element of civilized life. But there are always people who mistrust it
and dislike it. You find whole periods of history where humour is
completely choked off. For instance, if you look at the period from
about 1640 to 1660 in British history, you won't find much
humorous writing in it. The people down on humour then were the
same people who are down on humour now. The Puritans, the
people who are terribly touchy about any kind of criticism or
evaluation that isn't made exactly on their terms.

T: Are we experiencing a New Puritanism in a liberal age?

Davies: Oh, yes. It's a very puritanical age. It's not puritanical
about some of the usual targets of puritanism like sex, but it's
extremely puritanical about human rights. And children. All sorts of
things like that.

T: Do you put a value judgement on it?

Davies: I think it needs exploding. But it's going to take a very
good man to explode it. He's going to have all the blacks, all the
Jews, and all the minorities down his neck, chasing him with knives.

T: Do you have any desire to become that man?

Davies: I have to see if the opportunity presents itself. Any group that becomes too serious about itself, and this means most minorities, needs reminding of the ordinary humanity that encompasses us all.

T: In your essay on Stephen Leacock you say humour is the result of tension in the mind. Are there particular tensions in Canadian society that form the basis of a distinctly national humour?

Davies: I think we do have something which more or less approaches a national humour, and it's something that Stephen Leacock evolved with great brilliance. The characteristic of it is a kind of patterned innocence which covers a very great bitterness. Never is it so sharply shown as in Leacock's *Sunshine Sketches*. You analyse what he says about the little town and it's a snake-pit. But he says it with such charm! The charm is convincing because it probably seemed charming when it happened.

T: What about the tension of Canada feeling itself a dutiful daughter of the British Empire in jealous competition with the undutiful daughter, the United States?

Davies: That was the case. It's not the case any longer. Canada is no longer a dutiful daughter. It hasn't been since at least 1945. You see the whole British world-wide connection began to crack up about the time of World War One. By World War Two it was already becoming tenuous. When Britain served notice on Australia that whatever happened in the Pacific they shouldn't expect any help from Britain, that was the end of a great sentimental link with the Mother Country.

Now Britain's cultural influence is very much on the wane in Canada. But it's always been a one-way thing. It's been our feeling towards them, not their feeling towards us. They couldn't care less about us.

T: In your play, *Hunting Stuart,* Henry becomes Bonnie Prince Charlie and in your Deptford trilogy Boy Staunton is killed essentially by his desire to be like the Prince of Wales. As a young person, were your role models essentially British?

Davies: My relationship to Great Britain was not as strong as that of a lot of Canadians because my family was not English. Part of it was Dutch and American.

T: Would you agree the Canadian public thinks of you primarily as a man of intellect and education; whereas you think of yourself primarily as a man of feeling and intuition?

Davies: Yes.

T: Doesn't this variance limit people's appreciation of your work?

Davies: I think that it does. This business about me being so elaborately educated isn't true. I am very spottily educated. This is both because of the kind of schooling I encountered and because I was not capable of assimilating a fully rounded education as it existed at the time. Now I tend not to think my way through problems but to feel my way through them. I judge them on intuition and values. That's a feeling person rather than a thinking person.

T: Is this why you turned away from a career in psychiatry?

Davies: Oh, yes, I think so. The extreme tightrope-walking involved in psychiatry would have been too hard for me. As a psychiatrist, you've got to keep your cool all the time. That's very, very hard work.

T: Also psychiatry is a banishment of wonder. It's basically putting explanations on sensations.

Davies: [amused] Yes. And when you become a professional explainer, you're in great trouble.

T: This would explain why you've developed a fascination with insanity. It emphasizes the frailty of reason.

Davies: Yes. Attempts to explain what is happening in the mind of the insane person are often very wide of the mark.

T: Didn't Freud once say that neurosis is a form of creation?

Davies: Well, yes. But other people have said physical illness is also a form of creation. You can say those things and they sound very fine. But when you start to analyse them, sometimes they're not up to much.

T: I suspect you've also been curious about the possible benefits of mind-altering drugs.

Davies: I've thought a good deal about it and I've seen instances of people who have tried it. The thing is, their minds are altered but not enlarged. Attempts to gain some sort of instant enlightenment are apparently rooted in the idea that the drug is going to extend the mind. It doesn't really. It may clarify it or make it possible to observe something which is not ordinarily accessible, but people don't have

wonderful visions under the influence of drugs which are beyond
their power of imagination. And it can be frightfully destructive.

The road to enlightenment is hard, hard, hard. You can't do it with
pills or needles.

T: Perhaps the popularity of drugs over the past few decades has
something to do with advertising. The promise of instant gratification.

Davies: Precisely. Happiness can be yours!

T: Magnus in *World of Wonders* says he grew up in a world where
there was much concern about goodness but little love. Is that a fair
description of your environment?

Davies: No, my family was more highly temperamental than that
statement would suggest.

T: What about your society?

Davies: Oh, my society was very cagey about using the word
"love." But there was a great concern about goodness or what would
win approval.

T: And with this concern for goodness, there was a lack of giving
the Devil his due?

Davies: Yes. A lack of recognition of what the Devil might be.

T: *World of Wonders* can be read entirely as an exploration of the
nature of evil. Do you think our writers have been leery of that in the
past?

Davies: I think they have. Though now they're getting to it.
Margaret Atwood's latest book [*Life Before Man*] is interesting in that
regard. And Marian Engel's *Bear* was an attempt to come to terms
with the primal aspects of life. On the surface level, that novel was
absurd. Any attempt like that to form a relationship with a bear would
probably be impossible—and if possible, highly dangerous. But as a
dream, as an allegory of the relationship to the size and spirit of the
country, it's something very different and very powerful.

T: Did you become dissatisfied with mainstream Christianity
because most Christianity is concerned with Good, whereas Art is
concerned with Good and Evil?

Davies: Yes. I think that is perfectly true. Also anything that
becomes a mass movement is reduced by the mass. I am essentially a
cradle Protestant. I feel that your devotion to God has to be personal
and individual. To do it with a great gang who are really trying to get
away from thinking about God but want to do a lot of good for the

Boat People may be very fine but it's not a religion. It's an escape from a dire confrontation with whatever is beyond.

T: A great many people would violently disagree with you there.

Davies: Yes, I think they would.

T: About the Boat People analogy, I mean.

Davies: Yes. It's all very fine. But it's so easy. You get out and cheer for the Boat People; you're so obviously doing good and you can congratulate yourself; you can mix with a lot of people who think as you do. But just facing your relationship to what is ultimate in life, quietly, is much harder. It's not so self-honouring.

T: Ah, but what happens if you have faced yourself and then decide to say, to Hell with the Boat People.

Davies: Fine. But again you may not. You might just as conceivably say, to Hell with the Boat People.

T: You're probably most out of step with the times when it comes to your opinions on education. I look at Canada and I see a country that has made great progress in terms of developing a fairly high median level of education. Whereas I think you look at Canada and see how our middle-class society has discouraged excellence.

Davies: My opinion is very much conditioned by the fact that I teach in a university. I'm perpetually meeting young people who are products of our Canadian system of education. Sometimes I am shocked and alarmed on their behalf by the things they have not been introduced to and which I think they need if they're going to do the kind of study and work that they want.

I feel that in the yearning to make education acceptable and possible to everyone, certain tough things have been omitted. We have gone for breadth of education rather than depth. You can't really have both because there's only a limited amount of time you can spend going to school.

In the old days, when education was somewhat narrower, I think that it was in certain respects more effective. To come down to an example, I think that the modern training in history is not nearly as effective as it used to be. You get people trying to study something like literature who haven't really any notion of the historical background of what they're reading. This is shortchanging them. People like myself have to give them a quick course in history before they can get to literature.

But all systems of education are riddled with faults. The plain fact is that we are not enjoying the fruits of a splendidly organized and completed educational set-up. We are still in the midst of a great educational experiment which began about a century ago. It was decided everybody ought to be made literate up to a certain standard. We're still trying to find the most effective way of doing it. So no wonder we've got problems. We're in the middle of something, not at the end of it.

T: "We have educated ourselves into a world from which wonder, and the fear and dread and splendour and freedom of wonder, have been banished."

Davies: Yes. I was recently visited by a young man who was obviously a very good high school student. He wanted to talk to me about the Deptford trilogy. He came in and he sat in that chair where you are sitting now. He looked me right in the eye and he said, "What do you think is the chief structural flaw in your trilogy?"

I laughed heartily. We began to discuss this thing and it turned out he had been taught by his teacher to find flaws, to see through things rather than enjoy them and find what they had to say to him. I thought—that boy is a very good boy who has been given a very raw deal by the educational system. He's not been taught to blossom and enlarge. He's been taught to zero in on something he can understand because it's negative. It's very hard to understand positive things. It's pretty easy to understand negative things.

T: You also hold the unfashionable view that art is aristocratic, not democratic.

Davies: What I mean when I say art is aristocratic is that it is selective. It's not a mass thing. There never is a mass art that lasts very long or explains very much. But I don't mean aristocratic in the sense that it's produced by high-born people for high-born people. I just mean it's produced by special people for people who can understand.

T: Do you feel you were born with an artist's temperament?
Davies: Yes.

T: Can we assume then that artists are born and not made?
Davies: I think that's true. All kinds of people come to see me and want advice on how they can become writers. But if you're a writer, you know it. You can improve what you are and become a better

writer. But if you come to me and ask how can I become a writer, there is no answer.

Yet many people have this curious notion about writing. They know perfectly well they can't be a painter but everybody thinks somehow they may be a writer.

T: That's because everybody can write on a certain practical level of efficiency.

Davies: Yes. And a lot of technical writing or writing on factual matters may be very good indeed. But when you get over the bridge to what is imaginative and intuitive, then either you can do it or you can't. Nobody can teach you.

T: How far along were you in your writing career before you came to the conclusion that the function of literature is equivalent to the function of dream?

Davies: I don't think I ever came to any such conclusion.

T: It's in one of your essays.

Davies: Well, all art has some association with dream because it arises from the unconscious. Novels, poetry and plays and so forth are not exceptions to the general rule. So virtually everything that is written seriously, and isn't simply manufactured out of whole cloth, has some relationship to dream.

T: Does it follow that Canada is not going to have a great theatre until we recognize our collective dreams?

Davies: No, I don't think that is so. The collective dreams of a tribe don't mean the collective dreams of a political unit. One of the great collective dreams of our tribe is *King Lear.* That's one of the great collective dreams of western culture. We can't slough it off and say it's not Canadian, it's not ours. We'd be left with very little.

T: You once said Chekhov and Ibsen are our two great Canadian playwrights. Is that because they both explored self-satisfied small-mindedness?

Davies: Yes. And also because they explored a northern consciousness with an intensity that has not been equalled in Canada.

T: Are you pleased so far with the growth of Canadian theatre?

Davies: Yes. Though I think that it's shortly going to get sick of what it's doing and try more ambitious things. At the moment it's involved in a theatre of discontent. Of protest and underdoggery. It will have to get rid of that because it's not a sufficiently big theme to engage a whole theatre community for a long time.

T: I would agree that the underdog theme is prevalent. But what do you see replacing it?

Davies: Upperdog. Because the underdogs run the country. This is one of the things artists have always to bear in mind. It is interesting to explore the consciousness and lives of the dispossessed. But if you're going to talk about a whole nation, you've got to also talk about the people who make it work. That's not the underdog.

T: Who amongst the new playwrights do you see as particularly interesting?

Davies: I think [Michel] Tremblay. I wouldn't want to express an opinion beyond that.

T: It appears you're content to have moved out of the playwriting sphere.

Davies: Pretty much. Because I have been more or less successful in achieving an audience as a novelist. Although my plays did very well in their time, they're now old-fashioned. I'm not particularly interested in trying to establish a reputation writing in the new line. I've had my shot, as it were.

T: What do you make of that tag, "The Bernard Shaw of Canada"?

Davies: I think it's absolutely absurd. Nobody who had any notion of what Bernard Shaw was or what I am would ever use it. Canadians can be so shallow in their judgments! Any man with a beard is the same as any other man with a beard.

T: One similarity is that you've both emphasized that revolution is rarely a path towards freedom.

Davies: [laughing] It's usually the path towards another form of tyranny!

T: And you've both examined the pretensions of the middle class and decided roguery functions as readily within the law as outside it.

Davies: But you see, my outlook on life tends to be romantic. That certainly was not applicable to Shaw.

T: As the emphasis of your career has shifted from humour to drama, then from drama to novels, have these changes corresponded with changes within yourself?

Davies: Well, those changes of emphasis are not so great as they might appear on the surface. I think novels contain a great deal of humour and drama. Inevitably themes are broader in later work. So it's more a question of development than total change.

T: But the talents of a playwright and the talents of a novelist are quite separate.

Davies: Yes.

T: Wasn't it difficult making that switch?

Davies: No, I don't think it was. It seemed to be more or less inevitable. At the time I was writing plays in Canada, the opportunities for getting them produced were not very great. Productions were often unsatisfactory, for reasons that were really nobody's fault. It wasn't a time when we had a theatre that could work very well with a new script. The temptation was therefore to write a novel where you can control the whole atmosphere.

T: Do you wish you had applied more time to writing novels at a younger age?

Davies: No.

T: Would you agree with Liesl in *World of Wonders* that man isn't a good animal, but a noble animal?

Davies: Yes, yes, I agree with that one hundred per cent.

T: Even if it isn't true, it's a noble thought.

Davies: Of course. Better a noble lie than a miserable truth.

T: You once described Canada in Jungian terms, saying we had a "shadow" which was our habit of emotional repression. Does having such a strong shadow help Canadian artists or hinder them?

Davies: I think it has helped them. It gives a nation one appearance externally and something very different inside. That has evidenced itself time and time again in our history. And in our literature. For instance, in the work of writers like Margaret Laurence and Hugh MacClennan. It's there with the people who have written seriously about Canadian life.

T: You said back in 1972 that Canada expects nothing of its writers. Do you think that has changed?

Davies: Not really. Nobody pays any particular attention to the opinions of a writer about Canadian affairs. It is really quite extraordinary. We haven't got any writers who are really looked up to and whose word is awaited about public affairs.

T: Why is that?

Davies: Because their opinions are not immediately applicable. When you're asked an opinion about politics in Canada, it's "Do you think Joe Clark is going to make it in the next hundred days?" You're not asked, "Are we doing what we should to create a coherent nation?". The questions are always these Johnny-on-the-spot things.

T: And yet in the process of doing this book, it seems to me that our writers possibly know this country better than politicians.

Davies: That is quite possible. A writer hasn't an awful lot to gain except his own enlightenment when making his acquaintance with the country and its people. A politician is always looking for some kind of advantage, some kind of angle. So their perception is likely to be shallow. The perception of the writer is not. Nobody cares what he thinks so he's able to look more intently.

Also the politician is always on the spot. There's always somebody pushing a microphone in his face and wanting to know what he thinks. He probably doesn't think anything but he has to say something.

T: Writers are essentially tuned into the psychology of a nation.

Davies: Yes, but it's very hard to persuade a country like Canada that it has any psychology. Or that a psychological observation may be a weighty one.

There are things which people in the main regard as trivialities which I think are extraordinarily interesting and important. For instance, when Mr. Clark formed the government, he immediately began redecorating the Prime Minister's residence in Ottawa. How did he do it? He had all the red removed from the decor. It was replaced with blue because that's a Tory colour. Now what kind of a man thinks of decorating his house in terms of the colour of his political party? It tells us a great deal about him.

The Prime Minister's house is the place where our most important visitors to Canada, not the Tory party, are entertained. To decorate it in political colours is to narrow the office of Prime Minister and the head of state absurdly. But just try to get people to consider that as important and you'll have your work cut out for you.

T: I think this comes near the root of why your work is refreshing. You give the reader a sense that self-analysis can be pleasurable as well as painful. Do you yourself ever recall experiencing any memorable moments of personal insight?

Davies: Nothing like a flash of lightning. It's more a matter of a thing that happens in the course of a few weeks.

T: So it's a comparison of before and after.

Davies: Yes. You can't say on such-and-such an afternoon I came to a conclusion about something. At least I don't.

T: Do you think psychology is on its way to becoming our new religion?

Davies: Psychology and religion have always been very closely linked. Nowadays people are extremely cautious about committing themselves to any sort of religious statement so they tend to put psychological tags on what might formerly have been considered religious insights. But I don't think that it matters very much. Basically it's the insights that are important, not the tags that go with them.

T: Can you articulate the connection for yourself between a sense of wonder and religious feeling?

Davies: A sense of wonder is in itself a religious feeling. But in so many people the sense of wonder gets lost. It gets scarred over. It's as though a tortoise shell has grown over it. People reach a stage where they're never surprised, never delighted. They're never suddenly aware of glorious freedom or splendour in their lives. However hard a life may be, I think for virtually all people this is possible.

This is very unhappy, very unfortunate. The attitude is often self-induced. It is fear. People are afraid to be happy. Puritanical parents used to say, "If you laugh before breakfast, you'll cry before night." This sort of thing has been driven into us so much that we're almost terrified to rejoice. Or to think we're lucky.

How lucky people are! Look out of that window. An absolutely superb autumn day. Both of us are sitting here, neither of us are experiencing any pain. We're not hungry. We're aware. This is happiness. So many people tend to think that happiness must be a kind of glory which is absolutely unrepeatable. But it's an endlessly renewing thing.

A Conversation with Robertson Davies

Ann Saddlemyer/1981

From *Canadian Drama*, 7 #2 (1981) pp. 110-116. Reprinted by permission.

We met in his new study on the third floor of Massey College, overlooking the quadrangle of the institution he had served for eighteen years, its first Master. He seemed relieved—almost pleased—when I reported the break-down of the tape recorder I had counted on for support, and gracefully led me to the most comfortable chair. The room, somewhat austerely furnished, would now serve as the only formal link with the College and the Graduate Centre for the Study of Drama which he had helped found and influenced still. Here, surrounded by the warmth and fellowship of spirits past and present, he will continue to write. But, sadly, no longer for the Canadian theatre.

A.S. Let us begin by assuming a knowledge of your replies to Geraldine Anthony's questions in *Stage Voices,* and go on from there. You speak of your predilection for the comic style, and elsewhere you speak with approval of irony. Many have labelled you a satirist. Do you consider yourself primarily a writer of satire?

R.D. No. To me a satirist is a person who dislikes the world as it is and stands apart in judgment. I am an observer, but not a remote and unappreciative one. A satirist is self-righteous. I trust I am not.

A.S. Yet in a lecture to the Royal Society you speak of "the really serious business of comedy". It has frequently been observed that two spirits informing your work are those great comic masterpieces, Don Quixote and Mr. Punch. Indeed, they appear in several plays and are evoked in others. What is your attitude towards them?

R.D. I am devoted to both. Don Quixote is the ultimate romancer who dares all, unaware of ridicule. Punch is of course unredeemed man, whom all the theorists are constantly trying to bottle up. I regret

to say that Punch does not get much of a look-in at the Drama
Centre, or anywhere else for that matter. You see, the theatre is an
anarchic place where wonderful things can happen; it is no place for
theorists. I try to give Punch a chance, in all his facets; for he is a very
wicked as well as an admired and loved individual. He hates fools, is
an egotist—in fact, he is all the things lying at the root of art, vital,
and alive. It was Goethe's Mephistopheles who commented that all
theory is gray, but that art is a living, green tree. Punch is an
important part of that mystery.

   A.S. "Romance, mystery, and the higher hokum", as you yourself
once described the subject matter of drama. Do you distinguish
between material more suitable for the novel form than for the
drama?

   R.D. No. I am dancing a jig right now at the success of the
dramatization of *Nicholas Nickleby* in London—there's great melodrama for you! All of those nineteenth century novelists and
dramatists knew how to feed the audience with wonder. But a play is
conditioned by the time it takes to perform it—there is a limit to the
amount that can be fed to an audience. There is the great charm, of
course, of seeing a play with others, but the concentration is different.
A novel is more generous—there is time to fill things out.

   A.S. Is the purpose different between a novel and a play?

   R.D. The novel can provide narrative in a splendid inclusive
sense, not just tale telling. What grips in the theatre can be given
more concentrated feeling and perception by the novelist. But the
purpose remains the same.

   A.S. Although it is dangerous to try and identify the authorial
voice, I cannot help but feel that Major Rogers' speech in *Pontiac and
the Green Man* about the playwright's desire to make his audience
"feel as he does" and the description in *World of Wonders* of theatre
"showing people what they wish were true" are your own sentiments.

   R.D. Yes, that is mouthpiece writing. Of course, all literary art is
an attempt to buttonhole the audience as Coleridge's Ancient Mariner
does. One tries to offer a different perception of life. For example, the
girl who works at a switchboard all day goes to a Neil Simon play to
see life as she would like to believe it can be led—is led—by
someone else. I try to offer some of that magic.

A.S. Do you find it difficult to reconcile your love for melodrama with the comic perception?

R.D. Not at all. If the story of Mr. Punch were treated a little more seriously, it would be a melodrama of crime and retribution. Very like Dostoyevsky's *Crime and Punishment,* in fact. In that book a man commits a murder, as Punch does, because he thinks himself superior to the common run of mankind, and unlike Punch, has to admit at last that he was partly mistaken. My point of view is rather unfashionable now. I believe that tragedy, except in the hands of an extraordinary genius, is a ludicrous mode; it doesn't reflect life in a recognizable world. We can all sympathize with aspects of *Hamlet,* but for most people life is lived in the mode of melodrama, for a few people in the mode of comedy, but for very few in that of tragedy. Most critics don't sufficiently recognize the melodrama and the morality in my work. A satirist is a disappointed idealist; I am rather a moralist. The moralist looks at life and says that certain courses of action lead to certain consequences—here are people who are pursuing a dead end path, people who have put themselves in chains.

A.S. Life-denying rather than life-affirming, as you have expressed it in *Overlaid.*

R.D. Exactly.

A.S. You appear to have treated the range of sexuality and sexual activity much more sensitively and thoroughly in your novels than in your plays. Is there any particular reason for this?

R.D. I wrote plays first, before becoming a novelist, and sexuality is more easily dealt with in the novel. You can't tell what actors and a director are going to do with a play, so your view cannot be presented very carefully. Look at what the modern theatre has done to Shakespeare—there are far too many barefoot pregnant Ophelias dragging rag dolls behind them. One of the points I am perpetually trying to make is that sexuality is not nearly such a commanding element in most lives as we are taught to think it is today. This is of basic importance—so much modern literature and art suggest that we are in a perpetual state of frying lubricity. They can't imagine a purpose in life other than sex. Take the two of us here in this room at the present moment—we couldn't get on with the business at hand— nobody could—if we were to behave as modern literature suggests. I was delighted to read recently of Bernard Shaw's statement that he couldn't have been more pleased when in old age he was freed at last from the tyranny of sex. In my books and plays I try to indicate the other things that are influential in the sexual realm. In teaching, for example, it is extraordinary how difficult it is to make students realize that social distinction can be important in affairs of sex. Love on its own conquers very little.

A.S. What other subjects have you found more suitable for a particular form?

R.D. The religious, mysterious, and numinous area of life is difficult to cope with on stage where so many are hostile to it. One hears a great deal from directors, for example, about the "nuisance" of the ghost in *Hamlet,* the witches in *Macbeth.* Yet these things are a part of life. My novels, as in life, are full of ghosts. I am aware of the perpetual presence of the dead behind us. Everybody has experienced this—my youngest daughter recently commented that when she spoke to her son, she suddenly heard her mother speaking to her. And I could tell her that that was because her grandmother had spoken to her mother in the same way. These are the real ghosts. My next novel will deal with this perpetual recurrence of ideas and predispositions in families. That is tough to deal with on stage. Wilder's *The Long Christmas Dinner* succeeds, and few realize what a great play is. The third act of *Our Town* is too often misunderstood and performed sentimentally, stupidly. There is a fearful irony in the scene where Emily says to her mother-in-law, "They don't understand, do they?" and she replies, "No dear. They don't understand." That is usually said stupidly, with a sob. The sweetness and splendour of life cannot be footnoted.

A.S. In your 1966 epilogue to *At My Heart's Core* and *Overlaid* you note that these plays deal with the "intellectual climate of Canada"; *Question Time* deals with many of the same problems. Is there a difference in your attitude between the later and the earlier plays?

R.D. Yes, immeasurable. The early plays were imitative of plays I admired and which were still considered "modern". I admired James Bridie enormously and attempted to write in his mode. *Question Time* is a newer form, and it is a great sadness to me that it did not work because it was misunderstood by the director. He wouldn't

attack it. I write expecting the director to cut and it is not as finely
honed as it ought to be. The same thing happened with the director
of *Pontiac and the Green Man,* which was under-rehearsed and
vastly overwritten; it should have twenty minutes cut out of it, and in
consequence it is not a good play. But I am sad that nobody has
wanted to do *Question Time* since. In addition, it was absurdly cast. I
was told an actor who was small, wiry, alert would be playing the
lead; instead, an entirely different type was cast. Similarly with the
Spirit of the Far North. The result was a bloodbath—extravagant
writing and unintelligent casting.

A.S. Do you usually have particular actors in mind when writing
your plays?

R.D. Not really—just the kind of person. I did, however, write
General Confession for the Davises. Donald Davis wanted to act a
romantic lover before he was too old for the role and asked me to
write a play for the Crest Theatre. Michael Langham wanted to direct
the play and it was actually in the works. But J.B. Priestley visited
Canada, fell in love with the Davises, and wrote them *The Glass
Cage,* which they produced instead. It was a flop. But *General
Confession* is my best play and my favorite; in it is my attempt to
explain what an artist is. It has never been produced.

A.S. Gordon Craig built a model stage for W.B. Yeats; Shaw used
a chessboard. Do you use anything similar in writing your plays to
define movement and design?

R.D. I draw little diagrams on paper as I go along, that is all.

A.S. You have spoken of the great challenge language poses in
writing a play. Are there others?

R.D. What the actor can do by gesture or bodily movement. But
one has to learn to trust the actor. I use as few stage directions as
possible. One has to trust the director. My ambition was to work
collaboratively in the theatre, but that was not possible.

A.S. Besides *General Confession,* what are your other favorites
among your plays?

R.D. I am convinced that *Hunting Stuart* is a good play, and full
of magic if done properly. I have always yearned for the nineteenth
century kind of theatre—melodrama interspersed with scenes of
comedy—which looks like a blend if done right. If melodrama is not
played for all it's worth it fails. I remember for example a scene in
Cyrano de Bergerac at Stratford which became cheap and tawdry,

yet could have been magical if played straight. A young servant girl, full of admiration for Cyrano, offers him an orange. The actor should have accepted her gift with the grace and dignity of the spirit in which she offered it; instead, he smirked at the audience. A wonderful moment was lost. Comedy also has to be played straight; it is not funny otherwise. But these elements are no longer wanted in the theatre. As a playwright, I am old-fashioned; in the past I filled a place, but that's gone by.

A.S. One of your plays, *Brothers in the Black Art,* was produced on television; was it written specifically for that medium? What differences did you find?

R.D. Yes, I wrote it for a specific series, although I have not yet met anyone who saw it performed. Television gives you freedom to move around as an author; there is less tight a structure, and so marvellous things can be done which are not possible on stage. For example, in *Brothers in the Black Art,* there was a superbly atmospheric glimpse of the CNE in the 1920s, and another scene in the printing shop when the Indian poet Pauline Johnson walks through. I drew for that play on my father's experiences as an apprentice to the printing trade, and he used to have visits from Pauline Johnson, whose poetry was published in the paper on which he worked. None of that could have been evoked so well on stage.

A.S. You mentioned earlier the vogue for adapting novels for television; do you think any of yours would be successful?

R.D. The Deptford novels as a series only; perhaps *Fortune, My Foe.* That play was once broadcast on radio. I received $300, but they gave Lister Sinclair $500 for adapting the script, and he didn't have to do much to the text at all!

A.S. You have elsewhere spoken of the great influence the writers of early films had on you as a boy; have you ever considered writing a film script?

R.D. No.

A.S. As a young scholar at Oxford, you wrote a thesis on Shakespeare's boy actors; do you think that study had an influence on your masques?

R.D. Yes, in particular my realization that a full rhetorical actor could take the women's parts. But my masques are written for young people to perform; I don't think they would appeal to adult actors.

A.S. Yet your *Masque of Mr. Punch* in particular has a great deal of appeal to audiences of every age. But can we turn to another important aspect of your work, its presentation of things Canadian and your own attitude towards Canada? You once said, in comparing Australian art with Canadian, that Australia had left its mark on the physique of its people, but that Canada has put its mark on the spirit. Do you find a similar difference between Canadians and Americans?

R.D. Yes. There is a recognizable type of Canadian and I can write for that. On the other hand, I have never found any two Americans the same. The southerners are vastly different from the Californians, and New Yorkers are a breed of their own. There is a continuity of history among Canadians that Americans do not have. This is now changing because of the influx of so many new racial groups into Canada, and they have brought with them subtlety of mind and sophistication. I have changed as a consequence. When writing a novel thirty years ago I could not count on an understanding of European background; now I can. Publishers and producers are still afraid of this. It is crazy to underestimate the intelligence of an audience. There is too much of a tendency to simplify in contemporary plays.

A.S. Has your attitude towards Canadians, as expressed in *Fortune, My Foe,* changed?

R.D. Yes, radically. University life in Canada has blossomed astonishingly in the past twenty years. Any revival of that play must be dated, presented as a period piece. Vanessa was a girl of the period immediately before World War II, about 1936, the kind who wore white gloves—you would never find anyone wearing gloves to go out today!

A.S. You yourself commented that *Overlaid* "reflects a situation we shall have in Canada for a long time"? Do you still believe that?

R.D. Yes, and it appears in many places. You find it for example in the provincial government's getting the wrong end of the stick in the 1960s, building all those universities that in the 1980s are absolutely unnecessary and an embarrassment. Just one more example of a determination to pursue a course without recognition of the spiritual necessity of a situation.

A.S. Which could lead us to a discussion of the Stratford Shakespearean Festival, in whose history you have played a long and honourable part. In your recent article on theatre in Canada for the

University of Toronto Quarterly, you wrote that Stratford "seems to rise to the challenge of those plays that call for understanding of their chronicle form and mythical suggestion". Does that have anything to do with something Canadian or is it merely the chance of choice of directors?

R.D. Both. Jean Gascon's production of *Pericles* was marked by a French sensibility and delicacy that was typically Canadian. We can do things with freshness because we haven't that accretion of tradition which so often haunts English productions and English actors. Stratford could have exercised more influence than it has so far—the Canadian playwrights who have been sought out for production there have often been chosen for the wrong reasons, their plays insufficiently polished, not seriously treated and given backdoor productions.

A.S. What about the Dominion Drama Festival? You had a long productive relationship with that organization also. Was it useful to Canadian playwrights?

R.D. There were many good things about the DDF, which I have referred to elsewhere, but I think it should be stated that it had a malign influence also. The DDF persuaded amateurs to think of themselves with unbecoming seriousness. The result was a repressive influence on playwriting, negative because it did not know what to do with original plays. I am grateful for the opportunities I had, but the governors too often played theatrical grandees in a manner not substantiated by their experience. They were no use to a writer, and actually had a freezing influence on young playwrights. The only place that was different was Quebec, and they were all mavericks there; but some of them were artists. Père Legault and his company made the rest of us look like rubes—and we were!

A.S. You once wrote of Canadians, "We are a particularly violent people". Does anyone recognize that today in our theatre?

R.D. George Ryga does, which may be why he too is now without a theatre.

A.S. What contemporary playwrights do you feel most in sympathy with?

R.D. None. I am an old-fashioned playwright and my kind of theatre is gone. But I want to be heard. I am not heard in the theatre, but I am in my novels.

Author Davies Puts 'Inner Life' Concerns First

Tom Harpur/1981

From *Toronto Daily Star*, 2 October 1981, pp. C1-C2. Reprinted by permission—The Toronto Star Syndicate.

"I *see* mankind's advance . . . to what he is today as an extraordinary success. I think that kind of success will continue."

Robertson Davies believes that as mankind nears the year 2,000, Christianity will be replaced by a new religious revelation.

The 68-year-old author, educator and critic says that religion touches every part of his life, but that those who feel God is solely or even mainly concerned with mankind are flattering themselves.

Davies, who has just published his latest novel, *Rebel Angels,* also holds that the sexual revolution is largely a myth, and that marriage has very little to do with romance. He spoke intimately of these and a range of other topics in an interview with *Star* religion editor Tom Harpur at Massey college.

Q: Dr. Davies, people in our society define success in a whole range of ways. How do you think of it yourself?

A: I have never thought of success entirely, in a worldly way. Success with yourself and in the inner life is the success that counts.

Q: In any self-assessment, what do you think your weaknesses would be?

A: That is extraordinarily difficult to say. I am not very good with people, I mean in human contacts. I am not as genial and warm and understanding as perhaps I would like to be. There is a kind of a satirical streak in my nature which interferes, but I don't think that is entirely bad. People who are enormously warm and outgoing towards mankind, unless they are saintly people, are often not very interesting.

Q: Would you describe yourself as an optimist, generally speaking?

A: I am certainly not a pessimist. I think I try to hold the balance as evenly as I can, and that prevents you from being a pure optimist. I am a long-term optimist, not a short-term optimist.

Q: What would the long-term optimism be based on?

A: The long-term optimism is based on the experience of mankind in the past. A great many people who take a very short view say that mankind is an unsuccessful experiment and likely to be obliterated, as something that hasn't quite worked. But I don't see it that way. I see mankind, its advance from a protoplasmal, atomic globule, to what it is today as an extraordinary, wholly unpredictable kind of success. I think that kind of success will continue.

Q: Are you a religious person?

A: Yes, I am. It takes a total part of my life, because nothing I do is untouched by what I suppose has been defined as religion. That is, awareness of what is not immediately and superficially obvious in common life.

Q: I was wondering what content you give the word God.

A: I haven't any particular definition or view of what God is, but as a student of the work of Carl Jung I am aware of the God archetype. That is, the necessity which asserts itself in one way or another in the human psyche for an ultimate value.

But, the nature of that ultimate value I am not clever enough to speculate about in any very useful way. Infinitely more able people than I have done so, and it seems to me they have made rather a mess of it. The fact of God being all-encompassing ever-present is really about all that I can say about it. But the people who regard God as wholly good in terms of what they believe to be good, I think, are flattering themselves.

Q: Do you think then of God as some immanent force within us rather than some deity over and above the universe?

A: As both. Simply to say immanent within us suggests God is somehow the property of mankind and/or of the animal kingdom, I think God is immanent in everything that we know. I hesitate to say immanent in nature because the minute you say that, a lot of rather sentimental people say, "Oh yes, I am nearer to God in my garden than anywhere else in the world," and I think that is hooey! The idea that God is solely and gloatingly concerned with mankind is very self-flattering.

Q: Would this awareness of the religious dimension in your life
lead you to actual worship or prayer?

A: Yes. Though I regard them not in a way that would be wholly
gratifying, I think, to Christians. I consider them as symbolic
observances, to put you in touch with something which is not totally
expressed in, or encompassed by, or evoked by the ceremony. For
instance, the Sacrament of Holy Communion I take with the greatest
seriousness. But I do so as an assertion of one's unity with the rest of
mankind on the deepest level rather than simply as a solely Christian
service.

Q: Talking about the future of religion, do you see changes
coming?

A: Yes I do. I think a very decisive, radical change is imminent,
because in the psychological history of mankind there has been
something which you can call a new revelation about every 2,000
years. The 2,000 years of Christianity, what might be called the Age
of Pisces, is running out, and something will come to replace it; and
perhaps to build upon it, as the Age of Pisces built upon the earlier,
tremendous intellectual probing of the Greeks and also the extraordinary moral force and authority of the Hebrews. I think we are headed
for something new.

Q: Is your work your meaning largely, do you think? Is that what
gives you the reason to get up in the morning and go on?

A: No! I wouldn't say that it was. My work is enormously
important to me; but I think the mainspring for the kind of thing you
are talking about is an absolutely ravening curiosity. I want to see
what happens. I don't use the word curiosity trivially; I think curiosity
is one of the things that ties mankind together. Without curiosity we
would all just perish in our own miserable little holes. This curiosity
expresses itself in all kinds of forms which people think foolish, like
gossip. People despise gossip, and often gossip is trivial and
sometimes malignant; but it is better to gossip than not to care what
other people are doing.

Q: What makes Robertson Davies angry when he looks around at
the world?

A: Stupidity. That is a very wide-ranging definition of an enormous
amount of human action.

Q: In terms of the world scene, is it still stupidity?

A: So frequently it is stupidity, yes. And stupidity, of course, includes so many of the things which are, or used to be, defined as among the Seven Deadly Sins—pride, wrath, covetousness, etc. All those things are, if carried to any kind of excess, stupidity. Within reason, they are human; beyond a reasonable quantity, they become stupidity and are infinitely harmful.

Q: In your thinking of values and of right or wrong, what kind of framework do you work with?

A: I never was very good at making that sort of judgment, and I have become much less good at it as my life has progressed. I have seen so many instances of what looked like very bad behavior having good consequences and behavior which was widely praised bringing a lot of grief and trouble in its wake. It is most difficult to say what kind of action is going to bring about a good result.

Just on a very superficial level, I think that you can say about human conduct what you can say about trying to mend a machine; if you force anything, you are probably going to wreck it.

Q: The ultimate mystery in life is death and I wondered what you make of that as you think about it.

A: What I make of it is, I think, very simple-minded. It is simply this: You were nowhere before you were born; you were a possibility. And I think it extraordinarily unlikely that all that possibility, after 70 or 80 years blooming in this particular kind of life, disappears totally. So, therefore, as there was a life before birth I think it is absurd to suppose that there is not a life after death. Precisely what its nature is I do not know. Certainly we seem to be moved by whatever you want to call it, a spirit, or an energy, or something which if it's no longer moving us as individuals is hardly likely to disappear completely. When you turn off the switch, electricity doesn't go away.

Q: What about traditional belief in some sort of afterlife in terms of reward and punishment?

A: I don't know. I thought at one time that people had their reward and punishment here on earth. But I am not perfectly certain that is necessarily the case. I begin to wonder whether an afterlife is necessary to sort of even things out; but I certainly don't believe it is this Sunday school notion of heaven and bliss, because heaven and bliss, as lots of people have pointed out, would be wholly unendurable. The idea that the afterlife is totally free from pain or from experience of one sort and another, or involves some complete illumination, I cannot believe. But I think it is going to be uncommonly interesting. I won't say I can't wait to find out. Because I can! I can hold off; but I don't regard death as the ultimate horror by any means.

Q: Is there anything that frightens you? When you wake up in the night, what do you fear?

A: I fear oblivion in this life—that is, the loss of one's wits or a decline of one's senses into senility or something of that kind.

Q: Could we talk just a bit about family life? The pessimists say that it is going out and something else will have to take its place.

A: I think that the family idea is on the way toward some sort of evolution towards a different attitude. We no longer, for purely social reasons, money inheritance, and so on, work on the principal that parents own their children and determine their destiny by economic pressure or by moral pressure or whatever. We have got to find some way of coping with that, because it is also quite intolerable for the parents that children should enjoy a total freedom or even a great deal of freedom when they are still dependent and when they are still in a sense emanations of the parents and the family group.

I see a great deal of this kind of thing, especially in my work as a teacher. It is the old story that children want to be free and independent until something goes wrong, and all of a sudden they are their parents' child all over again. If they bring disgrace upon themselves and are in serious trouble, it is not they alone who suffer. There has got to be some recognition of this, some sense of a shared responsibility. But the old notion that children were just chattels and you formed them in your own image and either wept or stormed when they didn't take that image is ridiculous and has to go. I have seen it bring too much misery and destruction in its wake.

Q: Do you think in the area of sexuality, where there is so much talk of liberation, that some kind of revolution or change has taken place and has been for the better?

A: I don't think there has been nearly so much change as is popularly supposed. Young people, when sex begins to be important to them, experiment with it and sometimes they come to grief and sometimes they enjoy extraordinary happiness. I think they have always done that.

Q: In terms of sexuality today, are there any broad moral principles that you think apply?

A: Yes. If sexual adventures are undertaken just for kicks, with people you hardly know, I don't think it can work out well because it's just frivolous, and frivolity is a form of stupidity.

Q: What about the traditional ideal of marriage as one man, one woman, one lifetime?

A: I don't know that it is ever going to work very well, or more than perhaps 50 per cent, because the sexual impulse urges people to get together very early in life and they marry very early. They grow apart, and there are innumerable painful examples in very high circles. You know what was said during the last war, that Washington was full of brilliant men and the women they married when they were very young. And this is a sad, cruel, but true thing. The pretty, squeezy, delightful girl in the haystack is very different from the middle-aged, stupid, unambitious, frightened woman of 45 that she may develop into. This is frivolous talk and probably stupid, but nature hasn't changed her ways.

I don't have any inordinately romantic view of marriage. I think it is a much more serious partnership than what is called love. Love may well enter into such a partnership, but there's no guarantee it will, and I have seen, passionate love between people; who if they married, would have been cutting one anothers' throats in a year.

Q: If you were faced with a group of young people, and they were asking your advice, what would you say?

A: It is the advice I have given time and again to young people, particularly the ones I like best, and trust most, and it is: Don't plan your life too much. Let things happen to you. Much more interesting things will happen to you than you can devise for yourself. And, although you should not just swing around loose and have no sort of plan or ideas about life, don't shut out the element of chance. I have seen as a journalist and a teacher at the university, the young people, and some of them planned their careers right down to the last detail. And they were punished: They got what they had planned and how dull it was!

"Sunday Morning"
Elizabeth Hay/1981

Transcription from CBC Radio, 11 July 1982 (recorded October 1981). Copyright 1982 Canadian Broadcasting Corporation. Reprinted by permission of the CBC and Robertson Davies.

EH: This is Elizabeth Hay in Massey College at the University of Toronto, for 18 years Robertson Davies' home and still his haunt. When he retired as Master of the college last June, he kept a room which he uses as a study. He guides visitors to it through narrow halls, heavy with the smell of tobacco.

[Sounds of people walking]

RD: . . . and through that glass door.

EH: It's like a rabbit warren in here, isn't it?

RD: Oh I think that's a harsh way of describing it. It's an academic atmosphere. Come in.

EH: The study is simple, a wall of books, a few chairs, and a desk. It's a room with a view. One window looks on to a busy Toronto street, the other into the College quadrangle, grassy and quiet. Robertson Davies checks a gold pocketwatch before settling into an armchair, pillow at his back, to talk about his new novel and what its based on, the University he's observed for nearly 20 years.

RD: I watch all the time. That's what being a novelist is, a novelist is a watcher, and you watch all the time whether you're intensely conscious of it or not but of course I do make notes, and I keep a little notebook so that I won't forget anything that crops up that I might want to jot down, and things that I encounter in reading I make notes of because then I put them in a sort of file catalogue and keep them that way.

EH: What was your last entry?

RD: I've forgotten what it was, now let's see. Maybe it's something I shouldn't—Oh yes, here it is, "In former ages we clothed our fighters in colors of blood or the sea. In our age in uniforms which are the color of shit," and the point of that is I think we're living in an age which despises humanity and despises bravery and doesn't need

214

bravery because modern warfare has rather gone beyond bravery. It is a kind of warfare where people are finding enemies they never see, killing people of whom they know nothing.

EH: How might that thought turn up in your writing?

RD: Well, it might or it might not. On the whole I like to write about people who are in other kinds of difficulties. Canadians are still a people who don't want to admit that they are a people who are frequently torn by passion and driven by feelings that they frequently can't control.

EH: What made you first believe that there was hidden passion in Canadians?

RD: I used to notice it very much when I was a child with the children I played with. They were country children, and they seemed to me to have two characters: there's the character they showed at Sunday School and to superiors—teachers and so forth—and there was their dreadful brutality to animals and to anything or everybody who was very weak. I fortunately was not weak or I would have suffered greatly, but I saw people who were weak suffer frightfully. I went to school with a girl who disappeared, she ran away. And everybody wondered why Anna had run away. Anna was an orphan and in those days, orphans were let out of the orphan asylum, as at that time it was called, to work for people who would take them in and be foster parents to them. Anna had run away and when she was found and brought back, some people took a look at Anna and her body was entirely covered with tiny, tiny burns, and the reason she was burned was that the good Christian, fine-souled, woman who had taken her in used to teach Anna to do her work better by tipping her with the electric iron, and Anna was a mass of burns. Now what happened to Anna I don't know. If she ever grew up sane, it was a miracle.

EH: How would that kind of story work on your imagination as a novelist?

RD: It was horrifying. It was horrifying to me then, it is horrifying to me now. All kinds of things that I heard when I was a child and was aware of among the people with whom I grew up, sexual things, acts of cruelty, and so on and so forth, ate into me very deeply and I became very early aware that what people pretend to be and what they really are are two very, very different things.

EH: One of the characters in your new novel says that what shapes a person is the child he once was. What kind of a child was Robertson Davies?

RD: Well, I was a very lonely child because I lived in a community where my parents had not lived for very long. We only lived there five years when I was between the ages of six and twelve, and that was not long enough to form any real association with a community like that, which was one of those ingrown Canadian places. So I was very lonely and I became very much aware that the things that interested me did not interest other children, and I watched them and I took in what happened to them and I've watched what's happened to them since. And what is astonishing is that some of them who were so bright as children became so horrifying dull when they grew up.

EH: Do you have a good memory for the past?

RD: Yes, excellent. I can almost remember the day I was born.

EH: What do you remember?

RD: What do I remember? Oh, my earliest recollections were when I was a very small child indeed and being outdoors in my mother's garden and looking at plants and things, and I don't wish to make this sound dramatic as though I were a lovable little fellow who went around smelling the flowers, but I was astonished by them because they were so big and they were as tall as I was, and I remember what they were. They were peonies and if you're only as tall as a peony, you're not very tall but I was watching the peony and very interested and thought it was fascinating. The color was what interested me. Also lilacs. There was a lilac bush in the garden in which I had a secret place and I thought that when I was in there, nobody knew where I was and I expect they did but I thought I was hidden away. But I used to watch people doing interesting things. I used to, when I was a small boy hanging around the blacksmith shop, watch the blacksmith.

EH: In coming closer to the present you gave a reading from your new book. What did you notice about the audience there?

RD: I noticed that they were very quiet, and I kept looking out there to see who was really listening and who might be inattentive because if they had been I would have shot a few words out there to wake them up. That's part of what being a public performer is.

EH: Professor Davies, as you've gotten older, have you been able to write more frankly about what you feel?

RD: Oh yes, absolutely.

EH: What sort of process happened to you that made that possible?

RD: People died. It's very difficult if you've been brought up as I was to write with full frankness until your parents are dead, not because you want to say anything about your parents but because you don't want to say anything that might worry your parents.

EH: And it wasn't that you suddenly saw things in a new light, it was simply that circumstances made it possible for you to talk.

RD: Yes, that's true and people are very sensitive, you know. Relatives are very sensitive, and they tend to think that you're drawing portraits of them in books which I do not do but I don't want to have to explain that I'm not doing it.

EH: What intrigues me is your interest in passion and in the bizarre, in grotesque events. Why do you have that interest?

RD: Well, is there anyone who isn't interested in grotesque events? It's really, frequently the case that they simply don't see them and don't notice that they're grotesque. Every night on the television news, you'll probably see a picture of something which really if you think about it is grotesque. You see a reverent-looking old man casting a vote for himself when you know that just a week before he has condemned a number of people to have their right hands cut off. What's he voting for? Interesting, grotesque if you consider it that way.

EH: And yet you have the reputation for being a practitioner of civility, of the civilized life, you're known for your love of ceremony, and when you were Master here at Massey College, you would have High Table where people would wear gowns, there would be snuff and sherry, and so on. On the other hand you do have this interest in gypsy life, tarot cards, and so on. Is it the contrast in a way that appeals to you?

RD: I'm interested in the wide variety of life, and I'm always interested that so many people will settle for so little in life, they don't want any ceremony, they don't want anything that is wild, or enchanting, or grotesque, or vivid. They're astonished when young people have rock concerts which provide some elements of this sort of thing, but they don't seem to understand why the young people have it. It is that they want to extend their range of feeling and to have some sort of experience which isn't the common experience of every day. Incidentally, when you say that we went in for a lot of ceremonial here at Massey College, it is true, indeed, that we wore gowns at dinner, but you know the gown is the national dress of educated people. [Laughs] If we'd worn kilts, nobody would have thought it was very queer.

EH: Some of the other things like snuff and so on.

RD: We just had snuff because a friend of the college gave us a snuffhorn. Now I never take snuff, can't stand it, it bothers me, it gives me something rather like hay fever, but some people liked it and some of the young people liked it because they wanted to try it. They'd never had it before so that was something new for them.

EH: So the criticism that you were practicing traditions that were dead before you were born, you would answer how?

RD: Well, I don't think that they were dead before I was born. They are living now and they are living because they are being practiced in all kinds of places though not necessarily often in Canada. But you know because we will not permit ourselves really interesting and fascinating ceremonials, we try to make up for them with junky ones, and consequently, we have endless parades in honor of cancer and muscular dystrophy, and this, that, and the other. I remember one time when I was living in Massey College and I went outside to my front door and there was an enormous parade being formed on the street outside and there was a girl who was almost naked—she had a few things on, but she was shivering, she was blue with cold—and I said to someone, who is that poor girl in the car? And they said, "Oh, she's Miss Muscular Dystrophy." And this poor wretch was a beauty queen who was having to go around showing herself practically stark in order to raise money for charity. Well, this is a ceremonial, but it seems to me it could be one that could be bettered. We could have more fun than just celebrating diseases with big parades.

EH: In his study at Massey College, Robertson Davies handles his correspondence, the letters from children asking what should be done with old men who aren't of any use, and the letters from old men who want to know what should be done about all this youth. This is the spot where he does his writing about the theatre, the books on the shelves are about English drama and represent only a few of the books he owns.

RD: Never give away a book, it's bad luck.

EH: Bad luck?

RD: Bad luck, yes. You'll want that book within a month if you give it away.

EH: Is that the only bad luck it is though?

RD: Well, I don't know. I think the book resents being given away. Books have personalities, you know.

EH: On those shelves right now, which book has the strongest personality?

RD: Well, now, I'm looking at a book which is in six volumes, is a history of theatre by Karl Mantzius. It's translated from Danish and it is of extraordinary interest because Karl Mantzius was not only a historian, he was a very fine actor and one of the things that interested me most when I visited Denmark a few years ago was to go to the national theatre to find a handsome bust of Karl Mantzius in the lobby, and I thought, now there's the way to use your theatre historians.

EH: If there were to be a bust of Robertson Davies somewhere, where would you like it to be?

RD: Oh, in this College, I think. I spent a long time here and did a lot of things here and I think that would be interesting.

EH: Robertson Davies' place is secure in the hall of Massey College in the annals of modern literature and in the legends of Canadian life. At 68 he believes his best work lies ahead. He has plans for another novel, not a sequel to *The Rebel Angels,* but one that will continue the story of some of the same characters. He'll write it in his country home in the Caledon Hills outside Toronto working from 9:30-12:30 every morning with a pipe between his teeth, the white smoke curling around his white beard. For "Sunday Morning" this is Elizabeth Hay at Massey College in Toronto.

Robertson Davies: Beyond the Visible World

Terence M. Green/1982

From *Twilight Zone*, July 1982, pp. 19-25. © Terence M. Green.
Reprinted by permission of the author.

TG: I discovered that you are planning a volume of ghost stories. Could you tell us something about the book's genesis?

RD: Well, it's a collection of ghost stories which I wrote for consumption in this college, where every Christmas we have a party, and every party for seventeen years we've had a ghost story, and I provide it.

TG: I've read several of them, and they're quite humorous.

RD: An amusing ghost story is very rare. Most of them are straight tales of horror. I just thought it would be interesting to have some ghosts that weren't entirely solemn.

TG: I've read some of your critiques and speeches where you distinguish between "solemn" and "serious." Could you tell us a little more about that?

RD: So many ghost stories attempt to be solemn, by which they want to frighten you, make your flesh creep, and make you afraid to go to bed and afraid of the dark, etc., and they become very portentous and very solemn indeed, but they're not very *serious*. The ghosts are essentially rather trivial. If you want to read a really serious ghost story, you have to read one by one of the great masters, and I think the greatest master of the ghost story was Henry James. His ghost stories are magnificent because they are deeply psychological. The ghosts are not horrors that appear and scare people; they're ghosts relating to personal dreads, fears, things not done or things done that should have been left undone, and that sort of thing.

TG: You've also said that ghost stories are somewhat neglected by literary critics. Why is that so?

RD: They don't think that they're serious. Literary critics are rarely people who admit to an interest in such things as ghosts. And this functions also in the theater, where time and time again you see plays

220

of Shakespeare produced—*Hamlet, Macbeth, Julius Caesar,* etc.—
where a ghost is very important, and the director tries somehow or
other to get round the ghost. I saw a production of *Hamlet* in London
a couple of years ago in which Hamlet was his own ghost; he spoke
the ghost's lines. There was a production here in Toronto in which
Richard Burton appeared, where the ghost was never seen; he was
just a voice from off-stage. And in *Macbeth* they get into terrible
trouble because they won't admit the reality of the witches, and they
won't admit the reality of embodied evil. So they get into dreadful
trouble with these things, because Shakespeare quite obviously
believed in them *deeply* and put them in his plays for the very best of
reasons: he felt that they affected his audience powerfully, and that
they were part of the common experience of mankind. It's only
intensely intellectual people who are antighost. As Dr. Johnson said,
very wisely, "All reason is against it, but all belief is for it."

TG: You just spoke of "the reality of embodied evil." Could you
elaborate on that?

RD: Well, this gets you into rather deep water, but it is inevitable.
There are a great many people who will not believe in the reality of
evil. It is a theological doctrine—the doctrine of the *privatio bone*—
which insists that there is no evil, there is merely an absence of good,
or a diminishing of good; that the world is essentially good because
God is good, and that if something appears that is evil it is a tem-
porary falling away. Now I think, and a very great many other people
think too, that this is the most manifest nonsense, and that things
appear in life and have appeared in history, ever since we had any
records of the doings of mankind, which are directly evil, contrary to
the good of either one person or perhaps a hundred thousand people
or several million people, and that they are to be explained only by
the existence of an element in life which is definitely evil, and which
is the enemy of what we regard as best and most hopeful.

TG: Are you thinking of any specific historical events or
phenomena?

RD: The whole of history teems with them. The extermination of
several million people—Jews, Gypsies, "intellectuals," and other
minorities—during the 1939-45 war is a very, very potent example.
The Nazis attempted to wipe out whole races—not simply the Jews
alone; they also pretty nearly wiped out the Gypsies in Europe. And

the gypsies are a small, powerless minority. They hunted them through the woods as you would hunt animals, shooting on sight. If this can be explained in any way except by the existence of an evil principle which sometimes manifests itself, not only in a single man, but in hundreds and thousands of people at a time, perhaps in a whole nation, I don't know what the other explanation would be.

TG: Are you suggesting, to use the word loosely, that they are "possessed" by some kind of evil?

RD: Yes. If you have a power which is totally and wholly good, I think that it posits also a power which is wholly and totally evil, or there is no balance; everything is jerked in one direction. The sort of psychological principle that we can discern in human life suggests that there is a balance and a perpetual pull one way or the other. There is a polarity between good and evil, an you must give evil a name. You can *call* it "Evil," you can call the principle that animates it "the Devil," or you can call it what you like; but you've got to identify it in some way.

TG: In your novel *The Manticore* there is a group of adolescents that destroy a cottage in Muskoka, Ontario, and one of the boys defecates on a photograph that he finds in the cottage. If I recall you correctly, you said that that was an example of manifest evil, and that he seemed to be possessed at that point. Am I understanding you correctly now?

RD: Yes. It is mindless, unmotivated malignance—the desire to hurt somebody in a particularly disgusting way, for no reason. It's somebody you don't even know. It's just the desire to be as ugly and miserable as you can.

TG: You don't think it can be explained in psychological terms?

RD: Of course. But you see, everything is explained in psychological terms. The fact that you and I are sitting here talking is a psychological experience.

TG: Returning to ghost stories *per se*, you have also said that they're extremely hard to write, and I'd like to pursue that a little further. Why are they so hard to write? Is it because the tendency is to make them overly solemn?

RD: Yes. And you've got to be very, very careful in a ghost story not to indulge in any of the sidelines or distractions—the sorts of things you might be able to make use of in a different type of story, one in which the atmosphere does not have to be kept mounting in intensity all the way through. A ghost story must mount from the first word till the climax, and then a little bit of tailing away to finish it. Consequently, they're generally not very long. A novel about a ghost is a great rarity.

TG: We tend to laugh at the supernatural nowadays, but you still see long lines for films on the subject. Is this all some kind of quest for what happens after we're gone?

RD: Yes. We don't laugh at Shakespeare; we don't laugh at *Hamlet,* if it's well performed. The ghost is not terrorizing, it is *awesome,* because you know that something very frightful is happening in Hamlet's life—something that makes him see the ghost of his father. Which means that a very deeply held fantasy and conviction of his is projected into the outer world so that he actually sees the figure of his father and hears his voice. But what his father says is rather what Hamlet expects to hear, or what he fears may be true.

TG: So it can be taken as almost his subconscious talking?

RD: Yes, exactly, it is. Ghosts and apparitions arise from unconscious psychological disturbances. This does not explain them away, but it does put them on a rather different footing than pretending that they come from the grave or something of that sort. But what you were talking about—the yearning that people have to see a story with some supernatural background or something that is a link with a former life—is tremendous. Religion has lost its strong driving power; we are in an age when, if you look at the movies that one can see during an evening, there are sure to be quite a few science fiction or horror tales or ghost stories or something of this kind. People are crazy for some sort of assurance that the visible world is not the only world, which is an almost intolerable state of mind.

TG: I see that theme in most of your work: that we're only scraping the surface of reality.

RD: Well, it is a thing which you cannot help but see in the world about you. People are very, very hungry for some kind of contact with a greater world than the one which they can immediately perceive. And where they find it depends to an enormous extent on the quality of their desire and the quality of their intelligence. Quite a large number of quite intelligent people are kept happy with science fiction films or tv programs of this kind, and then there are people

who want something rather more substantial and look for it elsewhere. But it is very important to see what *children* want, because
children are less tied down by convention, of course, than adults.
And the popularity of these science fiction films, stories, magazines,
and so forth with children from ten to sixteen, eighteen, or whatever,
is very great.

TG: Even younger. I have a little boy who is four years old, and
he's quite interested in something like the *Star Wars* stories.

RD: It's very interesting about the *Star Wars* business. When it
made its appearance, my two oldest grandsons were quite small
boys, and I was astonished at the Christmas after the film when one
of the little boys gave me a very special Christmas card. It was a card
on which there was a very strange face. He said, "I'm giving this to
you, because I think it's like you." I said, "Who is it, Christopher?
What is this strange figure?" He said, "That's Darth Vader." And he
meant to give me a great compliment. I was astonished that he knew
Darth Vader but that, when I was trying to question him a little bit
about Christ, he didn't know very much about him at all. And I don't
find immense fault with that, because it's very hard to make conventional religion real to a child nowadays.

TG: It's as though something like the phenomenon of the *Star
Wars* saga is the new mythology for young people, with Darth Vader
as the personification of evil.

RD: Yes. But you see, this is what interested me. I made enquiries
about it and found that this menacing figure was the one that had
most taken the little boys' fancy. They love the bad guy. Now Ben
Thingamajig, the good guy that Alec Guinness played, was not a
figure to grasp a child's imagination. And his wisdom was terrible. It
was like the wisdom that Peter Sellers gives out in *Being There,* when
he says things like "If the roots are strong, the garden will be
healthy." That's all these good people in the films ever have to say—
cheap stuff like that. The drive and the impulse and the energy are
with the evil people.

TG: Having watched my own little boy's fascination with Darth
Vader—what he is, why he is—I've seen this extend into Disney
films—the witch in *Snow White,* for instance. Unless a child watches
a fantasy in which there is a very evil figure and some very great
danger, he or she tends to become almost bored.

RD: They *do* become bored. They *want* danger. And this is reasonable enough; this is psychological adventure. There's nothing, to my mind, wrong with a child being fascinated by these evil characters. They must dare, they must adventure, they must become acquainted with this element in life. It is, to me, extremely funny that in the modern world, where governments and other groups are falling over themselves to protect us from dirt in the air and from this, that, and the other, people have to seek their danger in these fantasy worlds. The world of ordinary life doesn't provide very much that is challenging and menacing for them.

TG: I've felt that fairy tales simplify a lot of the complexities of life for children in a helpful way, and I wondered if you felt the same. Or do you feel that they *over*simplify them so that they're *not* helpful?

RD: I think that is possible to be too simple and to underestimate the intelligence of children. But I think that it is also possible to reassure children in direct and positive ways. I remember an instance when my children were small. My youngest girl slept in a room which had a door in it which gave access to a stairway which led up into the attic. I became aware that she was extremely frightened at night, and I asked her why, and she said that there was a witch up there and that she was afraid the witch was going to come down in the dark. Now, you can say to the child, "Oh no, there's no witch, she won't come down." Instead, I said to her, "Where's your school Bible?" She fished it out and I said, "Now, look. We're going to put this on the third step of the stairs, just inside the door. She won't dare pass it. She's trapped up there." Well, it worked like a charm! I have no objection to using the Bible as a kind of talisman, and it reassured the child in a way that no reason or laughing at her would ever have done. It would have been stupid to laugh at her. That just makes children secretive about their fears. And that she should fear a witch seemed to me entirely natural, because when I was small, I used to read stories about witches and I was scared to death.

TG: You've said that myths and fairy tales are popular because they contain all the elements of real drama and all the archetypes of real stories. Perhaps you could elaborate on that for me?

RD: They do, you know. They're very fulfilling. This is why we recognize that in certain fairy tales, like Cinderella, the morality is a very primitive sort which, in the grand language of literary criticism, we have come to call "poetic justice." When, in the old story of Cinderella, not the cleaned-up version, the wicked sisters try to force their feet into the slipper, they can't, so they hack off their toes, but still their feet will not fit. *This* is poetic justice. Their vanity, wickedness, and cruelty bring a terrible retribution, and that is what happens in so many myths and in so many fairy tales. Cruel and frightful punishments are visited upon the evil, and the good prosper. And this is very satisfying to children, because they have minds like Ayatollah Khomeini—they don't think that cutting off a robber's right hand is wrong at all. Large numbers of them are great enthusiasts for capital punishment, because they haven't yet been brainwashed about how the triple murderer is really just "sick," or has premenstrual tension, or some other reason why you're not supposed to deal with him as if he were a nuisance.

Mind you, I must explain very carefully that my own feeling about capital punishment is by no means open and shut, and I certainly am not an advocate of cruel and brutal and degrading capital punishment. But it seems to me that if we can put a man on the moon, we can certainly take a man out of this world without making an unholy shameful mess of it.

TG: This seems to be one of the themes in your own work: that there are acts we are responsible for, such as the stone in the snowball (in *Fifth Business*), and that we must be willing to face the consequences.

RD: Yes, you've got to face the consequences of your own actions, and with most of us that's difficult and painful. But if one's own actions become too dreadful for other people, something has to happen somewhere along the line. The rights of the rest of society are being subjected to your whim—which, in a world which has doubled its population since the beginning of this century, is something that can very quickly become an impossible situation.

TG: You have spoken highly of Mervyn Peake and his *Gormenghast* trilogy, which at one point you said even Poe cannot rival. Would you tell me why you make that statement?

RD: Because Poe works in the short story and the short poem, and he works by a kind of incantation and poetic method. And I just happen to think that Mervyn Peake is a finer poet than Edgar Allan Poe, and he is therefore able to maintain his world of fantasy brilliantly through three novels. It tails off badly in the last one; but in the first two it is *brilliantly* realized. It is a very, very great work, and it will be recognized as a classic—perhaps a minor classic, but a classic—of our age. Even now, it has its underground enthusiasts. It's amazing how those books are continually gaining new enthusiastic readers, though they put heavy strains on book reviewers, who are unaccustomed to reviewing books like that. Reviewers are very fashionable people. They can recognize a book which is in the modern vein, and they can deal with it. They can review a book which is about how tough it is to have your marriage break up, or how awful it is to realize that you're a homosexual and have to come out of the cupboard, or something of the kind. But they're no good when you confront them with a book like *Titus Groan,* which creates a world of its own and laws of its own, and exists by a kind of magic of its own.

TG: Is it, then, in essence, a sort of fairy tale for adults?

RD: It is. And it has some magnificent scenes. That big scene of the fight in the garret between the two almost mythically awful creatures is a *brilliant* piece of writing—sustained, wonderful writing, for pages and pages.

Incidentally, returning to Poe for a moment, it seems to me that Poe's most successful story is "The Cask of Amontillado," about the man who bricks his enemy up in a wine cellar and leaves him there to die. It seems to me that, in sheer horror, it goes far beyond the ones where ghostly maidens come down the stairs and fall at somebody's feet, because you don't really believe much in the ghostly maiden, but you certainly believe in that poor wretch who's being blocked up in the wine cellar. With Poe, you see, the intensity which he is able to get into that tale of hatred and revenge is much greater than the more ambitious pieces that attempt to deal with the undead and doomed families.

TG: You speak of hatred and revenge. I recall reading that you said that things like hatred and jealousy were in fact the realities of life.

RD: Yes. In the rose-scented world in which many people wish to place us, you can't admit to that. You can go to church for a year and you'd never hear a sermon about the wickedness of hatred or the sin of jealousy. Nobody wants to talk about sin. It's unfashionable. There used to be frightful sermons that would take the paint off a door about the Seven Deadly Sins, but they're not fashionable now. Sin has become merely a kind of psychological concept, as if that made it unreal.

TG: Is there, in your mind, somebody or something or some force that could be called the Devil?

RD: It's just shorthand for a power which is hostile to the good order of the world and to the happiness of man.

TG: Is your vision of literature and life primarily a religious vision, then?

RD: I think it has to be called that, though that puts people off terribly. You say you have a religious view on life, they think you're a sort of Holy Joe. But actually the word "religion" just means "law," the consideration of law and consequence. That's what interests me: what happens as a result of what people do. Also the reluctance people have to learn that certain actions will bring certain consequences. I was brought up by parents who were always quoting the Bible, not very reverently, I'm afraid. One of my mother's favorite quotations was that about how the dog shall return again to its vomit and the hog to his wallowing in the mire. (Chuckles.)

TG: To reap what you sow.

RD: Yes, Yes. And people don't learn. Over and over again they do the same stupid things without having learned what happens. I think we face this at the moment very much in our international situation, where both the USA and the USSR are projecting all the evil in the world upon one another. The self-righteousness on both sides is truly terrifying.

TG: Are you suggesting that the appellation *Homo sapiens* belies the reality?

RD: Yes. "Homo the Sap" is what he ought to be called. We are not wise because we are always looking for causes for things which are outside ourselves. I was very interested to read the other day, in a newspaper interview with Mr. Reagan, about the fact that he had refused, although he had promised to do so, to drop the registering for National Service. He said, "The Russians might get the wrong message." This business of being psychologically unaware—I'm afraid poor Mr. Reagan gives evidence of it every day of his life. I thought that remark that he made about how possibly a nuclear war could be confined to Europe was one of the most fat-headed, cruel, *stupid* remarks that any national leader could possibly make—as though people in Europe aren't real. When you blow them up in Europe it doesn't hurt.

TG: This is the tendency of anyone to dismiss what you're fighting with a label. The Vietnamese were just "the Cong." You end up fighting a word, an idea.

RD: The poor devils, they never seemed to think of them as people, and they did the most horrifying things to them. Though I must say that "the Cong" could do some pretty nasty things, too.

TG: It works in reverse, certainly.

RD: Absolutely.

TG: If I can return more directly to fantasy, I wanted to ask your reaction to some other popular fantasy films of late.

RD: One of the things that fascinates me, in the slight acquaintance that I have with these films, is the very strong sexual element in them. It ceases to have much fantasy about it. It's just the old well-understood common thing. I was fascinated last summer with *Clash of the Titans*. There was a terrible monster in that: the Kraken. It was released from the vault of the seas. And do you know what it was he wanted most? A blonde. It was a dumb girl who was tied to a rock—Andromeda. And there was the Kraken, who was about as big as a very tall apartment building, who was going to sexually get after this cutie. It was hilarious. I almost fell out of my seat with laughter. All they ever seem to be able to think about with King Kong or the Kraken is that he's going to chase a blonde. I remember seeing a film years and years ago that was just a cheapie, which nevertheless commanded quite a big audience, about a professor who had discovered a fish that everyone thought had been dead for millions of years [*Monster on the Campus,* 1958, directed by Jack Arnold.] When he was working on it in his lab down in Berkeley, he accidentally scratched his arm with one of the scales of the fish. He became infected with the blood of a primitive creature, so he became, every time the moon was full, a primitive man. He turned odd-looking, and hair grew out of his face, and he was a dreadful mess. As a matter of fact, he looked rather like Abraham Lincoln, but he was supposedly terrifying. And do you know what it was that this primitive man wanted above all? The president's daughter, who was a blonde. It's absolutely hilarious (chuckles), but it goes very deep, and I suppose one shouldn't laugh at it, because it just shows that mankind is as scared that his woman will be taken away from him by a powerful rival as he was three thousand years ago.

TG: This was part of the pulp tradition in American science fiction all through the thirties and forties. The covers all featured alien creatures approaching a voluptuous female, while a male with a blaster fended them off.

RD: But there's never been a corresponding female figure of equal power. There are these great moon goddesses who use men as toys and throw them away like smoked cigarettes, but they've never had quite the clout of the monsters who want the blonde.

TG: You have spoken of writing as a "vocation of unhappiness," and said that the characteristic of the artist is "discontent." What led you to make these observations?

RD: Experience. You're always wishing you could do it better, and that means a life of discontent. But it leads somewhere. It's not just trivial discontent, it's not just whining and wishing things were otherwise. It's a wishing that you personally could do a better job.

TG: Can't the writer or artist be happy or contented?

RD: It's very unlikely that he will be, because what he's perpetually trying to do is to say as clearly as he can what he feels to be most pressingly important. And he can never say it quite as clearly as he'd like to. It is complicated, it doesn't lend itself to simple statement. And trying to say complicated things clearly is hard, hard work.

TG: Maybe a few general questions to finish . . . From what or from whom have you learned the most?

RD: (Long pause.) I have learned very important things from people that I have met during the course of my life. None of them were literary people. Many of them were women. Women tell men things that men are not very likely to find out for themselves. Of course, I've learned quite a lot from books.

TG: Has there been a turning point in your life?

RD: Yes, at the age of about thirty-five. It is a very common turning point that millions of people encounter, when you just have to realize that you've found out what you do and how you do it, and what you think the world can give you, and you've established your way of living, and you probably have children. You know roughly whether you're going to be rich or poor or in between. Then you've got to find out what you're *really* going to do—what you're going to make out of all that. Are you going to be just a kind of walking monument to a job, or are you going to have some kind of really significant inner life of your own? Because just the external things—the job, the mate, the children, the house, the this, the that—do not really fill the place inside.

TG: Let's end on a lighter note. In *World of Wonders*, the three characters, past middle age, enjoy getting into bed together. You make a point of discussing how bed is not just a place for sleep or sexual activity, but how kings held court from bed, and what a wonderful place it was for having philosophical discussions and the like in comfortable surroundings with friends. I wanted to ask you: If you were convalescing in a hospital for three months, whom would you like in bed with you?

RD: The hospital wouldn't permit it! (Laughter) I think that the answer would have to be nobody. You couldn't stand having anybody in bed with you for three months. The ideal companion in bed is a good book.

Robertson Davies on the World of the Occult
Terence M. Green/1982

From *Books in Canada,* December 1982. © Terence M. Green.
Reprinted by permission of the author.

TG: In your novel *The Rebel Angels,* a character says "never hope to find wisdom at the high colleges alone—consult old women, Gypsies, wanderers, and all manner of peasant folk, and learn from them, for these have more knowledge about such things than all the high colleges." Is this advice that you personally offer?

RD: The character is quoting Paracelsus. And yes, it is advice I would offer. Paracelsus was one of the very great astrologers; he was a very, very wise man. He was a Swiss. He hadn't much use for the high colleges, because one by one virtually all of them in Switzerland and Germany threw him out, because he was a nuisance. He was a physician, and he said "stop talking to me about Aristotle." Aristotle hadn't looked inside the human body. He asked for a corpse, to rip it up, to look inside it, to show them what it seems to do. They thought this was horrifying. Dissection of human bodies was utterly unheard of. Aristotle had said that the body worked in a certain way, and that was it. He kept saying you won't believe what's in front of your faces—you just believe authority, and I'm trying to tell you what you can yourself observe. And he was a very great man.

TG: I hadn't planned on going into this, but your mention of astrology leads me to it. You've mentioned elsewhere that your own birthdate is August 28, the birthdate of St. Augustine, Tolstoy, and Goethe. Do you thing there's anything to all this?

RD: I like to tease scientists about it because they're so convinced there's nothing in it. But they're just exactly the same kind of people, who, if they'd lived 300 years ago, would have been astrologers, and they'd have been hog-wild for astrology. They're people who believe in authority; they believe in the fashionable knowledge. Now, astrology is an attempt to project upon the stars a kind of intuitive knowledge of what may relate to somebody's life. Astrology as you get it in the newspaper is, of course, pretty rubbishy stuff. But there have been very interesting astrological predictions, which have a substantial amount of truth to them. The question is: how did they come about?

I think quite obviously they did not come about by reading the stars; they came about by intuitions. Reading the stars is a way of making intuition take some kind of form in your head. I do not profess to be a believer in astrology; but I don't jeer at it either. Because, you know, a good many years ago, I was hounded by a friend of mine in New York to visit a specific astrologer. I went, in a calm state of mind. He read my chart very carefully and said that within a year I would alter my occupation, I would work in a place where I would look out over water, and that I would be very much among young people. And within a year, I'd been asked to come to this university and to set this college going, and to work in a study which at that time was in the quadrangle looking out over the pool. That does not make me a friend of every tea-cup reader. But it makes me feel that it's unwise to brush it aside too noisily.

TG: G. K. Chesterton said, "Coincidences are spiritual puns." To what degree is it coincidence, to what degree is it something else?

RD: When I was just a lad I was visiting my father in Wales, and I went to a church fête. There was an old Welsh woman who was reading fortunes from teacups in a tent, and I went in and had a shilling's worth of fortune, and she told me all kinds of interesting things. I remember she said that I was going to have such a happy time next Christmas that I'd wish it was now. Sure enough, Christmas came along, and I had an extremely happy time. She said you're going to come under the influence of a man who will affect your life very profoundly; and within the year I met a very notable psychiatrist, Dr. R. D. Gillespie. He was killed in the war; he was head of psychiatric services in Great Britain. He did influence my life profoundly, because he told me some very extraordinary things, and he was a very strong and influential character in a positive way. You can't brush aside these old Gypsies and old teacup women and astrologers.

TG: What you're saying is that the world is just too incomprehensible to think that you can comprehend it.

RD: I know. The real superstition is thinking that you can reject things unexamined.

TG: You mentioned that you recently saw the film *Ghost Story*.

RD: I think it is exceedingly well done. It is about a past action that returns to haunt some living men, and they are totally in its grip. It was very well performed. I think people wanted to believe in it, they *want* to believe these things. You see, we live in an age where religion is very much suppressed, and what used to find a sort of home in religion and religious teaching now is in the psychology of most people just wobbling around loose, looking for something to attach itself to, and it attaches itself to the supernatural. What is happening now is what happened a couple of thousand years ago when the religious beliefs of the Romans were running into the ground; they no longer had very great faith in the rather peculiar religion they had at one time made their own. And the history of Rome, two or three hundred years before the birth of Christ, is one of ghosts and apparitions and spooks and bugaboos of every possible kind. They were always having spooks and horrors and trying to come to terms with the fact that they had no channel for their feelings about the supernatural. Their religion had failed them, just as ours has, rather, lost its strong driving power.

TG: You have said that many people who reject God have a sneaking acceptance of the supernatural, and the Freudian revolution offers them little comfort.

RD: The trouble with the Freudian attitude toward the world is that it is essentially a deeply pessimistic one. You know Freud's statement that he could not cure people of neurosis, he could only enable them to exchange their neurosis for ordinary unhappiness. Well, that's a big deal, isn't it? He offers no possibility of change, happiness, of a meliorative world—nothing of that sort—it is all downhill, all reductive. And I don't think that everything related to mankind does run downhill.

TG: From what I know of your background, you've found a much more satisfactory reflection of life in the psychology and teachings of Carl Jung.

RD: Yes. Because it allows for hope and change and development in a positive manner. It offers a much greater scope for mankind to live some of the time happily, a great deal of the time with satisfaction to himself and other people.

TG: You've quoted Ibsen in *The Manticore* and other places:

To live is to battle with trolls
In the vaults of heart and brain
To write: that is to sit
In judgement over one's self.

Who or what are the trolls?

RD: Oh, they're complexes and archetypes and all the things that well up from the unconscious when you're trying to write, and that have to be conquered and countered, and made for a moment to yield up some secret. They're part of the inner life.

TG: What have you meant by the phrase "the writer's conscience"?

RD: It is the commitment to his work and to his art, which must come before everything else. And he must not yield to the very great temptation to write solely what is cheaply popular. He wants, of course, to have people hear him; but he won't do anything to have people hear him, and he won't write propaganda. He won't write to push a moral system, or to whoop it up for a particular nation or something of that sort.

TG: Let me suggest a quote that isn't yours: "The best literature has a deep and intense moral concern." Is that something you would agree with too?

RD: Yes. But when I say a moral concern, I don't mean the advocacy of a particular kind of morality, but a deep concern with certain basic things. What you do bears consequences you are somehow or other going to have to face, or else, by not facing them, you will involve yourself in very painful consequences, even if it is only a sort of halflived life, a kind of stupid, knownothing life.

Dr. Robertson Davies
John Milton Harvard/1984

From *Waves*, 12, #4 (Spr. 1984) pp. 5-9. Reprinted by permission.

Keats wrote much of his best poetry while staying with a friend in a residence at Oxford. Dr. Davies keeps a room at Massey for writing, in much the same way as Keats wrote at Magdalen College. Dr. Davies has the same agile look in his eyes as one sees in the photographs of Anatole France. On the windsor knot in his navy blue tie there is a single red lion—the symbol of Wales. He dresses quietly and comfortably with grey slacks and a sweater. The room, facing the inner quadrangle of Toronto's Massey College, has part of a wall of books. "This is not my book collection: these are the books I work with every day." The volumes are very dignified. Over the door he has two full-sized University crests, one of Balliol College, and one of Oxford University—symbols of ancient learning. He offers the most comfortable chair to the reporter, and sits by the window.

Harvard: Why does a person need time to himself every day?

Davies: You need the opportunity each day to look deep inside yourself, at what you like and what you don't like when you look. It's a kind of concentration.

Harvard: A number of people are so afraid of public speaking they never do it. Is there any solution?

Davies: What on *Earth* becomes of a person who is afraid to speak in public? A person has to have common sense about these things. There are things a person simply has to do—and he should just do them.

Harvard: Does higher education help common sense?

Davies: Common sense means balancing things. If a person denies an aspect of himself, then that aspect will get back at him—and express itself in a weakened way. In the short story "Rain," by

Somerset Maugham, the protagonist reviles a prostitute. He didn't
need to be harsh on her. He ends up marrying her. In the case of
people with Ph.D.'s, there are as many as any other people who
don't have common sense. Education doesn't change that.

Harvard: There is a form of psychotherapy developed in Europe
called Guided Imagery, in which the therapist tells the therapisand a
story under hypnosis in order to bring about emotional change. Is
literature therapeutic?

Davies: The purpose of literature is to enlarge the reader's world,
to add missing elements so as to balance. Yes, the story-teller is
something of healer.

Harvard: There is a great deal of discussion in the press now
about how to deal with anger. Do you have any suggestions?

Davies: A person needs to examine himself very closely if his
anger gets him to the point where he is striking other people or
creating ugly scenes. Anger is a part of living. A certain amount is
inevitable. The reason people worry about things like anger is that we
live in a protected, affluent society where we can afford the time for
it. Still, I am *not* saying that hardship is a good thing.

Harvard: What do you think about the Stephen King horror
movies?

Davies: A large part of a person is irrational. With the deep
emotion of religion lost, there is still the need to be moved strongly.
George Bernard Shaw said that he quit believing in God when he
was a child and prayed for something and didn't get it. He was trying
to startle people. That's not the idea of God. Praying is a chance to
come to terms with the good and evil inside yourself. It's not just
trying to get something you want.

Harvard: How do you feel about censorship?

Davies: Pornography is boring reading. There would be no
pornography around if it were made legal. The fact that it is
forbidden is what makes it sell. If Shakespeare were forbidden except
to people who had completed University, he would be much more
widely read.

Harvard: What's the secret of good book reviewing?

Davies: The task involves understanding, being sympathetic,
looking at what the person has set out to do, and then telling the
reader whether or not the author has accomplished his aim. Some

reviewers give only their *own* ideas, and don't really get down at all to discussing the book in question. Critics have too much work for too little money, and this can make them bitter. They get caught in the hurry of their work and end up in a contest of one-upmanship with the author. Reviewers just don't have enough time.

Harvard: What is required of a literary critic by today's readers?

Davies: No skill at all is required. He doesn't need to know how to use his tools. With Margaret Atwood it has become fashionable for critics to say that she isn't as good as she used to be. Many music critics will sit in an auditorium and defiantly demand great music.

Harvard: Do literary critics help an author?

Davies: No. Creative writing and literary criticism are two different forms of art. A great many people are afraid to change, to grow as people. If you open yourself up to a work of art you will change. Many critics will jump on a piece of art because they go to it demanding to be moved. They are too egotistical and feel that they know it all before they even see it. A critic should approach a work of art with sympathy and respect.

Harvard: The craft of interviewing is frequently discussed in the *Columbia Journalism Review.* Would you have any suggestions?

Davies: To be a good interviewer you have to read up thoroughly. You have to be a good listener. I had one interviewer recently who wouldn't let me get a word in edgewise.

Harvard: Do you think that a person should read a certain group of books—say President Eliot's "Five Foot Shelf" of classics?

Davies: You have to read a certain amount of trash. You cannot have only one note on a piano: you have to go the whole range. A rich diet of anything will kill you if that's all you have. (Dr. Davies put his finger on an imaginary piano to demonstrate the range above and below the middle notes.)

Harvard: Is there such a thing as a consensus of taste?

Davies: Taste is something that is individual, and people disagree on what should be on the list of classics. I don't feel that a lot of the books on the Canadian classics list are old enough. Dr. Eliot has his five foot shelf of books, but books have to be *shared* between the reader and the author: the reader has to be ready to understand, or it's not a book for him. You can't just fill your needs by going to someone else and asking him. It is personal. Euclid as an example is considered a classic, but geometry says nothing to me.

Harvard: I understand that Oxford has a strong tutorial system.

Davies: I had a great number of wonderful teachers. My tutor would discuss what I had written and he would comment on what was deep and what was shallow. Then he would give me something else to write. He always had a clear idea of how I was thinking and how I was progressing. Experiments in television teaching haven't worked, because you have to have a real person so that you concentrate. There needs to be someone that the student can identify with and emulate—not copy in a childish sense as in mimicking the actions and mannerisms—but in the sense that you emulate a teacher's quality of thoughts. You cannot teach the same lesson twice: you have to fit it to the needs of the people who are with you right at the time.

Harvard: What do you think about the infusion of new words into the language?

Davies: Because the French Academy limits new words coming into French that language is dying. The three great languages, Chinese, Russian and English are all cannibals: they take in words from wherever they find them. A friend of mine at Oxford was questioned as to where he got the word "motivate" in an oral examination: the word has no Latin origin. I don't like the word "prestige" because it really has a different meaning than most people give it when they write it. Be neither first nor last to use a word.

Harvard: How does one become a good reader?

Davies: My tutor (at Oxford) once said to me, "You want to have read things." By that he meant you have to experience what you read as a present reality, to be infused with it. There is a big difference between a process and an acquisition, and reading is an experience. Also, you have to see things in context: I quoted an author to my tutor and he said, "If that's what he said then he's a fool and you are a fool too." What I had to understand was that he was an Aristotelian and to Aristotle it would be foolishness.

Harvard: For those of us taking creative writing courses, do you think that formulas help?

Davies: A person is his own best teacher of creative writing.

Creativity is something which cannot be harnessed. Without being critical of anyone, I mistrust any sort of formula for teaching writing. A problem-plus-three-complications-crisis-and-climax such as you mention might help at first, but in a great author like Somerset Maugham you see infinite variations, from the very light to deep psychology.

Harvard: Before writing I read Isaac Bashevis Singer or Alice Munro to warm up.

Davies: I am glad Isaac Bashevis Singer got the Nobel Prize. He is a strong narrator. A story should have resonance. It should start the process of emotional growth in the reader. You couldn't have anyone better than Isaac Bashevis Singer and Alice Munro for your warm-up reading before you write.

Harvard: I understand many people consider your major area of reading esoteric.

Davies: A lot of people think that nothing happened in the era which I cover. But the playgoers got something out of it. What they got out of it is important.

Harvard: Has acting helped?

Davies: When I was writing plays people accused me of being a novelist, and when I started writing novels people accused me of writing plays. My work with acting helped me to develop a sense of scene and setting.

Harvard: Your books have a very strong plot, as compared with the *New Yorker* stories which are mostly impressions.

Davies: With the *New Yorker*, you enjoy one of the stories, and you put it down on your desk. A week later you go to talk about the story with someone and you don't know what it said. Great literature always has plot—and there are always plot as well as impressions all around you.

Harvard: According to one business study a person's efficiency drops off after eight hours of work.

Davies: If you love what you are doing you can work almost any number of hours in a week.

Harvard: With divorce statistics in North America soaring, how can we understand marriage?

Davies: Constant love is not possible. Passionate love is not always possible. You can't live only for this man or that woman.

Marriage is a framework to preserve friendship. It is valuable because it gives much more room to develop than just living together. It provides a base from which a person can work at understanding himself and another person.

Harvard: Will mankind survive?

Davies: I don't think the world will come to an end. I just *can't* see the end of civilization. It's an idea which comes up in cycles. There's the Platonic millenium of two thousand years. I think that there will be a new age in 2001: people will be much gentler. This last millenium has brought in the idea of human well-being. How many hospitals were there when Christ was born? The turn of the century will be fascinating. I hope to be there.

Harvard: Is there anything we can do to prevent having another *Chariots of Fire* situation where the majority of a class is killed in war?

Davies: If I knew how to solve the nuclear arms problem I'd be the wisest person in the world—and probably very few people would listen to me. (Dr. Davies winced as the reporter talked of the billions of dollars flowing into nuclear arms.) Several hundred people run the country, but U.S. presidents are just figureheads. Better leaders are needed. The nation to the south has been run by peanut farmers and retired movie actors. The people who are in power are frightened. They don't think enough.

Harvard: What do you think about industry being sent off into space in the next century?

Davies: Such problems simply cannot be gotten rid of. Someone will have to look after industry and we can't just ship that off to Mars. Our problems are here and we have to face up to them here. We can't put people on Mars and leave the problem with them while we have an Eden here on Earth.

"Morningside"
Peter Gzowski/1985

Transcription from CBC Radio; 20 October 1985. Copyright 1985
Canadian Broadcasting Corporation. Reprinted by permission of
the CBC, Robertson Davies, Anthony Burgess, and Peter Gzowski.

PG: My next guest is Robertson Davies and perhaps the most fitting
introduction should come from someone who has never met
Robertson Davies but who has high regard for his work. This is the
British novelist and critic, Anthony Burgess:

　　AB: Robertson Davies *is* one of the most important of living
novelists, I may say this, now, I think, to Canadian ears. I've just
come back from Stockholm where I've been trying to persuade the
Nobel Committee to at least *read* the work of Robertson Davies and
consider him as, I think it must be, Canada's first Nobel Prize man.
The trouble with the Nobel committee is this: they're not omniscient,
they don't read everything. They ought to be told what to read, and
it's the function of writers like myself who tend to be—I think I am a
fairly omnivorous reader—to tell them what they ought to be doing.
Of course I mention myself, too, [Laughs] but don't take my own
claims very seriously. I think Robertson Davies' claim to world renown as expressed in the Nobel laureateship, I think, is undoubted.
There we have Canada's greatest living writer, greatest living novelist,
who must be universally acclaimed.

　　PG: Those comments came in an interview with Anthony Burgess
last month on Robertson Davies. Was that news to you? Had you
heard that he said that?

　　RD: No, I hadn't heard that. I knew that Anthony Burgess had
said some very kind things about me in his book *Comments on
Ninety-Nine Novels,* but I hadn't heard that piece and nobody had
mentioned it to me. That's very Canadian, isn't it?

　　PG: Are you slightly embarrassed by that lavish praise?

　　RD: Well, I don't know, it's the sort of thing that you have to take
with not a grain of salt but with care because you see when there are

so many people who are very fitting recipients of the Nobel Prize, much more fitting I think than I, like Borges, Graham Greene, and Robert Graves in especial, I think that the line is reaching [Laughs] a very long way from Stockholm.

PG: That's international acclaim that you're getting from Anthony Burgess, and I look back and I think of the way you have been received critically and also popularly in this country as well. Is this a very Canadian act too? Do you feel that we've waited for Anthony Burgess and others to discover you? Have you been properly received in your own country?

RD: It would be wrong to say that I have not been properly received but I have not been received on that sort of level. It began in the United States when I received a good deal of warm praise, when for instance *Fifth Business* appeared, whenever it did appear, I think it was 1970, and that seemed to change the attitude toward me in Canada but it hasn't changed totally. I was just reading last week a piece by a critic in the West who says my notion of wit is like an elephant on a trampoline and I write undramatically and I can't put a novel together and my characters are absurd and, you know, lots of things wrong with me. Very, very distressing.

PG: Doesn't seem to be bothering you very much today.

RD: Well, you have to expect that sort of thing, critics being what critics so reprehensibly are [Laughs].

PG: You've been a critic from time to time.

RD: Yes, I have been a critic from time to time, but you know when I was a book reviewer, I made it a rule only on the very rarest occasions to review a book which I could not speak of positively. There were only a few books that I thought had to be really given a sharp smack and then I did it, but most of the time I wrote about books that I could praise and a very large number of them were Canadian books. And I like doing that, I don't like knocking people's work, I know how painful it is for the author of even a very bad book to have it pointed out that it is a bad book.

PG: Are you patient with Canadian readers? Do we get you all the time?

RD: Well, you see this is one of the difficulties and a rather sensitive point, but I know you like to explore sensitive points. Canadians do not think of themselves generally the way I think about them and

the way I write about them. I think the Canadians are people who
like to live very much on the surface. It's as if they were a giant
wedding cake and they thought that they were just a big block of
icing. They're not. When you get down below the surface and you
get into the fruity bits and the rich bits and the dark bits and the bits
sometimes, which as in a very good fruit cake, taste just as if you had
been licking a piece of iron. That's where the real Canadian is and
that's what I want to describe, and recently, a Canadian critic said that
I was both a fantasist and a realist. And I think that that is true, but
the fantasy is rooted very firmly in what I see in Canadian life which
is very strange indeed, no stranger than life anywhere else in the
world, but much stranger than the average Canadian is prepared to
admit.

PG: To what degree do you have to be read to be appreciated
most fully by someone who is conversant with the Canadian
vocabulary in all levels of vocabulary? I mean we've just heard, or we
began, and I hope this will be my last reference to Anthony Burgess
this morning, but here's a man who appreciates you splendidly but
cannot possibly read all the subtle keys and the overtones, the
resonance for the Canadian reader that exist in much of your work
and I suppose specifically in *What's Bred in the Bone.*

RD: Well, it's very kind of you to say that and I hope that Canadian readers do appreciate some of the things that I say, not merely
usages of words but illusions and sorts of, shades of meaning which
are very Canadian indeed. I must say though that Mr. Burgess, who
is a great student of language, probably gets that better than most
readers do.

PG: Is it important that your novels, working as they do at so
many levels and dealing with so many fundamental ideas as well as
so many subtle ideas of philosophy and psychology and the
mysterious, that they touch real life? Is it important that there be
elements of detectable reality in there?

RD: Oh, absolutely, absolutely, and they *are*, because always in
really good fantasy, there is a very strong reflection of life. It's just life
seen through a prism. It's not unreality. It's not invention. This is what
is disappointing about a great deal of science-fiction and a sort of
invented fantasy. It has no relation to life at all. The best fantasy is
right there in life. The great fantasist was E. T. A. Hoffman, the
German writer. You know there's an opera about him—it hasn't got

much to do with him—called *Tales of Hoffman,* and the realities that appear in his stories seem fantastic but they're all rooted right to the things that happen and even the way they happen, which people often are unwilling to see. Very strange things happen in Canada, very strange things have happened in Toronto. Do you remember any witchcraft trials in Toronto?

PG: No.

RD: There was one about ten years ago. Do you remember an incident in which a lady asserted that she was going to bear a child, the father of whom was the spirit of Bernard Shaw? You don't remember that? Well, it was in all the papers, you just have to keep your eye peeled, you know. It's astonishing what crops up in our national life.

PG: I just read Robertson Davies and that fills me in on all the things.

RD: Well, then you get it all boiled down, you see.

PG: Could you read a bit from *What's Bred in the Bone?* The passage you've chosen raises some most interesting questions.

RD: Well, I've chosen a bit to read—because you warned me that I was going to be asked to read something—that relates to the hero of the book, a man named Francis Cornish. One of whose troubles that bothered him all his life long was that he was brought up partly Catholic and partly Protestant, and this is just an incident, one incident, from his childhood because he had a nursemaid who was a devotee of the Salvation Army and his great aunt on the other side, Miss McRory, was a devout Catholic, and this is an instance of the two sides of his upbringing crossing and how rapidly and how decisively that kind of thing could happen. Now this is about his nursemaid, Bella Mae:

[Davies reads an excerpt from *What's Bred in the Bone,* the first chapter of Part Two. In the excerpt, Bella Mae chooses her Salvation Army headgear and marches about the nursery singing in order to impress young Francis Cornish with Protestant religious values. The segment ends with Francis kissing Bella Mae's cross: "He held the cross in his hand, reluctant to let it go."]

And all his life he never did let it go.

PG: Now curse you, Robertson Davies. I could, I could. . . . There are enough matters in that short passage to occupy this program for the remainder of the season.

RD: Would you like me to sing some more?

PG: Yes, I would. But you know, that's the old ham, that's the old actor from the Old Vic. But here we have Francis Cornish, one Catholic parent, one Protestant parent, nursemaid, choosing between hats—the hat of the Salvation Army, the ultimate Protestant, if you will, sect, in a hat which is the symbol of the church in Quebec. There are fourteen different ways to come into this particular passage. Am I reading about Canada? Are you telling me something about Canada?

RD: Yes, yes. Because the first part of this book *What's Bred in the Bone,* is laid in the upper part of the Ottawa Valley, where I spent a great part of my childhood and you were very much aware there of the pull devil, pull baker feeling between Catholic and Protestant French and Scotch, basically, and the tension which it created all the time.

PG: In the religious part, too, which is very important, Francis never does, as you say, get rid of it. It echoes through his whole life. Is that going through mine right now? I was not in the Ottawa Valley, but I went to church, I was there, I was a Canadian kid raised in an ecclesiastical framework. Is that in my body, in my head right now?

RD: Of course it is; it's bred in the bone, and that kind of concrete is bred in my bone, too, because when I was a boy there were whole months when I couldn't get home from school, after school, without encountering a group of lurking Catholic kids who beat the socks off me, literally with bookbags filled with heavy books, and believe me the fact that I am not now a raging Orangeman I think points to the splendor of my character. [Laughs]

PG: How much of the aspects of Robertson Davies are there in Francis Cornish, in particular? I have to explain of course. Francis Cornish becomes an artist, who's very skilled at restoring, weaving the elements of his own life in time into the great artistic modes of another life in time. Is that Robertson Davies?

RD: Well, yes, I think you might say that it is, because of course I have to work out of what I am and what my experience has been but I try to relate sometimes to other times and other manners.

PG: Francis Cornish has a very-important-to-him teacher who is very dissatisfied with modern painting, who finds no meaning, finds it superficial and finds it too private, lacking a language of mythology. Would Robertson Davies say the same thing about modern writing?

RD: Well, no, I don't think you could say that about modern writing any more than you can say that about the writing of any period when, as a general thing, writers don't hitch up much to a mythological background or much that goes below the surface of life. But I think really serious writing in any age does that and that is why it seems so fresh when you read it now.

PG: And the writing that will survive now must have, therefore, those other levels of mythological symbolism and depth?

RD: Yes, it must have something to preserve it for people who do not live in the time when it is directly relevant and descriptive of the time as they see it.

PG: Are you conscious of putting in the layers as you write? The little beyond, the moment, the glimpse, that the people who have not yet met the whole book have just had of *What's Bred in the Bone*: that gives them an opportunity to see two things, one is how many levels it can be looked at, and I've only mentioned one or two right now, but also it stands on its own, it's a good little story, it's nice little bit. I wonder when you write that nice little bit, are you aware of all the echoes in it?

RD: Well, I don't know. You see, before I begin writing, I do a lot of sketching and notemaking, writing little letters to myself, and thinking about things, and I become preoccupied and when people are talking to me, I am not listening as carefully as I ought to, and I'm really sort of getting the feel of a book. And then eventually the book is written but by that time, all the overtones and layers and things are likely to be present.

PG: Is your subconscious putting them there?

RD: Yes, yes.

PG: The novel quotes Picasso which has caught the eye of a couple of us here and I want to repeat the quotation to you and ask for your comments on it. Picasso says in the book:

I don't think of myself as a great artist in the great and ancient sense of the term. I'm only a public entertainer who understood his times and exploited as best he could the imbecility, the vanity, the cupidity of his contemporaries. Mine is a bitter confession more painful than it may appear but it has the merit of being sincere.

That's Picasso.

RD: Yes.

PG: You too?

RD: Yes, I would agree with that thoroughly because you see the judgment on what Picasso does as an artist is for other people to make and the judgment on what I do as a writer is for other people to make. I think it is very, very serious, a very, very serious mistake when you begin to think of yourself as an important writer. It makes you venture into a kind of writing which my wife, who is my most important critic, calls life-workical and masterpiecical. And you begin to write rather grandiosely, and this happens even to writers of very great quality like Thomas Mann. I think that toward the end of his life Thomas Mann began to believe his own publicity, and he wrote splendidly and magnificently and because he was a fine writer, it works out very well but I think he would have been so much better if he had remained private and been a little less enchanted with his own abilities. It's fatal when you begin to approve of yourself and say, by gosh, that's a good piece of work and gloat over your own doing.

PG: It's also a bitter confession as Picasso says himself, "mine is a bitter confession"; it's suggesting that it hasn't been worth it, that I have not done as well as you think.

RD: Ah, yes, but only a man of Picasso's stature could say that and regard it as bitter; a little man wouldn't have said that.

PG: "What's bred in the bone will out in the flesh."

RD: That's right.

PG: English proverb, translated from the Latin circa 1290. Is it true, to what degree am I shaped by what is bred in the bone? Of course you can't answer that question in a— [Laughs] 42%!

RD: No, you can't. What is bred in the bone is to such an extra-ordinary extent what you grow up taking for granted, and they're the things that are never discussed, they're the things that are assumed, just to be true or right, or the lines along which one's life should be cast. And that is really what's bred in the bone and also, of course, there is a certain, I think, though I'm on very poor ground because I'm no scientist, there is a certain physical thing about it too. If you're born as I am, 6 feet tall and bulky, you're not going to write the same way as if you are four foot eight and weigh a hundred and twelve pounds. It just isn't going to be like that. I remember one time getting into some trouble when I was a book reviewer because I just wrote a brief note about a book which was very boastful, pompous, silly book. I said the writer writes as though he were very close to being a short man, and my gosh, it was proved that he was a very short man, and he was as mad as a hornet.

PG: Good thing he was a little guy!

RD: Yes, yes indeed. I just sensed that his writing was the writing of a short self-important person and that I think comes out.

PG: How tall was Charles Dickens?

RD: Charles Dickens wasn't very tall. I think he was about 5' 8", and sometimes he writes, well he was very muscular, very athletic and I don't think when you met you would've thought he was a short man. But he wasn't very tall.

PG: But he didn't write short.

RD: No he didn't. He wrote tall. But Henry James, you know, Henry James. . . .

PG: He wrote short.

RD: And fat.

PG: And fat, yes. What do we do here about free will to the extent that all of this is destiny through character? And also, and I'm leaving astrology out, the most fascinating passage about, all the astrological aspects of what's bred in the bone, enough again for twenty-two dinner parties.

RD: Ah, but you see, astrology is a science of the past and no science is utter trash, and some very, very clever people believed in astrology and found that it worked. But you say, what about free will? Well, our free will is very decidedly restricted by what we are. If you were born a man, you have a different sort of free will from if you were born a woman. If you were born a big man, it's different from if you were a small man; if you're born rich, it's different from if you're born poor; and if you're born with the capacity for education, it's different from if you're born stupid.

PG: But it does not follow as the night does the day, that if you were born at 7 a.m. on July 13, 1934, you have a different capacity than if you were born on September 4, 1926?

RD: Not necessarily, no. Astrology really hasn't got an awful lot to do with any of that. It's largely a way of constellating the intuitions of the astrologer. I have had astrologists tell me quite amazing things and it was quite extraordinary. I was aware that it was their intuition that was speaking rather than the stuff they saw on the chart. But you see I once had an astrologer tell me that I was surely going to change my job and that I would be doing my work among young people and that I would work in a room looking out over water, and within 18 months I was in precisely that, at Massey College where I had no notion at the time he told me that. . . .

PG: Massey College doesn't look out over water.

RD: My room looks out over the fountain.

PG: What about Canada? Now are we astrologically preordained hurdling toward a future set in the stars as someone comes close to suggesting in *What's Bred in the Bone?*

RD: If we fulfilled our real destiny, we could be, I think, a very important world figure, but not a figure of foremost importance because we wouldn't have the military or economic clout to do that. But we could be a very, very strong voice because we could be "fifth business," we could be to the North American continent what Switzerland is to Europe, but we lack the sort of guts and crust of the Swiss. We don't really believe in ourselves, we always play ourselves down.

PG: Do we?

RD: Yes.

PG: I'm wondering about that.

RD: Well, look at our politicians, look at them every night on television, clowning around, and talking silly and using stupid slang, and saying "You can bloody well put your seat on the line" and that sort of thing. It lacks the dignity of a man who really believes that he is a very notable figure. Isn't that awful? A lot of that goes on in our politics.

PG: We have to become more comfortable with our own limitations, or what?

RD: Yes, and we've got to stop saying when a man is appointed Lieutenant Governor that he is the son of a railway porter and a housemaid, and say that he is a notable man who is fit to represent the Queen and get down to it that way and stop always playing down and looking for the worm in the apple, or the trivial thing.

PG: Samuel Marchbanks is going to stride again this fall. Right?

RD: Yes.

PG: Now, I need to know a bit about, are you reworking Samuel Marchbanks?

RD: To some extent. You see what I am doing in the book, which is the three volumes boiled down into one, is editing Samuel Marchbanks as though I were an academic editor preparing the work of a rather difficult—

PG: Rather difficult!

RD: —rather difficult author, and I love doing that because I'm fascinated by academic editing and I love putting in footnotes and sort of trying to play the professor with Marchbanks.

PG: Was he ever wrong as you read him now? Does he ever get things wrong?

RD: Oh he was frequently wrong, yes.

PG: What do you do when you discover his wrongs?

RD: Well, I just had to explain it in a note.

PG: You don't correct it?

RD: No, no. I just explain that he must have misunderstood or something of that sort.

PG: I'm curious, as I haven't read him for a long time. What struck you about this cantankerous, disputatious gentleman as you read him again?

RD: Well, I'll tell you. I think it is a portion of me which could not find expression in any other way, a portion of my discontent with the world as I see it about me. It also is a portion of Canada, there's an awful lot of Samuel Marchbanks in Canada and when you really get Canadians talking, you hear that sharp, judgematical, discontented voice, and I think that's real.

PG: We're going to hear some of that voice on *Morningside*, I think. What a pleasure to have you here and want to thank you for chatting this morning. Robertson Davies' latest novel, *What's Bred in The Bone*, is published by Macmillan; *The Papers of Samuel Marchbanks* will be in bookstores soon, it's published by Irwin. Robertson Davies will be reading from that book for the rest of this week.

Robertson Davies in Conversation with Michael Hulse

Michael Hulse/1986

From *Journal of Commonwealth Literature*, Vol. 22, No. 1 (1987), 119-136. Reprinted by permission of Hans Zell Publishers, an imprint of K. G. Saur Ltd., London.

Michael Hulse writes: I met Canadian novelist, dramatist, essayist and wit Robertson Davies on May 6th 1986 in his room at Massey College, Toronto. Massey College is a new brick building, with concrete-floored passages and fire-doors, but an Oxford smell of cloth, tobacco and elderly gentlemen lay in the air and surely grew more Oxonian closer to the one-time Master's room. Unexpectedly, Professor Davies' room had a large open hearth; more expectedly, a portrait of Shakespeare hung on the wall with old playbills from the Old Vic and Sadler's Wells, the bookshelves were filled with volumes of and about theatre, Shaw was stacked on the table and papers piled on the desk, and bunched in a jug on the mantelshelf were a number of Palm Sunday palm-crosses. Robertson Davies, who can appear Mephistophelian and even harsh in photographs, proved gentle, white-haired and pink-cheeked, quick to smile, authoritative without being at all domineering, and possessed of a seductive gift for suggesting that he and his *vis-à-vis* were the two most agreeable members of a pleasantly exclusive club. The right lens of his spectacles was darkened, and he sat in a straight-backed chair. We began by talking about the reception his fiction has been given on the two sides of the Atlantic.

MH: Professor Davies, the novels you've written have met with slightly different receptions in the USA and Britain, and one has the feeling that in Britain there is something of a refusal to read them patiently, or with any willingness to admit that anything worthwhile could come out of Canada. Have you been vexed or disturbed by this split in the reception?

RD: Well, I have of course been somewhat dejected about it, but I became accustomed to it long ago when I used to write plays, and I would try to interest British producing companies in them, and they never were interested. I remember receiving one letter from the lady who was the secretary of a very famous British producing company, which said, "Mr. Davies, you must realise that nobody—literally nobody—is interested in Canada". This is a British attitude which I think is somewhat exaggerated in the literary world, because obviously a great many people in Britain are interested in Canada; but the reviewing and literary world seems to have a stereotyped notion of Canada as a dreadfully dull place where nothing interesting could happen.

MH: Could I suggest that maybe you've contributed a little to that yourself? Through the various masks you've been wearing, I notice that the adjective which you must frequently use of Canada—whether it's Marchbanks speaking, or Dunstan Ramsay, or David Staunton—is in fact "dowdy".

RD: Yes . . .

MH: It seems that this isn't only a reflex of scrutiny or self-defence; it seems to correspond to a nagging suspicion—in you, I would have felt—that maybe that is in fact what Canada's like.

RD: Well, yes. But to read about dowdy people is not necessarily to read an uninteresting book. There are scores of books, written in Britain and in the United States, about very dowdy aspects of society, which are very interesting books in themselves; and the British have for a long time loved to read novels about Ireland, about the dowdiest aspects of Irish society, by people like Brigid Brophy, for instance. To say that something is dowdy does not mean that it is uninteresting. *Why* is it dowdy? How does its dowdiness manifest itself? And I say that it is dowdy because I am a Canadian and writing primarily for Canadians, and I am trying to jolt them out of certain attitudes which are native to them. And, when I'm writing, my eye is not fixed principally on an audience in Great Britain, or in the United States, or anywhere else but Canada. That's why I'm a Canadian author.

An English author who is unfashionable, because a lot of Bloomsbury people disapproved of him, is Arnold Bennett; but I think he is an extremely fine writer, at his very best, and a great follower of the French realists—and the life he writes about is extraordinarily dowdy, but *how* fascinatingly he writes about it. *The Old Wives' Tale,* I think, is one of the remarkable novels of this century, in English, and is certainly not about a lively, vivid, urban society.

MH: What is certainly missing in *The Old Wives' Tale,* and never missing in your own work, is the dimension of the grotesque and the Gothic.

RD: I think that that plays a part in my books because I am a Canadian, and in this country, which is thought to be so dull, the grotesque and the strange are very present, and Gothic goings-on are to be found in every part of Canada—rural and urban, small town, large city—and I think that it is something to do with our temperament, which is that of a very northern people, a people who are perhaps temperamentally more like Scandinavians than like English people, or most Americans.

MH: I remember that Samuel Marchbanks complained that Canada was "unmonstered".[1] It's a lovely word, and it seems—given what you've just said about the presence of the Gothic and the grotesque if one only knows where to look in Canada—as if it may presumably be a matter of having the eye for it. Would you not say that your own particular vision is predisposed to find that?

RD: It *is* predisposed to find that because of my bias in certain psychological studies. I see things as being grotesque which a great many people pass over without examination. I feel that they don't see the grotesquerie because they don't look carefully enough.

MH: There's also a slight element of slapstick, isn't there? Aunt Mary-Ben's scalp being taken off by an owl![2]

RD: Yes! But, you know, like so much slapstick that is rooted absolutely in reality. There are instances which a colleague of mine— a scientist in this college—showed me, recorded in medical journals, of exactly that sort of thing happening: owls swooping upon women who were wearing those black-and-white hats and snatching them, to the terrible harm of their scalps. Everything in my books that seems most extraordinarily and improbable I can provide you with a reference for.

MH: That's wonderful . . . Can I link what you've just said to

---

[1] In fact I have misremembered this. In *Samuel Marchbanks' Almanack,* Toronto, 1967, p. 68, the crotchety wit observes: "Canada, I assert, is wretchedly undermonstered".

[2] In *What's Bred in the Bone,* London: Viking, 1987, Davies' most recent novel.

something which had struck me at times as an oblique defence of your own Gothic qualities—if a defence is what they need—? In *World of Wonders* there's a lovely description of Dunstan Ramsay's 'autobiography' of Magnus Eisengrim as "A splendid Gothic intervention from your [Ramsay's] splendid Gothic imagination"; and Ramsay himself then describes it as "a wonderfully good book of its kind. Readable by the educated, but not rebuffing to somebody who simply wanted a lively, spicy tale". Which seems to me to be excellent, and very unfashionable today. Do you think that that would also describe your fiction? It seems to me that it does.

RD: I sincerely hope that it *would* describe my kind of fiction, because I really believe that the formula for a good fiction is that it should be a tale for those who simply want a tale, that it should contain some degree of comment and have some irony for those who are aware of that and appreciate it, and that it should contain a very substantial amount of moral clout for those who are open to that sort of thing. If you get those three elements in a book, you've got a book that can be read on three levels. I know a lot of people read my books because they like the stories, which are lively and which they think are improbable and somewhat grotesque; but I think the comment, and the other two elements, suggest that if they would just look a little deeper into what lies around them they might see that they are not as grotesque as all that. I think that daily life lurches readily toward the grotesque.

MH: It's curious that you should say that we should look a little more closely at what lies around us, because that seems in fact to suggest the kind of fiction which you normally prefer not to accept quite so easily, the "dreary tales of adultery in suburbia, of the despair of illiterates who have never known hope, of pinheads who fear that they are incapable of love, or any of the other stock themes of modern fiction".[3] The defence of these kinds of fiction would be that they describe people as they are, as we can find them to be if we simply do look around as you've just suggested.

RD: If we look around with the disposition to follow the modern fashionable pessimism . . . I'm always being asked if I have any influences, and I'm not a great man for influences, but if I have any,

[3]*The Enthusiasms of Robertson Davies*, ed. Judith Skelton Grant, Toronto, 1979, p. 194. The remark is in a 1960 notice of Mervyn Peake.

one of them is certainly Henrik Ibsen, who's a great comic playwright. He watches his people suffering very very intensely; but they're suffering not necessarily because their fate is a black one but because they're disposed to suffering, they cannot see the way out, they cannot rid themselves of the shackles that make them sufferers. I am essentially of an optimistic nature, and I think that pessimism, at the moment, is a sort of literary and artistic and philosophic mannerism of people who are living in a world which in spite of many grave problems is an extremely favoured one: that is, the happy, well-fed, clean, well-housed world of the West.

MH: I wonder if I might briefly ask you about influences which I think I've seen in your novels at times—that is, the classic school of detective stories, from Conan Doyle through to Agatha Christie and Margery Allingham and Dorothy Sayers. This seems to have left its traces in your own work, and at times there seems a quite palpable influence. Parlabane's farewell letter in *The Rebel Angels* bears a resemblance to Justice Wargrave's in *Ten Little Niggers*. Are you a great detective story enthusiast? Would you say that there has been any such influence?

RD: Well, actually I never read detective stories, because I find them a bore. They're puzzles, and I don't care about puzzles. I don't really like Sherlock Holmes, though like everybody I fall under the spell of the character of Sherlock Holmes. And I like the writings of Dorothy Sayers because they're full of admirable writing: they're excellent novels, apart from the puzzles, which I find rather a bore. But I've never read a line of Agatha Christie. And I don't on the whole read detective stories. I don't *care* who killed Roger Ackroyd, you know. I want to know *why*.

MH: Your comment on puzzles reminds me of the distinction that Forster made in *A Passage to India* between muddles and mysteries. It seems to me that yours is a mind which is drawn—much more importantly—to mysteries rather than muddles.

RD: Well, I think that behind every murder lies a mystery, even if it is a very commonplace crime of passion—not that there's really any such thing as a 'commonplace' crime of passion. But that is what really interests me, rather than who done it. Usually there isn't much doubt about who done it.

MH: Agatha Christie would have been disappointed to hear you say that.

RD: That is what she founded her career upon: the solving of the puzzle. But she herself has told us that she wrote her books backward, or composed them backward: she got the murder and then she worked backward and created the mystification. But I just don't know, from what I read in the newspapers, that there's usually an awful lot of mystery about who killed somebody; but *why* is utterly fascinating.

MH: I had a slightly different mystery in mind when I mentioned Forster's distinction between muddle and mystery. I was thinking rather of the much larger mysteries of life—

RD: Ah, yes!

MH: —the Devil, above all, is very emphatically at the centre of the novels you've been writing in recent years. Again, you seem an outsider in our times in that you are the only novelist to take him very literally, or seem to take him literally. Maybe I just read your very sprightly caricature of the Devil—as Liesl Vitzlipützli, for example— too literally.

RD: Well, you see, the Devil is just a metaphor for negative forces that are at work in human destiny, as God is (generally) a metaphor for the—on the whole—benevolent, though often minatory, forces in human destiny. And I sometimes get in trouble with my theological friends, because they think that to believe in the Devil is an absurdity: you know, the Devil's almost banished in modern theology. But I think that the Devil is having a high old time laughing at just exactly that. I speak of him, you see, as 'he', but I really mean a very large force that intrudes itself into human life at almost every point and which creates the most frightful havoc. To be tempted by the Devil does not necessarily mean that a sulphurous demon appears to you and asks you to sign something in your blood; but he may offer you a job, or he may offer you a girl, or he may offer you some kind of apparent benefit which is really your destruction. And you've got to be on your watch for that.

MH: You seem often to like to interpret characters as a personification of Evil.

RD: There again I get in trouble with some people who do not believe that—but I have known evil people. They are not extremely numerous. It is as difficult—it requires as much energy and determination and resolution and, indeed, intelligence—to be evil as to be notably good. That is why I've written about saints and also about evil people. I have known some evil people; and John Parlabane, let me tell you, in *The Rebel Angels,* is not an improbable character. I could give the references, and tell you things I didn't use about Parlabane, because I don't think people would have readily accepted them.

[At this point we stopped the tape recorder and Robertson Davies told a story about John Parlabane's original model which was indeed nasty and scarcely credible.]

MH: Might I ask you about some of the rather fraught relationships between offspring and parents in your novels? In particular, the relationship between mother and son often seems a very problematic one—in the case of Dunstan Ramsay, and Paul Dempster, in particular, and marginally in the case of Francis Cornish as well. I wonder if this reflects in any way your own relationship with your mother?

RD: Oh no, not really. My relationship with my own mother was, I think, a perfectly normal one. Which doesn't mean there is always one of perfect unity and delight. But I have been very interested in the relationships of people with their mothers, and I've observed them, and I have seen mothers who literally, through their possessiveness and bossiness and strength of character, absolutely ruined a weak son. And I have been immensely impressed by the hold that some mothers maintained over their sons to an extraordinary age. I remember when I was at Oxford I used to be astonished that when I met with friends in the evening, quite often, about half past ten or eleven, two or three of them would get up and say, "Well, I have to go now, I haven't written my letter to Mummy". They wrote to their mothers *every day.* I met some of those mothers, and they were cannibals, and the effect on the sons was grievous. This is something which people don't like to see. I think that the relationship within a family is a particularly difficult and tricky one, and it's hard to manage it except by a combination of intelligence and instinct, if it is not to be injurious to both sides. Don't believe for one instant that I am suggesting that children are destroyed by parents and that it doesn't work the other way round: I have seen children who made their parents' lives a wreck. The family relationship is a very tricky one and you never get to the bottom of it.

MH: In *What's Bred in the Bone* you suggest two essential kinds of woman, the maternal on the one hand, the harlot on the other—and certainly there seem to be plenty of the second kind in your novels. We literally have a good number of prostitutes, who initiate young men, whether it's Francis Cornish, or David Staunton (we take Myrrha Martindale to be scarcely more than a whore), or Roly Ingestree in *World of Wonders,* who has his first magnificent failure at the hands of a prostitute. It struck me that sexuality in the novels is not always particularly pleasant—in fact, usually it's rather on the unpleasant side.

RD: Yes, I think that's true.

MH: There is this ritual initiation, isn't there? And also something of the peek-a-boo: Ramsay happening upon Faustina naked, or Leola's nude photographs—

RD: Yes.

MH: —and Francis Cornish drawing Ismay Glasson in the nude. This seemed to indicate a rather unsatisfactory side of sexual experience, which was much more present in your fiction, it seemed to me, than any more satisfactory portrayal of it.

RD: Yes, I think that that is undoubtedly true. But the portrayal of satisfactory sexual relationships is extraordinarily difficult to do. It's one of those very great problems that confront a novelist—like presenting a portrait of a really good and wonderful woman. It is frightfully difficult, and it's very very hard to bring it off. I've just been rereading Balzac's novel *Ursule Mirouët,* in which he attempts a portrait of a really wonderful girl, a pure, good, blameless girl, and my goodness! she's cold potatoes. And I'm no Balzac. And I don't think I could begin to present such a picture, nor—in the post-Freudian and post-Jungian world—could I perceive of a woman in that way. I regard women as human beings rather than as idealized anima figures. And that is perhaps why the mothers and the women in my books are not always models of discretion or perfection. But there are some very nice ones. I think, for instance, that Diana in *Fifth Business* is a charming girl, but she'd have been a disastrous girl for Ramsay to marry, for a variety of reasons which are apparent. But it doesn't say that Diana wasn't a girl of great quality, great charm, and fine character. And in *The Rebel Angels* I think that Maria is a wonderful girl—she's certainly intended to be so. And in an earlier novel of mine called *A Mixture of Frailties* there's a Canadian girl called Monica Gall, who had a stroke of luck because she had a good voice and a Foundation sent her away to study singing. I've been told by many people that they thought Monica a wonderful, delightful girl. Monica had some bad luck; and Monica's great problem was that when she came to a culminating point in her life she wasn't very courageous. But not to be very courageous is not to be a bad person. Monica—I thought—was a lovely girl, and I think Maria is a real charmer, and many other people have thought so too.

MH: She's certainly a charmer. I wonder, though, if you were being slightly disingenuous when you said that women in this post-Freudian, post-Jungian world must be real human beings. Maria's *name* seems to suggest that she is not only, or not even, a real human being. Maria Magdalena Theotoky. This is beyond belief, isn't it?

RD: My dear friend, you wait for the third novel! You wait for the end of that trilogy. And, believe me, I once knew a girl whose name was Maria Theotoky—but not Magdalena. The Magdalena was invented. Theotoky is not an uncommon Greek name.

MH: May I ask about the fathers in the novels? They seem to be on the austere side, rather stern, unbending characters. Major Cornish has "no poetry" in him.

RD: No.

MH: I wonder if this is the kind of father you had?

RD: No, my father was an entirely different sort of person. My father was a Welshman: a jolly, merry, capricious, mercurial man—a man you never knew, from hour to hour almost, how to approach, because his mood would change radically. But he was always extraordinarily amusing, and lively, and he could tear the most frightful strip off you or he could tell you something which you'd remember all your life long. He could give you advice which was—one would have thought—wrong advice for a father to give a son, but it was invaluable, and I'll give you an example of it. When I was a boy I was an absolute idiot at mathematics, a fool: I failed my entrance to university examinations twice in mathematics, scoring not just a low mark but zero each time. Well, I was desolate. I thought I would

never get to the university, and that my life was a ruin. And my
father, seeing how rotten I felt, said, "Now you know, I'm going to tell
you something which will be valuable to you. There are always
people who are good at mathematics and who for that reason are
disposed to be honest, whom you can hire to do it for you. *You* don't
have to bother with it!" And you know, that was dreadfully immoral
advice, in a way, to a boy who was struggling to achieve his right of
passage; but it was very true. And since then I've found all kinds of
people who, for a reasonable fee, will do any mathematics you want
done. And they are indeed honest. But that was the kind of man he
was. And he was also a man who loved poetry, loved fiction,
delighted in the theatre, loved music—a great man. My home was
one where there was a lot going on, as I now realise, that doesn't go
on in every home. There was a great deal of music. Both of my
parents were very fond of music and rather good at it: they both
sang, and my mother played the piano, and my father could play the
flute. There was a great interest in books, and literature, and very
much in the theatre. And so my relationship with my parents took a
great deal of colour from that; but there was also a dark side to it, in
that they were both moody people, and you had to learn to accom-
modate yourself to their moods, and if you were yourself a moody
person, sometimes there were clashes. But this is not just your
straight, blenderized American home, is it?—with dear old Dad, who
shows you how to make things down in the workshop. *My* father
didn't have a workshop. He was all thumbs. If you went to my
mother with your troubles, you might get sympathy or you might get
a thick ear—you never knew where you were. And that was an early
lesson that I learned very well!

Was that the answer to your question? You wanted to know about
my family background. Many people do. But that was it. It was
mercurial, and capricious, but immensely stimulating.

MH: There was perhaps a different thought behind the question,
and that was: to what extent you were going to disclaim autobiographical content in your novels. It seems that Deptford is based, is it
not, on Thamesville, Ontario; and I would guess also that Thamesville[4] had a canning factory . . . ?

---

[4]The small Ontario town, west of Toronto, where Robertson Davies was born in 1913.

RD: Oh yes!

MH: Deptford does, and so does Samuel Marchbanks' birthplace. The same motifs keep coming up. So plainly you pick out details that you can use, from actual, existing facts, but the broadest outline of your own life you haven't used . . . ?

RD: Well, you know, all I can say is what Flaubert said about *Madame Bovary:* "Madame Bovary, c'est moi". All novels are to some extent autobiographical. But I can tell you something about Samuel Marchbanks which I hope will surprise you—I think it may. He was born in a place called Skunk's Misery. Well, if you go to Thamesville and ask for directions, about a mile and a half from Thamesville you'll come to a swamp, which used to be called, and I believe is still called, Skunk's Misery. As I tell you, the weirdest things in my writing are straight fact.

MH: To return to the fathers for a moment, if I may. The most important fathers in your novels are not actually fathers but the 're-placement' fathers chosen by the characters; and Ramsay in fact comments, "every man who amounts to a damn has several fathers [. . .] The fathers you choose for yourself are the significant ones".[5] It strikes me that they're rather jesuitical characters, starting with one who actually is a Jesuit—Ignacio Blazon—and then we have Pargetter at Balliol, and in *What's Bred in the Bone* we have Tancred Saraceni. They're very magisterial characters, unbending: they know exactly what they can communicate, and they will do so, and they will suffer no nonsense from the man who is just willing to learn to the utmost of his capacity. They're disciplined. They're what would be called élitist now, because we don't *like* people like that in this time. I wonder if these characters represent people that you have met in your life, from whom you feel you've learnt, or whether they also, as I suspect, represent partly yourself, the way you would like to be seen in the role of teacher, which of course you've played as well?

RD: No . . . they represent father figures. I've had many father figures, some to whom I'm deeply grateful. When I was at Oxford, one of them was Sir Edmund Chambers, the great Shakespeare scholar, a marvellous scholar, austere and rigorous, but by no means dry. And I worked with Neville Coghill, who was an admirable tutor,

[5]*The Manticore,* Toronto, 1972, p. 261.

and much more genial, but again very rigorous in his demands in scholarship. I knew all my life, till his death, Tyrone Guthrie, the theatrical director, who was a father figure very much to me, and he was rather conscious of it and made rather a thing of it, and used to say, "Of course you realise I'm your father in Art". I used to think, "Well, yes, you're partly so, but not completely so". And later in my life, when I came to this college, the late Vincent Massey, the founder of the college, was very much a father figure in my life, and he was an austere man and often, in many ways, a difficult man; but he was a man for whom I was prepared because of my own father. If you could make him laugh, you could persuade him to see your point of view. Oh yes! Lots of father figures. And I know that various people, and sometimes students, have attempted to make a father figure of me, and I have always resisted it, because I know from my study of the work of C. G. Jung that nothing is more destructive to your character than to allow yourself to think that you are an archetypal figure. I am much too aware of my own variety of character and general foolishness to think of myself as a father figure to anybody. I'm very chary about giving advice.

MH: I wonder if these father figures always have a very salutary influence . . . ?—it seems that Saraceni is instrumental in making a faker out of Cornish. May I take up the matter of faking and art? I noticed in the *New York Times* on Sunday[6] that the Dieric Bouts 'Annunciation' is once again up for discussion—

RD: And I saw in the last few copies of the *Times* that I read about some man who has been openly faking the work of a number of quite well-known American water-color artists, and they finally ran him down. He's very cheerful about it.

MH: It's this cheerfulness which is quite perplexing, isn't it? Kujau as well, who faked the Hitler diaries, makes a very bright and chipper impression. He seems pleased as Punch about his faking. I came across a quotation, in that *New York Times,* from a work by Geraldine Norman called *The Fake's Progress,* published in 1979, where she says that the faker "stands outside society and should not be judged by conventional standards. A faker is creating art, not just something that looks deceptively like art". This seems to me to

[6]*New York Times*, 4th May 1986, p. 33.

describe very exactly the position that Francis Cornish finds himself in, with 'The Marriage at Cana'. I'm not sure, though, that you would subscribe to that. It seems that your standards are rather different from Saraceni's in this respect, and indeed from Geraldine Norman's.

RD: Yes . . . but not completely. Recently, when my wife and I were in London, we took great pleasure in visiting an exhibition of art fakes, and they were amazingly interesting. If you hadn't been told that they were fakes you'd have thought, "What an interesting collection of pictures that I've never seen before". But they were indeed fakes. Now: the problem which I put forward is, *why* is the fake not good art? If it is good enough to impose upon very able judges, why is it not as good as if it were by the man it pretends to be by? Well, obviously it is an imposture; because if you sign a famous name—Frans Hals, or something—to a portrait, you're trying to sell something which is wicked. But the picture itself, if you didn't sign it—isn't it fit to hang with Hals? That's the question that interests me. I'm very much interested in this curious line which is drawn between the true and the false, and it is something which interests me very much as it interested Thomas Mann, who was always concerned with this very thin line which divides the artist from the criminal.

Now of course these fakers are often very chirpy, like the man who did the Hitler diaries, because they think, "Well, if they were such fools as to accept them, I'm a pretty clever chap, am I not?" And that is not a very pleasing point of view, but it's understandable. There is always a great pleasure in fooling the experts—because the experts do take such grandiose airs upon themselves. I'll tell you . . . I had a letter, a delightful letter, recently from an old friend of mine who—an Oxford friend—who became a very noted artistic expert, and he said, "I read your book and it made me shiver, because I thought, 'How often have I been near to buying "The Marriage at Cana"?'." And I think that *every* art expert feels this. Of course the real crooks are the people—like the man in my book, Aylwin Ross—who just won't hear that it's a fake. He has no time for any nonsense of that kind. Too much money rides on the picture, and on his reputation. He is the real crook. There's no artist about him.

MH: May I pick up the words "money" and "reputation" and say that—without needing to be a Marxist—I would still feel that there are far too many privileged, or wealthy, or professional, or intellectual people in your novels. When I say "too many" I mean only that I feel that a large area of human experience has been passed over quietly, and I begin to wonder why; and I ask myself if it's because you're just not interested, whether you would rather pretend it wasn't happening.

RD: No . . .

MH: Why does nobody actually suffer in a less Gothic way in your novels? Why is there no rather boring poverty? Why are there no rather drab cities? It's all magisterial—Tyrolean castles, and so on. I'm exaggerating terribly, but this seems to be the split which exists, and, following the Gothic side of your imagination, you've moved over to one very lavish side which is available, haven't you?

RD: But you don't think that the brutal life of Deptford, or Blairlogie, is drawn from life?

MH: I think that it's very selectively drawn. I'm sure it's drawn from life—I'm happy to believe that everything, in fact, has its reference. And yet we're talking, after all, about middle class families, essentially, of some station, and with some idea of responsibility to a tradition in religion, in letters, in money and standing in society. We're not talking about down-and-outs. We don't *have* to—fair enough—I grant that, of course. It's simply striking that the 'low life' characters, as we used to call them in Shakespeare, don't get much of a look in; and when they do, for example Willard the Wizard's friends after he's sodomized—

RD: Yes, the boy—

MH: Dempster. I can never remember which name to call him: Mungo Fetch, Eisengrim. They speak in what I would have thought is a Shakespearean version of 'low life' speech; they don't seem real, working people—

RD: But do you know carnival people?

MH: No, I'm afraid I don't.

RD: Well, I think that they do talk like that. They don't talk like the kind of working class people that you're talking about. Carnival people and theatre people are generally very ready with their tongues. This brings me to something which I feel I must say if I'm to be honest with you: the reason I don't write about the kind of people that you are describing is that I can't. I meet them, I to some extent understand them, but they don't appeal to me as subjects for fiction, and I think that the reason for that is one which you will probably dismiss as foolish, but I am—as you are aware from my books—interested in astrology, and although I don't take it with great seriousness I think that is not entirely to be brushed aside. And I was born, as were both my father and my mother, when the sign of Mercury was at the highest point that it ever reaches in the heavens; and I really don't want to write about people who stumble and grumble and can't say quite what they think, and indeed don't quite think—I want to get on with it, I want people who say something, people who have tongues in their heads. You see, I am on my father's side of Welsh descent, and these inarticulate people who inhabit so many American and English novels . . . I don't understand them! And I don't appreciate what they're up to. I say, "Why the devil don't you spit it out? Tell me what ails you. Give me your hand and tell me what have you in your heart". But they don't. They just blubber. And I haven't got any time for that. I don't want to write about them. There are people who do it and do it marvellously, and so they can have it all. I want to write about the gabby folk.

MH: I'd like to ask about the structure of the novels. It seems that you unfashionably believe in the beginning, middle and end, and in that respect prefer a biographical outline because that seems to make some kind of a linear progression very much more accessible. And there are those who would say that that implicitly is a way of maintaining a political and social order as well, which has no longer any validity. The line of thinking, as I understand it, is that to interpret history as biography, in the way that Emerson or Carlyle did, is at core a 19th century way of legitimizing the emerging middle class. The middle class have had their day now—and here is this fiction of Robertson Davies which appears still to be doing the same thing, to be taking a structure which legitimizes these people of privilege and plenty, and which does it in a very traditional form. I wonder if you've ever felt drawn to question that biographical linearity and the premises which might be seen behind it?

RD: Oh yes, I think of it—but I adopt that manner with full consciousness of what I'm doing. But, you know, if you examine fiction today, or at any time, you find that remarkably little of it is about people who *work* in the sense of having a daily job—which I have done all my life. It's hard to make narrative and drama out of them. J.

B. Priestley attempted it, and attempted it with considerable success. So did Arnold Bennett. But it's very difficult, very rare. It's when you get away from the work-place that the really interesting things begin to happen; and my people generally have enough money, or are in some way able to avoid having to spend eight hours a day doing something which may be intensely boring to them, because I want them to get on with the adventures which I see in their lives, which interest me. That doesn't necessarily mean that I brush aside those people, or am filled with contempt for them—it's just that . . . it's like writing a play. If you try to write a play about inarticulate people, you'd better be very good or it's going to be a perfectly awful play. And if you write a play about people whose social and economic position cuts them off from virtually any adventures outside a very restricted circle, you'd better be very very good or it's going to be a dreadfully dreary piece of work. And you find that the great masters who deal with the middle class, of the kind that you're talking about, don't show them at their work. One of the great examples is Ibsen's play *The Wild Duck*. You never see the photographer taking any photographs. You never see the journalist doing any journalism. You never see the man who runs the factory running his factory. They're all doing something else. Becaue the plain fact is that our daily work may be fascinating in itself but it's not fascinating to readers; and you have to think about readers.

This is where I get into trouble with some of my academic critics. I am interested in having as many readers as possible, reaching as wide an audience as possible. And the man who does a nine-to-five job doesn't want to read much about a man who does a nine-to-five job unless he's a *very* unusual person.

My books are not novels in the sense of being artistic constructs formed on something which reaches back to a French origin, or Henry James, or something. They're romances. I just write romances, and when you write romances you have to be Scheherezade and bear in mind that if you do not hold the Caliph's attention he will cut your head off in the morning.

MH: I'd like to ask about the writing process, on the basis of two comments, one by one of your fictional characters and one by yourself, which seemed very similar. Eisengrim says in *World of Wonders,* "That was how I learned about never doing your damnedest; your next-to-damnedest was far better".[7] And in your own preface to the play Question Time, you say, "one should stop tinkering just before the play seems perfect".[8] I wonder how it is that you decide that your work has reached the stage just before perfection that you want it to be? Do you go through many drafts?

RD: Oh yes. I go through several drafts, and work over a manuscript very very carefully. But I feel that any work of art—and I try to make my novels works of art—are inevitably going to have some imperfections; but if you level off and grind down and polish and shine too much, you may get a very glossy novel but it may have lost its life on the way. And sometimes I wonder if that isn't what happens in the work of a writer whom I used to admire very much—not so much now—and that was Aldous Huxley. I always thought his novels were too finely honed. Much better to be Evelyn Waugh, whose novels present some obvious imperfections and infelicities and abound with life.

MH: A final question. Which contemporary authors do you read with pleasure?

RD: Well, that is a very difficult question, and one which I must perhaps answer somewhat at length, and indirectly. People in Canada are always saying, "What do you think about this, what do you think about that, what is your position or feeling about such-and-so's position in Canadian writing?" I read Canadian writing very carefully, because I feel that it is a bad idea to be too much influenced by—or to know too much about—your fellow-writers. I read some of them, for pleasure, not to inform myself and say, "Ah, Canadian literature's coming on very well, put on another little bud today" and that sort of thing. God, no. About other contemporary writers: I read a number of American writers, and one of them who I think is un-dervalued—because he's a remarkable moralist, and a very, very adroit technician—is Peter de Vries. He writes an awful lot, perhaps more than . . . well, if you were going to shape a career, which I'm sure he's not dreaming of doing, you wouldn't write so many books. But they're wonderfully well done and they have a kind of moral root which is brilliant. Among British writers, living ones, I read of course everything of Graham Greene's. A master. I read a lot of Anthony

[7]World of Wonders, Toronto, 1975, p. 271.
[8]Preface to Question Time, Toronto, 1975, p. ix.

Powell, whom I do not admire so much, but whom I am fascinated by because he's able to do just exactly the sort of things that I cannot do; and I'm not trying to find out from him how they're done, I'm just interested in seeing him do it. And I read Anthony Burgess, because he writes a type of novel which is in effect a romance: it's wildly high-collared and so forth, but when you look at it coldly it's drawn right out of contemporary life. And I read John Fowles. That sort of thing.

    MH: Thank you very much.

The Grand Old Man of Can Lit
Robert Fulford/1988

Transcription from "Realities" 8 February 1988. Copyright 1988 TV Ontario. Reprinted by permission of "Realities," and Robertson Davies. All rights reserved.

RF: More than a quarter of a century ago, in a pretty celebrated book called *A Voice From the Attic*, you called for the creation or the recreation of a class of people you called the clerisy. Why did you do that?

RD: Well, I felt that at that time the consideration of serious literature was passing entirely into the hands of academic critics, who wrote and taught for one another. And literature does not belong to academics, it belongs to everybody, and everybody should have access to it. And I wanted to give a signal that serious readers, whatever they did for their livelihood, were part of a very important group which I called the clerisy.

RF: Where'd that word come from?

RD: Oh well it's a very old word. You'll find it back into the 18th century. It just means not necessarily learned people but literate people.

RF: I think you said in your book that the mark of a member of the clerisy was intelligent curiosity, and a kind of endless curiosity too.

RD: Yes.

RF: A need to read and a need to go farther and farther into literature without ever becoming a professional.

RD: Right.

RF: Well that was more than a quarter of a century ago as I said. The book was much discussed at the time. How would you look at that argument and that warning?

RD: Well, I think, that things have changed substantially here in Canada, because there is a much larger serious reading public than there was when I wrote that book. And I attribute a great deal of that to the immigration into this country. When we read about immigration the press seems to concentrate on very unhappy poor people

270

who come here in desperation. But we've had a large immigration of very intelligent, middle-class professional, well-educated people who are interested in the new country and interested in the literature they find here.

RF: That's made a difference in Canada?

RD: I think it's made an enormous difference. I get a great many letters from readers, and a surprising number of them are from people with names that would not have been thought of as Canadian when that book was written.

RF: Americans, to whom you addressed the book—how did they change in that period, that quarter of a century?

RD: I honestly don't know. I think that there has been a substantial change, because I feel that there is a—not a revulsion—but a sort of revolution against the domination of radio, television, movies and so forth and that people are reading more, more than ever. Look at the extraordinary proliferation of book shops in Canada, and here in Toronto, and the great enthusiasm for paperback books. You can only account for it by a public, and a lot of those books in the paper-back area are serious books, they're not trash.

RF: So in other words, you would say, contrary to what one often hears in universities, that things in that regard have changed for the better since 1960?

RD: Yes, I think that they have. You see, the academic critic who writes for 2500 people in a journal or whatever it is that he writes for, rarely thinks outside of that and does not often value the opinion of people whom he calls patronizingly "laymen." Well, an author would be in a bad way if he relied on most professionals who—I shouldn't say this it's unwise—but do they ever read a book that they don't get free?

RF: Or do they ever read a book without a pencil in their hand?

RD: Yes, exactly.

RF: Books are things to be studied, judged rather than experienced. I think you once said that the heresy of the critic is that he is a judge rather than an experiencer of literature.

RD: Yes, and he tends to drift towards becoming an explainer. And a large part of the public adores explainers. And if they can get an explanation of a book, it saves them from thinking about it. As for my own books, I hope that the readers will have to use their heads and be collaborators, which is a thing I stressed in that earlier book. They should be collaborators in creating the work of art which is the book. It's just a script you know.

RF: I remember you saying it's like a scenario or something from which the reader operates or the reader actively works.

RD: Yes.

RF: You went even further. You said that the gifts demanded of a good reader are less than those of the critic than of the actor.

RD: Yes. Well, unless you visualize, and hear the voices of the characters, and more or less see what you're reading about, I don't know how you get the full content out of a really richly contrived book. And the notion that the speed readers put forward, that you shouldn't vocalize when you're reading, seems to me to be absurd. Because I think all the writers I know, and certainly I myself, take extraordinary pains to write as carefully and as well and sometimes as eloquently as we can. Well if people just grab up the words in gobs, and sort of get a bit of the meaning, what's the good of it? We might as well write in telegraphese.

RF: But there's something more than that going on though. More than a slow or careful look at the prose, you're imagining a kind of interior theatre in which the novel is being acted out.

RD: Yes. And it is extraordinary how that operates. It's always been so in my case. But not very long ago, I saw some of Trollope's Barchester novels on television. And I reread some of them because of it. And as I reread them, I heard the voice of Susan Hampshire, and saw all the admirable actors, and it contributed amazingly to my enjoyment of the book. They could do it better than I could imagine it, and I had wonderful pleasure from the combination.

RF: So contrary again to what was often said about *Masterpiece Theatre,* they're not lowering the value of those books as books, they are in that case enhancing it.

RD: Depends on the book. Some of the books that they do are pretty sorry stuff. Like *Sorrel and Son,* which was no good when it was written and it's disgusting now. But the fine books take on quality from fine acting and the imagination of gifted artists.

RF: I've often heard that denigrated as a way of making the book slighter, for instance Jonathan Miller on this program said that he thought the worst thing you could for for a good novel was to act it out, because the real novel is in the prose.

RD: Ah yes. Well, Jonathan Miller is professionally displeased. He is really a critic by trade.

RF: More than a director or a—

RD: Oh yes. And certainly as a writer.

RF: *A Voice From the Attic,* which the more I read it recently the more true it seemed in 1988 than in 1960, but there was one thing in it you said that is very clearly not true today. You assumed that the problem of illiteracy, narrowly defined, was vanishing. That everyone had learned to read and write, and you said we have only a tiny percentage of people who are now illiterate. Today of course, every time you open the newspaper you find out that there's an enormous number of our fellow citizens who can't read or write. Have you any idea of how that happened?

RD: Well, those people are called functionally illiterate. I think they can probably read a little bit. They can read traffic signs or things like that. But they cannot read and understand anything which is at all demanding, and by that I simply mean the directions on a bottle of medicine or something of that kind.

RF: Or a manual to fix a piece of equipment, something like that.

RD: Well, one of the problems is, of course, that we have under-taken this gigantic revolutionary idea of educating everybody, and we will not face the fact that a certain number of people are ineducable, and that you make it hard for the ones who can learn by bringing everything down to the level of those who can't or won't learn. Look at this problem which is now taking a lot of space in the papers about the schools in New York, where the kids are just revolutionaries—I don't know what you can do about that, I suppose something has to be done about it but it doesn't create a literate populace. And yet you know, sometimes among people in very humble circumstances, you discover marvelous readers. People who live out of books.

RD: So really, it has only a little bit to do with economic class—it is something else.

RF: I think it has nothing to do with economic classes. You know, everybody knows perfectly well that there are a lot of exceedingly stupid rich people. Well, it is also a fact, not so widely understood, that a lot of highly intelligent rich people and it's the same with the poor and it's the same with the middle group. Intelligence and enthusiasm for the kind of thing that the arts and literature bring are just not related to economic circumstances at all.

RF: But it seemed only a few decades ago that mass literacy was within the grasp of North American civilization.

RD: That was what the ambitious and optimistic people thought, but it has proved a solid disappointment, and for a very big variety of reasons.

RF: One of them as you say, there are some people who are in-educable, but what are the others?

RD: Well, I don't think that teaching is what it used to be obviously. And of course teachers put up great arguments about their professionalism and their psychological insights they bring to their teaching today. But there were things in the old days which were involved in teaching, when the teachers were not necessarily terribly bright, that were imposed upon them, and which were good for everybody. One was the necessity to memorize a certain amount of good stuff during the course of each school year. Another was that every day, every day of my life from the time I began to go to school as a little boy, until I emerged from school at the age of 18 or 19, I heard the Bible read to me and that meant that every day of my life I had an example of the finest prose in English read to me first thing in the morning. I didn't think of it as that, but that was what I heard, and it's amazing how it imposes itself upon you as a standard of expo-sition and concise expression. Because the Bible's written almost in shorthand, all of it.

RF: The strange thing is that the Bible was read to you presumably by people who thought they were giving you religious indoctrination.

RD: Yes they did.

RF: And so was I. And so were all the people of our generation and generations before it. But in fact, we might have taken religious instruction from it, or we might not, but what we did take for certain was an idea about writing.

RD: Well, no religious instruction was offered. We were simply read a passage from the Bible every morning, and you heard it, and it was not discussed or it was, and then you had to memorize things in the reading classes, and some of them, the really tough nuts, I remember as a boy of not more than nine if that, having to memorize a verse by Ben Jonson of all people, "It is now growing like a tree, in bulk doth make man better be, or standing long at oak, a thousand year. The lily of the day is fairer far than they," and so on. And what he said was that you can live a good life, even if it's a short one. And this was pumped into us, and we were made to memorize it, and that has grown in my mind. I've come from just hearing it as a child to realizing, in old age really, what it really means. The quality of life. Well, you see, that's big stuff in education. You give that to little children, and you have set a time bomb in their minds. Sometime or other they're going to wake up and think, *that's* what he said. And that's what education is.

RF: Even sixty years later, it's, the person still has it.

RD: Education is vittling a ship for a long voyage, not just getting people through examination.

RF: The idea of memory work though, has been out of fashion now for thirty years. What killed it? Why did it seem to be a bad thing, that one should memorize a poem?

RD: I think it was because a certain number of children found it burdensome, and certainly I can remember hearing things like, uh, Tom Moore's lyric, "Oft in the stilly night," and the sigh of children who hadn't a clue what they were talking about. It was silly, but maybe later on, something happened. This thing had been imprinted on their minds and later something very interesting might come of it. But there came a revolution in education which seemed to think that everything had to be done instantly, and there was a passion for what the teachers called creativity. They said everybody's creative. Well, everybody is. But any real creativity has to rest on a basis of an acquired technique and an acquired knowledge; you can't be creative in a void, or you just get mess. And they were so busy being creative, they forgot to lay the foundation, I think.

RF: The other thing they wanted was to teach people how to think.

RD: Yes.

RF: They would say, we're not teaching rote learning, we're not teaching facts. We're teaching these children how to think.

RD: Yes.

RF: Was that equally misguided as a theory?

RD: No, because children do think anyway, but in the old schools that I went to their thinking was somewhat repressed. Any idea that was not the orthodox idea was not to be expressed. Well, to give children a chance to express their own ideas is, I expect, a good one indeed. But there must also be some balance between just a gabby child talking and really using his head.

RF: But the problem perhaps seemed to be, after a while, that they were teaching children to think, without teaching them anything they could think about.

RD: Well, exactly. They weren't giving them anything to vittle their minds. You must feed a mind.

RF: And that became the problem.

RD: The schoolbooks broke down very badly, and things like scraps of Ben Jonson, and Dickens and so forth were supplanted by Dick and Jane, and Dick and Jane was an abomination. Dick and Jane was even racist.

RF: You taught at the University for a good many years.

RD: Yes, twenty.

RF: Twenty years. I guess, beginning around—in the sixties.

RD: Yes.

RF: You began to deal, day by day, with the products of the education system that followed your generation's system.

RD: Yes.

RF: How did it manifest itself in the students at the University of Toronto?

RD: Well, I was fortunate because I was teaching principally graduate students, and they were a very good group, very intelligent, and very well informed. But it astonished me how many of them thought that English literature had begun with James Joyce, and I used to nag at them and say, you know, you don't know anything about English literature unless you have some sort of chronological notion of how it works. And the two things that you must be acquainted with, even if only slightly, are the Bible and Shakespeare, because they lie at the root of so much that has been written. You'd better have a look at some Milton. You really must find out what you're measuring modern stuff against. And I think a lot of them paid heed to what I said. But I did have a very good group. They were very intelligent, but they were not always terribly well informed.

RF: I think they're probably nicer than they were a generation before.

RD: I think they very probably were. And I remember, I went to the university at Queen's, during the depression years, and the stress there on students was appalling. They had to succeed, they had to do well, or it was just the end for them, and that imposed upon them a kind of stress which I don't think was really friendly to learning.

RF: In the humanities today, in university you don't have that stress, so often, but certainly there is a great deal in medical school, law schools, business schools and so on, there's a terrific amount of competition there, so it, the element of stress has become almost vocational.

RD: Yes.

RF: Was that the way it was when you went to university?

RD: It certainly was in the professional schools, and I think that it is so today, even in the humanities schools, because those people have got to get jobs, and the humanities is the sort of study which consumes its own smoke. You study humanities for what? To teach humanities. I used to nag my students and tell them that an education was to fit you for any kind of life, it was to teach you how to approach life, and if you've got a moment, I can tell you a tale about that. There was a young man that was in Massey College, whom I'd talked to and who was having a good deal of trouble, because he'd got an excellent degree in history, and he couldn't find a job as a historian. So to keep bread in his mouth he took a job with a stock and bond company. Well, I met him 18 months later, and he was looking very sleek indeed. And I said to him, how are things going? He said, well I've made a great discovery. There's nothing about the financial world that a good history degree doesn't help. And I think that's what an education is.

RF: You said that the humanities devour their own smoke. That you study humanities in order to teach humanities. But something else has happened, and this is, I would say, a very big difference between 1960 when you wrote *A Voice From the Attic* and today, and that is that in the humanities—particularly English studies, but other areas too—the writing about them, discussion of them has become so intensely convoluted and almost private, so technical, that a large part of the world, or the largest part of the world is shut out from their discussion. Is that something that you watched happening in the university when you were there?

RD: It was something against which I and a good many of my colleagues worked as strenuously as we could, insisting that in English literature your approach to a book was an approachable work of art, and you experience it as a work of art and feel it as a work of art, and as someone capable of sharing something with the artist. And that after that you can haggle and sneak up and cut out and do all the other things if you felt you absolutely must, but first of all you must get hold of what the writer was really saying.

RF: But what about this mass of scholarship that is produced under the name of structuralism, deconstruction, and post-de-construction and all that sort of thing. All that enormous, hundreds and hundreds of books that have been produced in the university presses. What does that amount to? What does it have residual meaning for? For literature? Or for the public?

RD: Well, I take a rather tedious view of that. I say, those people belong to the avant-garde, and we all know what the avant-garde was. It was the group that was sent forward to encounter the worst of the fire, and to fall bravely in the service of their country, and then the real army came up and took over and won the battle. And I think that's what happens in literature. Those who want to be in it, are just inviting their destruction, because the avant-garde has changed its clothes and its uniform and its underwear three or four times in my lifetime. Who wants to get into that?

RF: The Bible we mentioned a little earlier. We mentioned Bible studies at school, Bible reading and so on. And that really is one of the biggest changes in your lifetime, as a reader and a teacher and a writer, what is the difference between a society in which the Bible is everyone's possession, and a society in which the Bible is the possession of ten percent or so of the people.

RD: Well, in my opinion, the latter society, the one from which the Bible is disappearing is a society which is moving toward barbarism. Because one of the elements of a civilized society is that it has a congruous body of common knowledge, generally of classic liter-ature. And that is what the Bible was, quite apart from what it had to say on religious subjects, which was another thing. It was a common classical literature which was known to virtually everybody. And it

was a literature which had its origin in Hebrew and in Greek, and
when you read it in English you were reading perhaps the supreme
classic of the English language. And everybody knew the allusions,
everybody knew what was meant when certain things were referred
to, and when my mother referred to people that she didn't like, as
the Tribes of Menassi, I knew exactly what she was talking about. And
this meant that there was a common frame of reference for
conversation, oratory and opinion, right from the top of society to the
bottom, and when somebody in parliament made a biblical reference, he was literally talking to a nation which understood him, not
making a classical allusion which went over the heads of most of the
people who might hear him. We have lost that great classic
background. And to have lost your classic background is to be very
much at sea. So—

RF: And to be splintered—

RD: Yes.

RF: To be pushed into tiny little groups, each presumably with its
own classic . . . or each presumably with its own set of references.

RD: Well, now there is education in some places, like near where
we are, that if one religious book is to be put forward in the schools,
several others must be—the Koran, the Talmud, and so on and so
forth. Well, very possibly so. I think if we had a compendium of writ '
of that kind it would be perhaps a good thing. But they are trans-
lations, the people who study the Talmud study it in the original, and
so do the people who study the Koran, and we have got the Bible in
the language which is supposed to be our principal language, and we
are abandoning it and casting away our classical background.

RF: In a certain way, you were writing about a clerisy twenty some
years ago in *A Voice From the Attic*. In a certain way, you've realized
that among your own readers, at least that is the sense I have. In your
books you called for intelligent, curious, energetic readers who would
work hard and expect a good reward in return for working hard. I
have the sense as I meet your readers, not only in Canada but in
Britain and the United States, that you've put together an audience
like that, for yourself, without necessarily transforming society and its
readership. How has that worked for you?

RD: Well, you pay me an enormous compliment which I would
hesitate to claim as a truth. But I do write for people who delight in

life and are curious about many aspects of it and are aware of its
tragedy as well as its comedy but who do not adopt a sort of glum
attitude which they think is realism. My books are not realistic, in the
literary criticism sense, but they do appeal to something I hope below
the surface of the ordinary perception of life, and I think a lot of
people are like that, and I know from the letters that I receive that
they do like it. It means that I don't have the gigantic readership of an
enormously popular novelist, but that was something I never hoped
to have, and therefore do not regret.

RF: Thank you very much.

RD: Thank you.

Index